Sexualized Media Messages and Our Children

Recent Titles in Childhood in America

Sexualized Media Messages and Our Children

Teaching Kids to Be Smart Critics and Consumers

JENNIFER W. SHEWMAKER

Childhood in America
Sharna Olfman, Series Editor

AN IMPRINT OF ABC-CLIO, LLC
Santa Barbara, California • Denver, Colorado • Oxford, England

Library of Congress Cataloging-in-Publication Data

Shewmaker, Jennifer W.
Sexualized media messages and our children : teaching kids to be smart critics and consumers / Jennifer W. Shewmaker.
    pages cm.—(Childhood in America)
  Includes bibliographical references and index.
  ISBN 978-1-4408-3333-5 (alk. paper)—ISBN 978-1-4408-3334-2 (ebook) 1. Mass media and children—United States. 2. Mass media and sex—United States. 3. Sex in mass media. I. Title.
  HQ784.M32U674 2015
  302.23083—dc23   2014037798

ISBN: 978-1-4408-3333-5
EISBN: 978-1-4408-3334-2

19 18 17 16 15   1 2 3 4 5

This book is also available on the World Wide Web as an eBook.
Visit www.abc-clio.com for details.

Praeger
An Imprint of ABC-CLIO, LLC

ABC-CLIO, LLC
130 Cremona Drive, P.O. Box 1911
Santa Barbara, California 93116-1911

This book is printed on acid-free paper ∞

Manufactured in the United States of America

For Rylan, Catherine, and Alexandra Shewmaker: May you always believe in your power to make a difference in the world.

Contents

Series Foreword

The rich diversity of cultures created by humankind is a testament to our ability to develop and adapt in diverse ways. But no matter how varied different cultures may be, children are not endlessly malleable; they all share basic psychological and physical needs that must be met to ensure healthy development. The "Childhood in America" series examines the extent to which U.S. culture meets children's irreducible needs. Without question, many children growing up in the United States lead privileged lives. They have been spared the ravages of war, poverty, malnourishment, sexism, and racism. However, despite our nation's resources, not all children share these privileges. Additionally, values that are central to U.S. culture, such as self-reliance, individualism, privacy of family life, and consumerism, have created a climate in which parenting has become intolerably labor intensive, and children are being taxed beyond their capacity for healthy adaptation. Record levels of psychiatric disturbance, violence, poverty, apathy, and despair among our children reflect our current cultural crisis.

Although our elected officials profess their commitment to "family values," policies that support family life are woefully lacking and inferior to those in other industrialized nations. U.S. families are burdened by inadequate parental leave, a health care system that does not provide universal coverage for children, a minimum wage that is not a living wage, "welfare to work" policies that require parents to leave their children for long stretches of time, unregulated and inadequately subsidized daycare, an unregulated entertainment industry that exposes children to sex and violence, and a two-tired public education system that delivers inferior education to poor children and frequently ignores individual differences in learning styles and profiles of intelligence. As a result, many families are taxed to the breaking point. In addition, our fascination with technological innovation is creating a family lifestyle that is dominated by screen rather than human interaction.

The "Childhood in America" series seeks out leading childhood experts from across the disciplines to promote dialogue, research, and understanding regarding how best to raise and educate psychologically healthy children to ensure they will acquire the wisdom, heart, and courage needed to make choices for the betterment of society.

Sharna Olfman, PhD, Series Editor

Acknowledgments

I express my deep appreciation to those who have helped make the writing of this book possible. I am thankful to all who allowed me to interview them and shared their thoughts through the "In Their Voices" sections. I am particularly grateful for the invaluable support of Amy Boone, Laura Carroll, Caron Gentry, and Heidi Nobles for their many thoughtful suggestions and unending encouragement. I could not have completed this work without the constant support of my husband, Stephen, and my daughters, Rylan, Catherine, and Alexandra.

Introduction

In a full window display, women manikins are dressed in scanty lingerie, their breasts spilling out of bustiers as they hold masks and tape made for binding partners during sex acts. A man manikin looks on, eyeing the women like so many delectable objects from which to choose. The words "Are you pleasure bound?" are emblazoned across the window. The captive audience for this scene: preschoolers in a mall's dedicated children's play area that happens to be directly across from the novelty store selling these products.

A megabrand famous for their sexy fashion shows and advertisements depicting lingerie-clad women creates a new line with products covered with the phrases "wild thing," "let's get wild," and "let's party." The target audience according to a statement made by one company executive: 15-year-old girls.

Her glossy lips shine with lip color, her eyes are large and doe-like. Her miniskirt hits at midthigh and is accompanied by sky-high heels. Her main interests are fashion, shopping, and boys. She is a doll, marketed to children as young as five years old.

I am a mother of three daughters, a psychology professor who has worked with hundreds of young women in my career, and an educator who has walked with children, teachers, and families through some of life's most difficult moments. But I have never been personally challenged quite like I was when my oldest daughter moved from being considered by marketers and media makers as a young child to a "tweenager." I began to notice a shift in the media and marketing directed at her. All of a sudden, she was bombarded by messages that struck at the core of what my husband and I had been teaching her about who she is. Instead of being strong, she was told to be flirtatious. Instead of being brave, she was told to be sexy. Instead of being smart, she was told to be beautiful.

I have seen the increase of sexualized media and marketing messages, and I am not alone. There has been great debate in recent years concerning the issues of sexualized products and programming directed toward children and adolescents. Parents and researchers argue that sexualized media have increased and is harmful to children.[1] In the past few years, scholars have proposed that childhood has become highly sexualized.[2] They contend that our society has exposed children to messages that advance the idea that their primary value lies in their sexuality. Several government and professional organizations have released reports on the sexualization of childhood, including the United Kingdom's *The Sexualisation of Young People* and *Letting Children Be Children*, the Australian government's *Inquiry into the Sexualisation of Children in Contemporary Media*, and the American Psychological Association's *Report of the APA Task Force on the Sexualization of Girls*.[3] Much of the blame for such exposure has been placed on the mass media.

The key to understanding the problem lies in the meaning of the term *sexualization*. Sexualization is not the same thing as healthy sexual development. Healthy sexual development involves a child learning to identify her own desires and coming to see herself as an agent, with power to make choices and navigate relationships built on mutual respect and equality. This definition is based on that of the World Health Organization, in which sexual health is defined as including a "positive, respectful approach to sexuality and sexual relationships and the possibility of having pleasurable and safe experiences, free of coercion, discrimination, and violence."[4] Sexualization, on the other hand, is the consistent depiction and understanding of a person primarily as a sexual object. Whereas healthy sexual development provides room for complexity, sexualization does not. It is the shallow representation of a person as an object of desire.

Through the use of images and narratives within advertisements, movies, television, music, and products developed for children and adolescents, the media industry has introduced children to the importance of physical appearance and sexual attractiveness at a very young age. Olfman contends that children are "growing old younger" due to new social norms that encourage children to move very early into dressing like adults and seeking entertainment in media that focus on romance, sex, and gender stereotypes.[5] Durham discusses what she terms the "Lolita Effect," which is promoted by the media's construction of an understanding of sex and sexual development that provides children with very limited narratives of sexuality.[6] Both scholars and those who work with children have become increasingly concerned about the way sexualized media influence children. Media ranging from the Disney princesses to hip-hop videos have been analyzed to examine the kinds of effects they have on children. Researchers have also focused on the progressively more aggressive marketing campaigns aimed at children, from candy-flavored lip glosses developed for girls under the age of 10 who have been labeled as "pretweens" to Burger King's commercials for children's meals featuring an altered version of the song "I Like Big Butts." All of these studies have attempted to understand the way that increased sexualization in media impacts children's attitudes and behaviors. Strasburger, Wilson, and Jordan recommend studying the interpersonal context of the child.[7] To understand how sexualized media influence children, we must find out which factors within a child's life impact the way that he navigates the sexual depictions that he sees in the media.

Young children are overwhelmed with the pink and blue marketing that promotes rigid gender stereotypes, while adolescents are struggling to establish their identity as they live in a culture that encourages them to use their sexuality to gain attention and power. It is imperative that families and communities confront sexualization head on. In my work and research with adolescents, I have heard time and again that children desperately want to be able to talk about sexualized and stereotyped media messages with the adults in their lives. They long to get some guidance, to be able to ask questions, to see how others deal with these pressures. When we avoid talking with children and adolescents about sexualized messages and how they feel about them, we leave them vulnerable and without guidance.

Families and communities can help children and adolescents navigate our sex-drenched culture and prepare them to stand up for their own values and share their own perspective with others. As caring adults, we can help children see the great lie of sexualization: that their value lies in sexuality.

This book takes a unique approach to understanding how sexualized media impact children. I agree that children's media have become increasingly sexualized and no doubt have a negative impact, especially in the areas of self-concept, body image, and sexual behaviors.[8] However, I submit that important interpersonal variables in a child's life mediate how she responds to these images and narratives. These variables include the child's connection to the culture of celebrity, family, gender, and community systems.

Understanding the importance of these variables and the part they play in how children engage with and respond to media is essential to understanding the impact media have on their lives. Although the "external blocking" paradigm has been popular in trying to control what children are exposed to through media, ranging from television to the Internet, I take a more ecological approach. Throughout this book, I will build primarily on the bioecological model,[9] with a focus on the interactions between the child as an active learner and his or her environment. The important thing to remember about this perspective is that rather than being a passive victim to media, the child is powerful and active.

I do believe that external filters, rules, industry regulations, and laws are important and have a role to play in controlling the media content to which children are exposed. The difficulty is that many times children and adolescents are quite adept at working around filters on the Internet, ratings on computer games, movies, or music, and so forth. In the end, quite often it is very young children and adults themselves who are foiled through the external blocking paradigm rather than older children and adolescents!

Thus, I believe that the approach of teaching caregivers and children to become critical consumers of media is vital in dealing effectively with sexualized media. This book explores the interpersonal variables that mediate how a child responds to media while providing strategies within those contexts to encourage a more active and critical relationship with the media. The first three chapters will set the stage for understanding the context of child development and media influence, focusing on exploring the ways media shape children in general. In the chapters examining the mediating variables, I first present information about how media impact children in a particular area and then begin to unravel the ways the interpersonal context of the child's life works to engage the child in learning to process media messages. I also provide positive examples of the way that media can be used to encourage children and adolescents to examine their own understanding of sexuality and its development. I believe that children and adolescents are powerful in their ability to interact with the world around them, and with guidance from their families and communities, they can learn the skills needed to respond effectively and decisively to sexualized media.

Understanding the ways that individual children and adolescents navigate sexual media portrayals and the interpersonal contexts in which each child operates is key to grasping the way media impact children and in building successful experiences that advance media literacy. Within the context of each individual child's personal experience, an opportunity exists to become an empowered media consumer and even an activist. In order to harness that potential, the caring adults in a child's life must understand the ways that the particular child is experiencing media.

Media messages are prevalent and powerful. The increased sexualization in these messages influences children and adolescents in many ways, but they do not occur in a vacuum. They shape children within a context. I provide an analysis of the interpersonal mediating variables that affect the way children engage with, interpret, and adopt the sexualized messages from media. Each variable is examined in light of how it influences the way a child learns to cope with and either internalize or reject these sexualized messages. I also share strategies to engage youth in the active examination of media that allow them to enjoy and learn from it, noting examples of both positive portrayals of sexuality and individual value and those that are sexualized. Not only can children learn to be active media critics, but they can also become media makers. This book provides strategies that involve children in becoming active consumers and makers of media.

I will explain how understanding four mediating variables has the potential to dramatically change the way those who live and work with children respond to sexualized media. These variables provide several avenues to lead parents, caring adults, and children toward becoming critical consumers of media rather than passive ones. My goal is not only to educate you about the factors discussed, but also to provide you with practical strategies for dealing with each one in order to help children become critical consumers of media who are willing and able to critique and actively respond to the sexualized messages that are presented to them. I will give specific examples of things you can do to help children begin to see themselves as empowered and behave in ways that challenge the status quo. This book will focus on helping children and adolescents to see themselves as people who can make a difference in the world.

In each chapter you will find a section called "In Their Voices," which provides a personal perspective from a parent, adolescent, or professional on an issue addressed in that chapter. I see this book as the beginning of a discussion that will continue to impact the way parents, professionals, and communities help children understand and respond to media messages for many years to come.

IN THEIR VOICES

Melissa Wardy is the owner of Pigtail Pals Ballcap Buddies, a small business designed to promote a broad view of what it means to be a girl or boy growing up today. She is also the author of the book Redefining Girly *and the mother of two children.*

The thing about elevator music is that you don't hear it until it is too late. You didn't notice it when you stepped on the elevator because you had a lot of little tasks to do right at that moment that preoccupied you as you set about doing them. Then you looked up at the closed doors, and let your thoughts wander. Somewhere between the 19th and 20th floors, you realize you've been listening to some awful music the entire time. Or worse, you've been humming along to it without even knowing it. You didn't hear it, because it was everywhere around you and you had so many other things going on.

The sexualization of children is the children's rights issue of our time. We need to wake up and hear the music. The tune goes something like this: The vast majority of girls are indoctrinated into Princess Culture by age three, teaching them largely to focus on their appearance and acquiring things, the greatest of which is a prince. By elementary school, these girls have make up, shoes, fashion, music, toys, and media coming at them from every direction and all of it is telling them to be hot, sassy, obsessed with shopping and beauty, act older than they are, and to be boy crazy. The message oftentimes not so subtly underscored by these products is that "looking sexy" will be their greatest achievement. Cue the orchestra, music crescendos.

So in addition to the loss of childhood, one starts to question what happens to these kids as they go through puberty and start down the path of romantic relationships. We know the stats on low body image, self-esteem/depression/anxiety, bullying, teen pregnancy, teen date rape, etc. But what happens to them emotionally? I wonder if the issue of sexualization is largely ignored because most of the damage done is emotional and therefore unseen. What if instead sexualization manifested itself as a purple horn and started growing on the heads of kids who are sexualized, and the worse it got, the bigger and purpler the horn got?

So then I started thinking about all of these kids with various-sized purple horns, all bumping into each other because the horns weigh them down and change how they move and act and think. Wouldn't some, for the love of God, cry out, "What have become of the children?"

I remain unconvinced that parents have to accept this for our children, and that we are doing the best we can. I think a lot of us are still listening to elevator music. Much like elevator music, once you are aware of sexualization, it is very hard to ignore it. The thing is, we can't ignore it, because our kids' emotional and physical health depends on it. Through grassroots education by parents on social media and in social settings, media literacy programs in school, and consumer pushback, we can change the tune our society is listening to and create a media culture and space in childhood that is more harmonic with the natural-born rights our children have to be happy and healthy. Because really, there is no better sound on Earth than healthy and happy children.

1

Mediating Variables

Children are both involved with and influenced by media. The images and narratives they absorb from media shape the way they see the world. Media provide a lens through which the child sees how the world is supposed to work; what makes someone valuable, what is important in life, what is expected of men and women. Children today have become media consumers to a degree that was not possible in the past. With the advent of mobile technology, children have access to media that is unparalleled in any other time in our history. They have also become targets of marketing campaigns, with experts aiming their power of persuasion at children to make products more attractive than ever. The combination of the accessibility and attractiveness of the current media messages aimed at children is important to understand. It means that they are being inundated with media messages to an extent that was not possible 10 years ago. With the increased sexualization of media, we see the introduction of these values into children's lives at an increasingly younger age.

In 2007, the Task Force on the Sexualization of Girls was formed by the American Psychological Association (APA) in response to public concern about the sexualization of girls within the culture of the United States. The task force worked together to

(a) define sexualization; (b) examine the prevalence and provide examples of sexualization in society and in cultural institutions, as well as interpersonally and intrapsychically; (c) evaluate the evidence suggesting that sexualization has negative consequences for girls and for the rest of society; (d) describe positive alternatives that may help counteract the influence of sexualization.[1]

Using the task force's updated 2010 report as a springboard, throughout this book I will use the term *sexualization* as occurring when:

- A person's value comes only from his or her sexual appeal or behavior, to the exclusion of other characteristics.
- A person is held to a standard that equates physical attractiveness (narrowly defined) with being sexy.
- A person is sexually objectified (made into a thing for others' sexual use) rather than seen as a person with the capacity for independent action and decision making.
- Sexuality is inappropriately imposed upon a person.[2]

It is important to note that, just as the APA's report does, this book will consider the latter condition as especially relevant to children. The task force says, "when children are imbued with adult sexuality, it is often imposed upon them rather than chosen by them. Self-motivated exploration . . . is not considered sexualization . . . nor is age-appropriate exposure to information about sexuality."[3]

This chapter explores the research on how children use media, the number of hours spent using them, the types of media they use, and the way media impact them in general. As we consider media's effect on children, key ideas that I will introduce are the way that images are controlled and the stereotypes that are perpetuated through media. I will present findings from several studies and from authors in the fields of psychology, education, communication, marketing, and more. I will then introduce the four mediating variables that I believe influence the way that children cope with sexualized media.

In our increasingly connected world, media have taken on greater power to influence children and early adolescents. In fact it has been labeled a "sexual super peer" because teens and preteens are so heavily influenced by the norms and expectations presented via this medium.[4] In this book, the term *media* is defined as mass media, which is a "medium of communication, such as newspapers, radio, television, and advertising designed to reach the mass of people."[5] All forms of media have been identified as important socializing forces that deliver messages to children and adolescents about identity and sexuality.[6] As media messages have become more easily accessible and persuasive, children and adolescents have been rendered one of the most helpless targets of manipulative messages. Developmental research has clearly demonstrated that until the age of eight, children cannot separate persuasive messages from entertainment.[7] Even preteens and those in their early teens are at a disadvantage in identifying advertisements when they are presented online rather than in television or print.[8] These facts make it more important than ever for adults to pay attention to the media that children consume and to consider how children can become active, critical media consumers.

ACCESSIBILITY

Research indicates that children spend more time involved with media than anyone or anything other than sleeping. Specifically, recent research has noted that 71 percent of children ages 8 to 18 and 36 percent of those ages 0 to 8 have a television in their bedrooms, 45 percent of children aged 8 to 18 live in houses where the television is "always" on or on "most of the time," 64 percent say that the television is on during mealtime, and 8- to 18-year-olds reported being exposed to media an average of 7.5 hours a day seven days a week, with 10 hours and 45 minutes a day when accounting for multitasking, such as watching television while surfing the Internet and listening to music.[9] Children aged 0 to 8 years spend one hour and 55 minutes consuming media. Young people spend more of their time engaged in watching television than with other types of media, with children aged 8 to 18 years old reporting watching an average of 4.5 hours of television per day and those 0 to 8 years old spending 57 minutes per day.[10] This increased exposure to media among children and adolescents has created the potential for increased exposure to depictions that sexualize women and girls, presenting the idea that females are primarily sexual objects.[11]

Children are more highly involved with media than ever before due to increased accessibility with the advent of mobile and online media,[12] making these messages even more powerful. Accessibility is a key issue when considering the way children and adolescents use media today. Fifteen years ago, if a child or adolescent wanted to watch media, they had to turn on a television, go to the movie theater, or rent a videotape. With mobile devices that access media, such as the iTouch, iPhone, BlackBerry, Android, and iPad, media become readily accessible. The past five years have seen an increase in the ownership of mobile media among 8- to 18-year-olds, with increases in iPod/MP3 player ownership from 18 percent in 2004 to 76 percent in 2009, cell phone ownership from 39 percent to 66 percent, and laptops from 12 percent to 29 percent. Ownership of iPads and other tablets has risen from 8 percent in 2011 to 40 percent in 2013, and 75 percent of children now have access to a mobile device.[13] In addition, cell phones have changed from primarily a vehicle for communication to a way to connect with media. Young people who own a cell phone tend to use it more often to play or watch media than they do for talking to another person.[14] As children access media more readily, they become a prime target for marketers seeking new audiences for their products.

ADVERTAINMENT

As anyone who has accessed a website featuring games for children can tell you, product advertisements are ubiquitous. In fact, companies have developed their own websites that lure children in with free games, while constantly sending them marketing messages. Consider the websites of such companies as Disney or Nickelodeon. Both sites have promotions for their most recent television shows, movies, and the products related to them. Both also have free games for children. Nickelodeon's site aimed at young children, Nick Jr., was a target of ire in 2010 from both parents and the Campaign for Commercial-Free Childhood due to the promotion of its adult gaming site, Addicting Games, on a website devoted to children.[15]

As access has increased, there has been a blurring of the line between entertainment and advertisement. Marketers hired by companies to promote their products spend $17 billion each year marketing to children.[16] In fact, marketers see children themselves as very influential in the purchasing habits of their families in everything from cars to vacations.[17] Children under 14 years old collectively spend about $40 billion annually. Compare this to the $6.1 billion 4- to 12-year-olds spent in 1989. Children under 12 influence $500 billion in purchases per year.[18] Child consumers are considered big business. In the United States, it has been estimated that children aged 6 to 14 years are exposed to about 25 hours of television every week and approximately 20,000 commercials every year on television alone.[19] Given the proliferation of advertising on the Internet through game sites, it is likely that this number has increased exponentially. It is important to know that this type of direct advertising to children is not accepted or allowed the world over. In Norway, Belgium, Greece, Sweden, and Australia, for example, there are specific limits about times, conditions, and shows during which children's products can be advertised. Not so in the United States. Since the deregulation of entertainment and food industry advertising in the 1980s, advertising to children has increased exponentially, rising from $100 million in 1983 to $17 billion today.[20] At this point in time, children in the United States are considered fair game to large marketing companies who employ techniques ranging from focus groups to neuroscience to determine what types of advertisements will get and keep a child's attention in order to persuade them that they need to buy a specific product.

Movies and television shows regularly feature products that are prominently placed in the story. In a move that was heavily condemned by parents and advocates for a commercial-free childhood, McDonald's Corporation launched HappyMeal.com, which has become a leading online destination for children. The site uses the power of advertainment to promote consumption of unhealthy food by extending a child's interactions with the brand through game playing and providing special access to areas that are only available by entering codes found on purchased food packaging.[21] This intrusion of advertisements upon entertainment for children is confusing to them. Children are not at the developmental stage where they can easily analyze and compartmentalize advertisements and entertainment when they are presented in unison.

Of course, television commercials aimed at children have long attempted to entertain. But these were clearly advertisements for particular products. What we see now is a combining of the two genres that is so ambiguous that children are often not aware which of the two they are seeing. In studies focused on discovering if children could tell the difference between commercials and television programs, it has consistently been shown that, while children know the two are different, they are often unable to identify the purpose of the commercial.[22] Not until the age of seven or eight years can children even begin to understand that advertisements are one-sided depictions attempting to persuade one to buy something.[23] Advertisements presented on the Internet are even more elusive to children. Oftentimes, children up to the age of 12 are unable to identify an advertisement as such.[24]

Television, movies, music videos, and advertising aimed at young people contain many gender stereotypes and sexualized images of women. Push-up bras have been marketed to girls as young as eight through stores such as Abercrombie Kids, while young boys are playing video games like *Grand Theft Auto* that portray women as objects. Even though *Grand Theft Auto* has a rating of M, which indicates that it is for mature audiences only, 56 percent of all 8- to 18-year-olds said they had played this game.[25] *Future Trophy Wife* is emblazoned across onesies for babies and T-shirts for young girls. LEGOs and Tinkertoys market two separate groups of products, one, clad in pink and purple and focused on cafes and cooking, is marketed toward girls, while the set marketed toward boys features primarily dark colors and focuses on fighting and aggression. Even science sets are marketed in a way that promotes gender stereotypes, with pink makeup creation kits for girls and blue or green slime-making kits for boys. At a time in their lives when children are forming important attitudes and impressions about sexuality and gender roles, the media have great power to lead them to base their ideas about sexuality on representations of value associated with superficial qualities and sexualized ideals. It is imperative that families, professionals, and communities be aware of these influences on children in order to help them learn to respond effectively.

IMAGE CONTROL

Not only are images presented by media highly sexualized, but they are also unrealistic. Through the use of makeup, lighting, and computer reimaging, even models and actors are air brushed to remove blemishes and change body shape and size. In 2003, actor Kate Winslet showed public outrage when she realized that a *GQ* magazine cover featuring her had been airbrushed and changed to the point that she did not feel that it truly looked like her anymore. She said, "The retouching is excessive. I do not look like that and more importantly I don't desire to look like that."[26] Media have distorted the image of beauty so that not even people who are well known for their physical attractiveness can meet the standards. This "image control" impacts children and adolescents as they view pictures they believe to be real and then compare themselves to impossible standards of beauty.

After discussing this topic in a class that I was leading with a community youth group, one young adolescent boy said of a woman in a magazine advertisement, "She's not real. That person doesn't exist." The recognition of this reality was startling for him. Yet, how many adolescents and preadolescents do not understand this? How many girls look at pictures in magazines aimed at teenagers or women and think "I wish I looked like that," without knowing that the models themselves do not even look like that in person? In a study conducted by Duane Hargreaves, almost 70 percent of the adolescent girls sampled said that pictures in magazines influenced their conception of the ideal body size and shape.[27] Forty-five percent of them also said that those pictures made them want to lose weight or otherwise change their body shape to match the ideal. Those adolescent girls who viewed commercials depicting unrealistically thin models tended to then feel less confident, angrier, and more dissatisfied with their weight and appearance. Research has shown that mass media play a part in body dissatisfaction for both young men and young women.[28]

Even preschool-aged girls have demonstrated the internalization of the thin ideal. In a study published in 2010, researchers looked at how much girls aged three to five had internalized the thin ideal (the idea that beauty in females is equal to thinness) and how they attributed stereotypes to others because of their weight (fat equated with lazy, stupid, has no friends, while thin equated with nice, sweet, has friends).[29] A strong research base shows that children as young as three years of age are already buying into the idea that for females, thinness is equal to goodness.[30] The little girls who were studied showed evidence of having already begun to internalize the thin ideal and to stereotype others based solely on their weight.

What was interesting about this study is that it had girls choose from several different game pieces (like those in the game *Candy Land*), which were identical except for their weight. The children chose pieces that represented themselves and a best friend. Up until now, research studies have shown that children do not tend to distinguish that much between thin and average weights.[31] However, in this study, the girls more often chose thin game pieces over the average-sized ones. The authors suggest that this may be due to the fact that in recent years, the thin ideal has evolved from focusing just on adults and adolescents and is now being presented to very young children through products and entertainment and even through antiobesity health programming.[32]

For example, if you compare a Barbie doll from the 1970s to one manufactured today, the proportions of the doll have changed to emphasize the thin midsection and curvaceous breasts and behind. In 1998, Mattel released a more streamlined body style for Barbie with slimmer hips that one critic labeled as "not so much more healthy or realistic as simply pubescent,"[33] while another compared the new body style as reminiscent of a stick-thin supermodel rather than a real girl.[34] There have been many recent makeovers of several well-loved children's characters, such as Rainbow Brite and Trollz, to give them shapes and appearances more in line with the thin ideal. This change in the characterization of positive characters is likely connected to the change in young children's opinion of thin versus average weight. One of the saddest and most startling findings in this study was what the girls said about the different game pieces. For example, they said about the fatter piece "I hate her because she has a fat stomach" or "I don't want to be her, she's fat and ugly."[35]

This unrealistic image of beauty impacts the way girls feel about themselves and their looks as well as the way boys learn to judge girls' attractiveness. When repeatedly presented with ideals of beauty and the concept that this is what makes one valuable, it is difficult for children and adolescents not to be impacted. In my own research and work with youth organizations, when I asked adolescents how they felt about themselves when they watched their favorite shows, listened to their favorite music, or read their favorite magazine, many of them have reported feelings consistent with that found in the research. They say they do compare themselves to those images, and they often find themselves lacking.

The pressure to meet unrealistic beauty ideals manifests not just in the way that young people feel about themselves, but also in the way they think about relationships. Rather than looking for someone with whom they have something in common, or with whom they enjoy spending time, they are likely to focus first on the person's physical appearance. As one 16-year-old boy at a youth group meeting said to me when we were discussing the topic of dating, "Even if I really like a girl and have fun with her, if I don't think other guys will think she's hot, I probably won't ask her out. There's a lot of pressure to date a certain kind of girl, a hot girl." This provides a pattern for superficial relationships as children begin to understand romantic connection, with an emphasis on physical characteristics, rather than inner qualities and common interests. This is perhaps one of the most disturbing outcomes of sexualized media, the promotion of a shallow understanding not only of oneself but also of what it means to be in relationship with others.

GENDER STEREOTYPES

Media also present children with highly stereotyped versions of what it means to be male and female. A perusal of any toy store or toy catalog will demonstrate this quite effectively. In a visit to a large, nationally known toy store, I took note of the fact that the toys were divided into sections by color. Blue indicated toys for boys, while pink indicated those for girls. Items that were considered "unisex" fell under either the green or yellow category. The toys in the blue section were predominately cars and sporting equipment. So if a little girl really loves race cars, soccer, or basketball, she has to go into the "boy" section to find the toys that she is looking for. One day I was at a toy store with my own six-year-old daughter, and she told me that she really wanted a certain race car, but she did not think she could have it because, as she said, "it's for boys." Even when parents attempt to mitigate stereotyped messages, it is impossible for a child not to absorb some of the stereotypes. If a boy likes to play with dolls or stuffed animals, he has to go into the "girl" section to find them. This type of gender stereotyping is played out consistently in media for children of all ages. Very limited constructs of gender are presented as acceptable.[36]

These are clear examples of what the research tells us about gender stereotypes in both advertisements and entertainment aimed at children. In their book *Media and the American Child,* Comstock and Scharrer provide a historical overview of studies that evaluate the ways males and females are presented to children, both in entertainment and educational programming and products.[37] They conclude that the majority of the literature indicates that television programs, advertisements, computer games, and even educational software promote the gender stereotypes that present boys as active, adventurous risk takers, while girls are presented as passive, subdued nurturers. This research is supported by more recent studies.[38] When children repeatedly see these gender stereotypes, they begin to believe them.

Children identify with activities that they see someone of their own gender engaging in. Comstock and Scharrer make a strong case that when children view people in the media engaged in nontraditional roles, they begin to see it as more acceptable in general.[39] They also argue that when males or females are clearly linked to a specific job or attributes, those characteristics or careers then become unattractive to viewers of the opposite gender. The case is clear; if we as a culture want girls to be able to see themselves being an athlete, doctor, politician, and so forth someday, then we need to be sure we are showing them examples of women doing those things. If we want boys to be able to see themselves as being a positive father, teacher, nurturer, and artist someday, then we need to be sure they get the opportunity to see men doing those things. If children are not allowed to dream of certain options, that closes doors for them and prevents them from pursuing their passions and gifts. Our children deserve the chance to follow their dreams, to cultivate their talents, and to fully examine how each can make this world a better place, in big ways and small ones.

KEY AREAS OF IMPACT

As we begin to explore the literature regarding sexualized media from fields as varied as education, adolescent health, psychology, and communication, what you will notice is that three areas seem to emerge as being especially vulnerable to sexualized media. These three areas are self-concept, body image, and sexual behaviors. This book will consider all three of these areas through the lens of positive youth development.

Positive Youth Development

The positive youth development (PYD) perspective grew out of the applied developmental science field.[40] The core idea of PYD is that adolescents have strengths that exist within themselves and the systems that influence their development.[41] These systems include family, school, and peers. The resources within each system work together to provide the child with what are called *ecological developmental assets.*[42]

These assets function with the child's individual characteristics to lead a child to thrive. What does it mean to thrive? In the context of PYD, it means a child displays competence, confidence, character, connection, and caring.[43]

Richard M. Lerner defines *competence* as having a positive view of one's actions in specific areas, such as social, academic, cognitive, health, and vocation. *Confidence* is an overall positive self-worth and self-efficacy, in other words, believing that one is valuable and able to effect change in his or her environment. *Connection* indicates those positive relationships with people and institutions that impact the child's life, such as family, peers, school, and community. *Character* is respect for societal and cultural norms or a sense of right and wrong. *Caring or compassion* is defined as having empathy for others.[44] Throughout this book, I will continue to come back to the five C's of PYD to consider how parents and caregivers can harness a child's assets to help the child learn to respond effectively to sexualized and stereotyped media depictions.

In the context of PYD, self-concept will relate to the concept of confidence. I will explore self-concept in more detail in later chapters. Body image encompasses the way one thinks and feels about one's body. It can relate to a child's satisfaction with her own body, but it also includes her beliefs about her body's appearance and ability to perform certain actions.

Risky sexual behaviors are a concern for parents, professionals, and a child's community for many reasons. For one thing, risky sexual behavior is an important health issue in many countries. These behaviors include engaging in sexual relations with multiple partners, inconsistent or nonuse of condoms and other forms of birth control, and lack of discussion of protection and birth control with partners. In the United States, unplanned pregnancies and births and sexually transmitted disease and infection are national health concerns, with 38 percent of all births being unplanned and approximately 19 million cases of sexually transmitted disease or infection diagnosed each year.[45] These issues lead not only to difficulties for the individual involved, but also to increased health care and education costs for both the adolescent and the unintended child who is born to her. For adolescents who engage in risky sexual behaviors, the likelihood of acquiring HIV/AIDS and other sexually transmitted diseases and infections is increased, along with the likelihood of having an unintended pregnancy.[46]

These consequences of risky behavior lead to long-term results. In fact, a study that examined long-term reproductive health has linked risky sexual behaviors as an adolescent with young adulthood problems such as an overall high number of sex partners, diagnosis with a sexually transmitted disease or infection, and unplanned childbearing.[47] This research builds the case that early risky sexual behaviors in adolescence may persist into adulthood, increasing the chances of long-term health problems. It is imperative that parents, professionals, and communities consider both the short- and long-term consequences for adolescents who engage in risky sexual behaviors.

Each of these areas is important developmentally. Identity development is impacted by self-concept and body image. The choice an adolescent makes to engage in or avoid risky sexual behaviors impacts his or her long-term health and emotional and social well-being. With this in mind, I turn to the mediating variables and examine how they shape a child's response to sexualized media.

Media Influence

As we talk about the ways that variables within a child's life can mediate her response to sexualized media, it is important to remember the ways this type of media itself influences children and adolescents.

Self-Concept and Body Image

Sexualized media consistently promote the worldview that a girl's value is found in her ability to attract romantic interest. For boys, the idea is that a male should care about having sexual relationships with attractive women, and with as many as possible. This one-dimensional depiction of female value and male power provides children and adolescents with a very narrow idea of where a girl's worth comes from and puts a tremendous amount of pressure on girls to conform to the images that are presented as ideal.

Several studies have examined the relation between the consumption of objectifying media and adolescent girls' tendency to think of themselves as sexual objects and worry about their appearance. Simply viewing media that presents the thin ideal seems to lead to body dissatisfaction for girls as young as 11 years old.[48] Exposure to media that present females as sexual objects has been linked to low body esteem, dieting behaviors, and symptoms of anxiety and depression in girls as young as 13 years old.[49] Body dissatisfaction was found in girls aged 11 to 17 who frequently viewed television, although the same was not found for boys.[50] A study conducted by Dohnt and Tiggemann found that by the age of six years, girls were already talking about wanting a thinner body.[51] The girls in the study who watched music television shows and read appearance-focused magazines were more likely to be aware of the concept of dieting and be unhappy with their own appearance. A pattern emerges that links the consumption of sexualized media with body dissatisfaction and negative body behaviors such as dieting for girls even down to the age of six.

Sexual Behaviors

Researchers have been studying the relation between the consumption of sexual content in media and adolescent sexual behavior. Associations have been found between the consumption of sexualized media and sexual activity as well as the intention to be sexually active in the future in people between the ages of 12 and 20.[52] Adolescents who are exposed to more sexual content in the media and who view the media as supportive of teen sexual behavior report more sexual activity and the intention to engage in such activity again.[53] Research shows that exposure to sexual content not only predicts sexual activity and pregnancy, but may also hasten it.[54] A national longitudinal study that was conducted in 2008 found that adolescents between the ages of 12 and 17 who viewed television with high levels of sexual content were twice as likely to experience pregnancy in the next three years than those teens with low levels of exposure.[55]

It is important to be aware of these connections between viewing sexualized media and adolescent attitudes and behaviors. Children and adolescents are being influenced by sexualized media in everything from the way they feel about their bodies to dieting behaviors to risky sexual activity. These are very real and very important effects, and they are areas in which families and communities can also have an impact.

MEDIATING VARIABLES

So what are parents, professionals, and communities to do? How do they address these issues in ways that make a difference? The truth is, media exposure does not occur in a vacuum. Children live within a complex environment with many different variables influencing the way they process information. Media messages are pervasive, and they are powerful, but they are mediated by strong interpersonal variables within a child's life. This chapter will provide a brief overview of the mediating variables, and the following chapters will provide an opportunity to take a closer look at them.

Culture of Celebrity

Increased accessibility has led children to be more exposed than ever to the lure of the culture of celebrity. Twenty-four-hour access to information about one's favorite celebrity means that an adolescent with a mobile device can surf the web constantly in search of new gossip or new photos. As opportunity increases for exposure, so too does the level at which celebrities use their sexuality to spice up their image and garner more attention. Children and adolescents who choose to become deeply involved in the culture of celebrity increase their chances of being exposed to sexualized imagery and its effects. It is vital that families and other caring adults are aware of the ways that a child's involvement in the culture of celebrity may be harmful.

Family

Family clearly matters when it comes to two issues. First, parents and other caregivers are the first people in a child's life who set boundaries on the child's media exposure. Although there may be a lot of sexualized media available to children, the parents themselves are in the primary position to limit how much of this type of media their own child engages with and to make sure that their child is exposed to positive, healthy media depictions. Second, parents who take the opportunity to do so are in a prime position to help their child learn to openly discuss the types of messages that media send and how to respond to them. Primary caregivers or involved adults can provide children and adolescents with the tools to become critical consumers of media as they work with them to evaluate the messages they are receiving and begin to consider if they will accept or reject each message. The place of family in helping children learn to respond to sexualized and stereotyped media cannot be emphasized strongly enough.

Gender

Although popular responses to sexualized media have often taken the perspective that it is extremely harmful to girls, I believe that it presents a dilemma for both boys and girls. As girls are bombarded with messages that tell them that their value lies in their physical appearance, it will be difficult for them to maintain their self-esteem and see their value in more diverse characteristics. For boys, the problem affects the way they learn to relate to females. With a focus on using physical appearance as the primary way of evaluating the worth of their female friends and acquaintances, boys miss out on the deeper relationships that can be built between those who share common interests and genuine liking. For both boys and girls, sexualized media messages emphasize romance and physical relationships over friendship and authentic emotional connection. Many products marketed toward children are the epitome of the sexualized stereotypes that are unhealthy for both boys and girls. Boys learn to emphasize physical attractiveness in females with whom they have a relationship, while the pinnacle of success for girls is to become valuable by showing off their bodies. This is a far cry from the goals that most caring adults have for the children in their lives.

Community Systems

Organizations that focus on building a community that advocates specific value systems may provide guidance in helping young people negotiate the sexualized messages they receive from the media. For example, communities that advocate working as a group toward similar goals, such as scouting and churches, can provide a positive community for children. Sports teams can provide shared goals and values that promote working together. The set of values that are communicated to adolescents in these communities, along with the accountability for their actions due to the encouragement of emotional intimacy, is an important piece of understanding the best way to help children learn to respond to sexualized media.

Each of these variables plays an important part in mediating the effects of the sexualized messages that are consistently directed at children and adolescents. Each of them works with the others to either help the child learn to respond to sexualized media or to leave him or her open to receiving these messages with little guidance. The goal of caring adults should be to provide the children and adolescents in their lives with the tools they need to become savvy media consumers. External blocking systems such as legislation, filters, and so forth combined with the approach of teaching children to recognize sexualized messages, talk about and analyze them, plan an appropriate response, stand up for their own values, and build a community of support lead children toward becoming active, critical media consumers. Children are vulnerable to sexualized messages, but by understanding and harnessing the power of these interpersonal mediating variables, caring adults can reduce that vulnerability and increase the child's ability to respond effectively. These are important tools in combating the sexualization of childhood.

IN THEIR VOICES

Brittany Huckabee is an independent filmmaker who most recently produced and edited Sexy Baby, *a documentary that follows a former porn star in the midst of an identity crisis, a young woman undergoing a controversial surgery, and a 12-year-old girl growing up faster than her parents can handle.*

> We're the first generation to have what we have, so there's no one to guide us. We are the pioneers.
>
> —Winnifred, 12

As a filmmaker I am most interested in stories about what happens in our rapidly changing world as old rules are unsettled and reconstructed. Thanks to the Internet and mobile technologies, sexualized imagery and messaging had become inescapable. And it seems to be filtering into the lives of ordinary people in unprecedented ways. From middle school to middle age and beyond, sexy has become the new imperative. As we delved into the lives of our characters and surveyed their influences, we kept coming back to one place: the adult-entertainment industry. Ours is a culture where porn stars double as American Apparel models, ménages à trois are standard pop-music-video fare, and sex tapes transform heiresses into celebrities. Call it the trickle-down effect—and it can be both overt and subtle.

In the film, 22-year-old plastic surgery patient Laura becomes obsessed with the appearance of her genitals based on comments from a porn-loving boyfriend. Nichole, a former stripper and adult film star, notes attempts by young women in nightclubs to mimic strippers, and by ordinary men to "pull porn moves" in bed. A friend of 12-year-old Winnifred describes her accidental introduction to sex via hardcore online porn, while Winnifred herself posts sexy photos to Facebook—images which, she confides, sometimes set the bar for real-life conduct. Such photos capture teens appearing to mimic the celebrities they see in entertainment magazines, who in turn seem to be mimicking poses and behavior straight out of strip clubs and porn sets. This infiltration has consequences: as we learn from interviews with young adults across the country, porn culture is radically reshaping expectations about sex and relationships among women and men alike.

When I was Winnifred's age, my conservative Christian parents could reasonably expect to protect me from unwanted media. I did my best to sneak glimpses of MTV at friends' houses and occasionally managed to check out a questionable book at the public library, but the options were limited. That is no longer the case for families who want to be part of the modern world. No matter where you live or what you believe, exposure is a given. Sheltering is obsolete. I would argue that parents no longer have a choice but to become part of the conversation. It is the only way we can hope to guide this generation of children as they navigate the ever-changing rules of our technologically enabled, sexually charged culture. Books like this one can help facilitate the interventions necessary to produce grounded, media-literate young adults like Winnifred—who, at the end of the film, still struggles with the sexiness imperative but recognizes its limits. "I do want to change people's lives," she concludes, "and I'm not going to do that by being sexy."

2

Development in Context

With adolescents being exposed to media an average of over 10 hours and 45 minutes per day and with media messages consistently repeating that females are valued primarily for their sexual attractiveness, is there any hope?[1] The answer is a resounding "yes!" The systems in a child's life can exert a powerful influence on the way that sexualized and stereotyped messages influence the child or adolescent.

As a blogger, speaker, and professor, I often hear from people who do not believe that media and marketing really impact children. These people seem quite certain that children can be exposed to any kind of media, marketing, or product and it does not affect them as long as parents are teaching their child specific values. For example, several commenters on blog posts, Twitter, and my Facebook page have stated that as long as a parent teaches girls that their value comes from within, no amount of exposure to sexualized and objectifying media or marketing will impact that girl's belief about where her value lies.

But I am not buying that. Parenting is not performed without context, and messages from the environment do matter. From a psychological perspective, it is important to understand how the environment impacts children and the long history of research that supports that idea.

CHILD DEVELOPMENT IN CONTEXT

The bioecological theory of development can serve as a helpful model to understand how the mediating variables of the culture of celebrity, family, gender, and community systems impact a child's response to sexualized media. Urie Bronfenbrenner developed this model, which is called the bioecological model, because he believed that both a child's temperament and the setting in which she lives lead the child to learn, think, and develop in particular ways.[2]

This perspective provides a way of looking at the forces of influence in a child's environment. I find the bioecological model particularly helpful in understanding what leads children to develop in certain ways. What leads to certain effective or ineffective behaviors? What causes certain values to be adopted or rejected? In all of my years of working with families, adolescents, and children, what I have noticed is that there are multiple forces that influence the way the child develops and the choices that he or she makes. In my experience, Bronfenbrenner's model provides the best paradigm for understanding development as it considers the many systems that influence a child and how those systems interact with one another.

Within this bioecological framework, there are four components that are crucial to child development:

- Process
- Person
- Context
- Time

In short, the acronym PPCT represents these components.[3]

This model suggests that a child develops through the process of interacting with things within the immediate environment, such as family and community, but also through interactions with things within the wider environment, such as media and marketing. Components of the person him- or herself, such as gender, race, temperament, and past experience, influence the way the child interprets and responds to that interaction. The context of the systems of influence, such as what the child is learning within the family, community, or his or her larger culture, will shape the child's understanding of and ability to respond to interactions with media and marketing. The time period in which the child is growing and learning influences the type of environment with which he or she will interact.

Children growing up today are living within a time that is different from any other when it comes to media and marketing exposure. From the car to the school halls, children are inundated with media and marketing messages. Both who a child is individually and the contexts within his or her life, such as family and community, will shape the way the child processes his or her interactions with sexualized media.

The concept of process helps us understand the idea that mediating variables, such as family, community, and gender, influence a child's response to sexualized media. Bronfenbrenner says that "development takes place through processes of progressively more complex reciprocal interaction between an active, evolving . . . human . . . and the persons, objects, and symbols in its immediate external environment."[4]

It is through these everyday interactions with other people and the environment that the child begins to make sense of the world and understand his or her place within it.[5] This is why it is vital for caregivers, professionals, and communities to be aware of the impact that sexualized media and marketing have on a child's development. Once the caregiver understands that sexualized messages promote the concept that female power comes from sexual attractiveness and that males are sexual consumers, they can begin to harness the strength of the family and community to promote media literacy. They can begin to provide the child with a context that supports an active rather than a passive relationship to media and marketing. This shifts a child into being actively involved in critiquing the messages he or she receives through media and marketing.

Bronfenbrenner viewed the process of development as one in which the child can learn to fit in to the existing environment and those expectations, but can also change the order of things through his or her own actions.[6] When we provide children with the tools to critique and challenge the messages from sexualized media and marketing, they can become change makers. Their actions through media literacy programs, activism, and creation lead to change in their environment. At the end of this book, I will present some specific ways children can become agents of change through media creation and activism.

The bioecological model provides a way to understand different types of systems that interrelate to influence development. The *microsystem* is the setting in which the individual behaves at any given moment.[7] Bronfenbrenner describes the microsystem as "a pattern of activities, roles, and interpersonal relations experienced by the developing person in a given face-to-face setting with particular physical and material features and containing other persons with distinctive characteristics of temperament, personality, and systems of belief."[8] We can think of the people who a child interacts with on a daily basis as belonging in the child's microsystem. This would include parents, siblings, and peers.

The *mesosystem* "comprises the linkages and processes taking place between two or more settings containing the developing person (e.g., the relations between home and school, school, and workplace)."[9] The mesosystems are just the interactions between the different systems that allow them to influence one another. For example, a child's home and school systems interact through homework assignments, parents volunteering in the school, and so forth. These systems influence one another as they communicate with one another on a regular basis.

Exosystems are influences that are felt daily but are less direct. Bronfenbrenner defined the exosystem as "the linkage and processes taking place between two or more settings, at least one of which does not ordinarily contain the developing person, but in which events occur that influence processes within the immediate setting that does contain that person."[10] An example of an exosystem would be the mass media, because the child is not usually directly involved in producing mass media, but the mass media interact with and influence the contexts in which the child lives, such as the home, school, and peer groups.

The last type of interrelated system from Bronfenbrenner's model is the *macrosystem*. The macrosystem "consists of the overarching pattern of micro-, . . . and exosystems characteristic of a given culture, subculture, or other broader social context."[11] Now let's take a closer look at each system and its part in influencing a child's response to sexualized media.

Microsystems

The child, as the person in the PPCT model, is a part of the microsystem. The temperament that she is born with, her emotional responses, and her abilities all influence the way she relates to those in her immediate environment.[12] The child brings three different types of characteristics into the environment to influence it:

- *Demand characteristics.* These are things such as age, gender, skin color, and physical characteristics.[13] As I will explain later in this book, gender is a mediating variable that impacts how a child responds to sexualized media and how that child is targeted by such media.

- *Resource characteristics.* These are the resources that a person brings to any interaction, such as past experiences, intelligence, skills, social skills, and material resources.[14] The family often impacts these resources. Parents can provide their children with either rich or poor resources for responding to the images and narratives of sexualized media and marketing. For example, a parent may leave the television on unmonitored and allow a child to consume media without any feedback. On the other hand, a parent may monitor a child's television consumption and watch it with her, providing prompts and questions that allow the child to build media literacy skills. The child in the first example approaches sexualized media with fewer resources than the second child.

- *Force characteristics.* These have to do with differences of temperament, motivation, and so forth.[15] These are important when we think about how sexualized media influence children because some children may be more prone to accepting the messages than others due to their own innate desire to fit in and please others. Children with a high need for acceptance may need more support in order to make critical decisions about sexualized media than those children with a lower need for acceptance.

There are many different opinions regarding the concept of temperament. However, the generally accepted definition integrates those different perspectives to provide us with an overarching framework. This definition views temperament as "early emerging basic dispositions in the domains of activity, affectivity, attention, and self-regulation, and these dispositions are the product of complex interactions among genetic, biological, and environmental factors across time."[16] Activity can be understood as a child's level of physical movement. Affectivity is a child's general emotional state, whether positive or negative, happy or sad. Attention is a child's ability to concentrate on his or her immediate environment and what is happening in it. Self-regulation is the child's ability to control his or her behavioral response to situations in the environment, regardless of the child's current feelings.[17] All of these traits play a part in the way a child interacts with his or her environment.

The first and closest system of influence is the child's immediate environment of the family. The child and the family function together to help the child learn to interpret the environment. The family is influential in terms of sexual socialization[18] because a child begins to understand sexuality through the beliefs that the parent shares about sexual behaviors, gender roles, and sexual values.[19]

Understanding this process means understanding not only what type of media is in the home, but also how the parent and child interact around that media. When a stereotypical gender role is presented through media, what happens within the home? Does the parent point it out and discuss it with the child? Does the parent ignore it? Does the parent endorse it? Here is an example of a conversation starter that parents and those who work with children and adolescents might use to promote active media consumption.

Conversation Starter

I went to see the Disney movie *Brave* with my daughters, who were 12, 11, and 8 years old at the time. The heroine of the movie is a princess named Merida. Merida is supposed to marry a prince who will win her hand in an archery contest. But Merida does not want to get married, so she enters the contest and wins her own hand. This pattern of behavior was very different from most of the other Disney princess stories that my daughters had seen, such as *Snow White, Cinderella*, or *Sleeping Beauty*. They noticed this and we talked about it. I asked my eight-year-old daughter a few questions and was interested to hear her thoughts about this different kind of princess. First, I asked a general question to get the conversation started, "What did you think about the movie *Brave*?"

It was different from other princess movies. Most of the Disney princesses don't look like real people, . . . they're too perfect. Merida is like a real person. She has freckles and hair that doesn't look perfect. Her hair acts like real hair! Her brothers have ears that stick out, all the people in the story look like real people, they're not perfect looking. I liked that. And, Disney princesses don't usually do anything wrong. I liked that Merida made mistakes but then was able to fix them and learn something.

I noticed that there's not really a boy involved in the story that goes to save the day. She's the one who's saving the day, with her mom. In *Sleeping Beauty* and *Snow White*, the prince saves the day. But in *Brave*, Merida and her mom save the day, and her dad works with them, so it's really about the family saving the day.

I then followed up with a direct question, "What did you like about *Brave*?"

I liked how Merida could shoot arrows and ride horses. Even though she was a princess, she didn't want to act all fancy and wear fancy dresses and things like that. I liked that she didn't want to get married because most princesses in the movies really focus their life on getting married and things. Merida was different. She wanted to be a princess but be a normal person who could do her own thing.

In most Disney movies, the girl has something bad happen to her and someone saves her. In *Brave* something happens but she learns a lesson and has to solve the problem. Disney princesses don't usually have weapons. Somebody else fights for them. Merida fights for herself, and her mom and family fight with her. I like that they stick together.

It is important to help children learn to think about the positives and negatives of any media, so I also asked, "What didn't you like about *Brave*?" My daughter answered, "I didn't like it when Merida and her mom were fighting. They weren't listening to each other. But, I liked that they learned that they needed to listen to each other. They learned to listen to each other and understand each other's ideas."

An important part of media literacy is helping children apply what they have seen in media to their own lives, so I asked, "Merida learned some important things in the movie. What did you learn from watching the movie? Are there ideas that you're taking away from it?"

For a long time people have been thinking that boys do the fighting instead of the girls. That boys are stronger than girls in lots of ways. That makes me feel like girls aren't strong enough to fight for themselves, to stand up for themselves, to be the hero who solves the problem. Seeing Merida fight for herself and her mom made me feel like girls can be the hero. As a girl, I see that people think girls aren't strong enough to stand up for themselves, but seeing Merida makes me feel that they can. *Brave* also shows boys that girls aren't just weak and pretty, they can be smart, they can be strong. Being a girl isn't just about being pretty. That makes me feel really nice inside, that this message is getting out into the world.

Hearing my daughter's perspective was eye-opening for me. Being an assertive girl herself, I thought she would like Merida's character because of her independence and strong will. What I did not expect to hear were the ideas about learning to work out difficulties in relationships. I was not even certain if she would notice that there was no romance in this film compared to other princess movies. But she did notice, and she liked that. At her age, romance is not high on her list of priorities, but identifying herself with strong characters is. The fact that she is beginning to see that media carries messages that can inform and persuade people is a huge step toward becoming a critical consumer of media.

Other structures that form part of the child's microsystem are school, religion, and community groups that a child regularly attends such as sports, scouting, performing arts, and so forth. These structures are considered prime areas of influence on child development. Companies have begun to recognize this fact and have started promoting their products and programming through different venues, such as sports arenas and even public schools.

In the past 10 years, schools have become fertile ground for product sales and direct and indirect marketing of products by advertisers. Large companies provide schools with money and other benefits if they choose to allow products to be advertised or sold on school grounds. These marketing maneuvers can range from a free book cover with a product advertisement on it to commercials on educational current event programs made specifically for schools to programs that provide children with coupons for free products if they achieve certain academic goals. For example, Pizza Hut has a school-based program that rewards children who read a certain number of books by giving them a coupon for a free personal pan pizza. Scholastic has formed partnerships for school programming with several brands such as Bratz and has used their school-based book clubs and fairs to sell products other than books, such as makeup and lip gloss.

It has been reported that over half of all primary schools in the United States participate in some form of product marketing program.[20] In the annual reports on "Schoolhouse Commercialism Trends," the authors indicate that advertisers have integrated schools into their marketing plans.[21]

Although schools may have the opportunity to promote healthy values for children, there is also the exposure in many schools to companies that are directly connected to sexualized media. Families can help children think about and respond to whatever they are presented at school. Marketers have clearly targeted children within the school setting, so we should not assume that every message a child gets at school is valid. Instead, caring adults must pay close attention to things like which products and companies are sponsoring activities, which reward programs are being offered, and how each of those companies are connected to sexualized media messages in general. Adults also need to know which toys, games, and movies are being used at the school. If the school is given "free" toys or books from a company, it is likely for marketing purposes. Being aware of this allows caregivers to watch more closely for the ways that children may be influenced while they are in the school environment and then respond as they see fit.

Community activities are considered an important part of the microsystem as well. For children actively involved in religious, scouting, sports, or other community groups, these often consume a fair amount of time and provide both a guideline for behavior and accountability in terms of publicly demonstrating behaviors that are consistent with stated beliefs. Later in this book I will revisit the place that community groups play in promoting specific value systems and influencing a child's response to sexualized media. Systems that promote specific ideals regarding individual value are influential in establishing a child's understanding of what makes a person significant. Scouting and other volunteer groups teach the importance of community service, performing arts groups promote achievement, religious groups foster shared moral standards and service, and sporting groups encourage physical prowess and teamwork. These different types of groups endorse a value system that aids children in seeing themselves as important as they engage with the world around them.

Another component of the microsystem that must be considered is the role of peers. Peers play a large part in the life of the child and have a growing influence as a child moves into adolescence. For example, Potard, Courtois, and Rusch found that peers influence both adolescents' sexual attitudes and behaviors.[22] This is no secret to those who work or live with adolescents. Developmentally, this is a life stage when we expect children to become more attached to their peers and seek their approval rather than looking to their family as the primary source of acceptance.

As children move into the adolescent stage, they begin to look to their peers for social guidance in many different ways. From choice of dress to involvement in romantic relationships and views on sexual behaviors, adolescents frequently follow the trends being demonstrated by peers with whom they most closely relate. This can be a disturbing fact when viewed through the lens of sexualized media, because in both dramas and "reality" television aimed at adolescents, teens are encouraged to identify with the actors or participants as peers. With promotional campaigns that state that teen stars are "just like you," networks promote these shows as extensions of friendships themselves, as representations of what adolescents are doing in real life. When sexualized media become an extension of what an adolescent views as his or her own peers, then the messages become much stronger and more influential because of the power of the peer relationship at this developmental stage.[23] In fact, some researchers have proposed that mass media may be considered a "sexual super peer" in providing large amounts of information about sexuality, which leads to more risky sexual behaviors in those adolescents who consume a lot of media.[24] This dynamic will be explored further in Chapter 4, which examines the culture of celebrity and how it influences a child's response to sexualized media.

Understanding the part that peers play in helping children and adolescents respond to sexualized and stereotyped media is vital for families and communities. Professionals who work with children and adolescents have opportunities to provide them with a safe place to talk with one another about sexualized popular culture.

Exosystems

These are systems that influence the child indirectly, such as mass media, social unrest, or the parental workplace. The function of the exosystem is to communicate the values of larger groups that are important to an individual's life. Within any given community, for example, there are certain values that are promoted more heavily than others, and this shapes the child's values as well. The bioecological model of child development is interactive, and the child can choose to accept the values associated with the exosystems or may respond by rejecting them. But whichever way she or he responds, these entities are closely aligned with the values that the child adopts. As a part of the exosystem, mass media often reflect prevailing beliefs and value systems about sexuality and gender stereotypes that are an element of the macroculture, or the broader influences within a child's life.

Conversation Starter

Providing a child with a guide for considering media messages allows the child to critically analyze the message and identify conflicts between the values he or she is learning within the microsystem and what is being promoted through the exosystem. In media literacy workshops, I have worked with children and adolescents to develop a way of looking at pieces of media and marketing that gives them a template for thinking about media. Using Hobbs's guidelines, we think about such questions as:

- Who is the creator of the piece and what is its purpose?
- How does the creator of the piece attract and hold your attention?
- What lifestyles, values, and worldviews are represented?
- How might different people interpret this message?
- What is left out?[25]

This is a great exercise to go through with children at home and in small groups in a community setting. For younger children, you may use simpler language, but these concepts are ones that even preschoolers can understand and walk through with guidance. Once you have given them this tool, they will begin to use it on their own.

For example, my family was walking through the downtown area of a large city. After having silently observed several billboards and advertisements in public places featuring semiclothed women, my then nine-year-old daughter, Catherine, asked me, "Why are women's bodies used as posters to sell stuff?" I asked her what she meant, and she said, "It's like companies put what they want to sell out there and put a woman's body by it, even if it has nothing to do with her. They use her body to sell their stuff." Without my prompting, Catherine had started to walk through the steps above to evaluate a media or marketing message. She had asked herself who makes these advertisements? What are they trying to sell? What techniques are they using to sell their product? How might different people feel about or be impacted by these advertisements? What is left out? From her perspective, the women in the advertisements were being portrayed as objects or "posters" to sell products that may not be related to women at all. This was a great opportunity for us to talk about how what she is learning in our home about what makes a woman valuable compares to the exosystem messages through these advertisements.

Macrosystem

The macrosystem can be understood as the culture at large. This is an influential force in the child's life that includes things like society and the particular culture and subculture in which the child is growing up. Culture is especially important in presenting the child with general belief systems, lifestyles and options, and acceptable patterns of social behavior.

I stated earlier that the bioecological model stresses the interactivity of the systems in influencing a child's development. A specific example can demonstrate how these systems influence one another in a child's life. In 2010, a viral video hit the Internet of a group of eight- and nine-year-old girls dancing to Beyoncé's song "Single Ladies" while dressed in what appeared to be a child's version of lingerie, complete with thigh-high hose, a bra-like top, and hot pants. Because the little girls were repeating some of the dance moves that the singer performed in the official video for the song, they were bumping, grinding, and shimmying. To many people who saw the video on the Internet, this was a clear case of the sexualization of children. And yet, in an interview with George Stephanopoulos, the parents of two of the girls defended both the costumes and the dance moves as appropriate, given the fact that they were in a dance competition.[26] These parents were using the context of the behavior to excuse it. One of the mothers even said she would not let her child wear that outfit anywhere else, but because it was at a dance competition, it was appropriate. Apparently, she was making a very specific exception to her own set of microsystem values to fit the behavior into the exosystem.

This example illustrates the interactivity of systems of influence within a child's life. The macrosystem of our culture in general has begun to accept sexualized behavior used to garner attention, and sexualized media are often used to promote celebrities in the pursuit of fame and fortune. The mass media send the message that it is appropriate for little girls to dress as sexualized grown women through television programs such as *Toddlers and Tiaras* and products such as Baby Bratz, which have baby dolls wearing makeup, low-cut skirts, and belly shirts. Clothes that are marketed to children are sometimes scaled-down versions of adult labels, such as Beyoncé's House of Dereon's children's line. The larger community of the dance competitions has promoted the idea that it is acceptable for children to wear revealing clothes when dancing. These are exosystem ideas.

Now we come to the place of the interactivity that occurs between these larger systems and the microsystems. Within these systems you have the dance school that these girls attended and their families and close friends. If anyone at this level had thought to critique the ideas being promoted by the macro- and exosystems, then the girls might have worn different costumes, performed different dance moves, or danced to a different song completely.

To really grasp the power of the systems within the bioecological model, we have to understand that they interact with one another and with the child to influence development. In situations similar to the one described above, I have seen the power of the microsystem in challenging the values of the exosystem. In one instance, a friend of mine, Marcia, complained to a large retail store about a T-shirt they were selling that she found offensive. This is what she shared with me about this incident.

When I saw the shirt at a large national retailer that said, "Boyfriends are fun to toy with," I got angry that this message about "toying" with men would be plastered across the chests of 10-year-olds like my daughter. I wondered if I was the only one bothered by this shirt. While I was standing there, an employee walked by and asked if he could help me. I told him that the shirt gave a message that was inappropriate and offensive and that it shouldn't be marketed to children. And I asked him to pass that on to the manager. Speaking with this employee was already more than I had planned to do. My plan was to put the photo on Facebook and discuss the terrible plight of our society and the awful message. My plans were to talk about it with those who were like-minded and not really do anything. When I got home, I called back to the store and asked to speak to the manager. After she politely listened to my concerns, she told me that the national headquarters had asked stores across the nation to remove this. I'm certain that I was only one of many voices, but it is amazing to be a part of this act of victory for my three daughters, ages 10, 5, and 3. At first, I felt that I was simply defending my own children. In retrospect, I think that I was speaking out against the dehumanization and sexualization of all females. By doing so, I won a victory for all of our children.[27]

This was a commanding stance on the part of this mother, and it made a difference! Had she not felt empowered to exert her own influence on the systems in which her children were functioning, things would not have changed. It is vital that caregivers understand that they have the power to interact with the systems that influence children. From signing a petition to talking to a teacher, it is a caregiver's right and privilege to be able to step in and be willing to speak up when she or he does not agree with something that is happening within a child's world.

The interactivity of the bioecological perspective means that the child and family have the ability to respond to the messages that are being sent by media and culture. When an adult takes this perspective, it makes sense to begin to think of both herself and the children in her life as powerful. We will continually come back to the idea that both caring adults and children must interact purposefully with the systems in which they function and see themselves as people who can change those systems. Parents and caregivers need to think of themselves and their children as world changers, people who can challenge and change systems with which they do not agree.

POSITIVE YOUTH DEVELOPMENT AND IDENTITY

The PYD system focuses on the assets that a child has and how those work together to help a child thrive. The following sections will consider the five C's of PYD and how each of these components of thriving relates to sexualized media and marketing.

Competence

Competence is how well someone does the things they consider to be important. Adults need to ask themselves, "What am I teaching the children in my life about what is important for them to do or be?" In order to help a child learn to respond actively to media messages, it is vital for caregivers to help children see themselves as competent. Caregivers must identify those important tasks in life. Many adults will have specific areas that they put more emphasis on than others, such as academics, sports, musical ability, and so forth. Think about this: What kind of skills does this child need to stand up to the media's pressure? When put up against these powerful, pervasive messages, what will help this child learn to critically evaluate rather than just accept those messages? The skills I want to see children master in this capacity are, at the core, about identity, values, and sharing their own message with the world. I want them to be able to identify their own values. How can children know that sexualized media value the wrong things in a person if they have not been taught where their true value lies? Open and purposeful conversations about what makes a person valuable and critiquing other representations of value provide children with a good background to begin to identify their own value system.

I want children to be able to openly and respectfully present their own values to others. That means spending time talking through what makes a person valuable and helping children learn to articulate their own ideas of value. Children and adolescents can learn how to share their own message with the world when given the opportunity. For example, a teenage friend of mine named Haley started a program to provide stuffed bunnies and bears to children in the hospital when she was five years old. She has now been spearheading this program for 13 years and has spoken on radio, television, and done multiple presentations sharing her message. She has identified what she believes to be important, why she believes it, and how to share her message effectively. I asked Haley to share the story about how she started her program, the part that her parents played in supporting her, and her thoughts on how parents can help their children make efforts to be world changers. Here is what Haley shared with me.

I started the program when I was five years old because I saw a commercial from St. Jude's Hospital about kids with cancer. I didn't really understand what a hospital was, I thought it was a bad place. My mom took me to Cooks Children's Hospital in Fort Worth for a tour so that I could see that it was where kids went to get help! While we were there I saw everything, but the one place that stuck out to me the most was the Prayer Bear room. This was where they kept all of the stuffed animals, mostly bears, to give to the children. I asked them what they did for Easter and they said they still gave them bears. At the age of five, I thought that was awful. I thought Easter was all about bunnies. That's when I told them that I would bring bunnies at Easter time, and it has grown ever since! My parents have been the most supportive and helpful people with the drive. My mom was the heart and soul behind it when I was younger. There's no way it would be where it is today without her. My dad has helped me with my corporate sponsors.

The program has grown more than I had ever imagined. We started out our first year with just my church and my school and donated 1,400 stuffed animals. Thirteen years later, we have been able to donate a total of 28,772 stuffed animals with the help of over 30 other schools and churches.

Honestly, when helping kids think about being world changers, I wouldn't say think big. I would say think small, because a small gesture can have a huge impact. The bunny drive was a very easy project for other people. All they had to do was put out a box and make an announcement to bring a stuffed animal for the hospital. It was very simple, but I know it touched the lives of many and has taught a lot of young kids how easy it can be to give back to their community.[28]

Haley's parents fostered in her the belief that she was competent to make the world a better place. That gave her the confidence to attempt to start the Bunnies & Bears program. Children need to be able to stand up even when it makes them stand out in the crowd. That is the kind of identity that fosters competence in children.

Adults need to have conversations with children and adolescents about the ways they can make a difference in the world. Caregivers need to be willing to listen respectfully to a child's ideas and then give the child their own in response. When Haley came up with the idea for the Bunnies & Bears program for sick children, her mother talked with her about what her goals were and then they thought together about the steps required to reach them.

Parents can help children begin to see themselves as competent by taking several specific steps. First, listen to find out what the child is passionate about and answer his or her questions honestly. What if Haley's mother had not believed that her daughter was competent emotionally to learn about childhood cancer? What if, instead of answering Haley's questions, she had ignored them or changed the subject repeatedly? The Bunnies & Bears program would never have served the thousands of children that it has. Using developmentally sensitive information and language, approach your child's questions about the world around him or her with the belief that your child is competent to consider the issue.

Second, help the child gather the information he or she needs to make a difference. Haley's mother took her to a local children's hospital to learn how sick children are cared for. She never imagined that a simple visit would grow into a 13-year project! But when Haley found out about the Prayer Bear project and wanted to develop an Easter project with bunnies, her mother was able to guide her through the process of learning what might need to be done to begin such a campaign. Third, help your child break the project down into small steps. As Haley so aptly said, the Bunny & Bear project is really about just asking people to share something small with a child in need. When Haley's parents were able to help her think about each step that needed to be accomplished in order to launch and run the campaign, it made it more manageable to her. And she grew in the belief that she was competent to effect change in the world, to make a difference in a real way.

Confidence

Confidence refers to an internal sense of overall positive self-worth and self-efficacy.[29] Albert Bandura defined self-efficacy as "the conviction that one can successfully execute the behavior required to produced the desired outcome."[30] Self-efficacy is a person's belief in his or her ability to succeed in specific situations and that person's evaluation of his or her effectiveness, competence, and causal agency.[31] We can think of self-efficacy, from a global perspective, as how much a child believes that he or she can influence his or her environment. But we can also consider self-efficacy in specific domains, such as sexuality. Sexual self-efficacy is the belief in one's ability to control one's own behavior and the key aspects of a sexual interaction.[32] Research has found that sexual self-efficacy is important in the areas of sexual risk taking, contraceptive use, and being able to resist pressure to engage in unwanted sexual acts.[33]

Confidence is connected to how well and to what extent a person can control him- or herself and his or her environment and influence others. To become world changers, children must perceive themselves as being able to effect change in the world around them. The adults in their lives need to give them choices first in little things and then greater things as they prove themselves able to make responsible decisions. For instance, if a parent allows a child to choose his own clothing for the day, it is not so important if his pants and shirt do not match exactly, is it? Giving a younger child the option to choose his own outfit, within reason, or choose which chore to do first, lays the groundwork for bigger choices later. It is not helpful to "fix" everything when the child makes a choice that is not effective or appropriate.

When caregivers allow children to experience negative consequences early on for small things, children learn that their actions have consequences. They are powerful! Whatever choice they make, it will lead to a consequence. Those consequences may be negative or they may be positive, but they will be there. Adults need to step away from shortchanging a child's agency by making all of the child's choices or fixing all of his or her mistakes. Teach children that they have the power to effect change in their environment! There is no stronger message to someone we hope will one day become a world changer. Children with confidence and self-efficacy view themselves as agents in their own lives. This means they believe they can act purposefully to achieve their goals. This is a far cry from viewing oneself as an object, which is the view promoted by sexualized media. People who view themselves as objects are those who think of themselves as primarily valuable for the pleasure they can give others. Caring adults want to promote a sense of agency in a child rather than an objectified view.

Confidence comes from experiencing challenge and success.[34] Bandura found that children developed self-efficacy as they performed a task successfully, saw others complete tasks successfully, and were assured by a trusted other that they could perform a task successfully.[35] How can parents provide a child with the opportunity to try new things and to grow through experience? Let me share a personal example.

When my daughter, Rylan, was in first grade, her teacher had the students in her class make bath salts for Mother's Day. Rylan became fascinated with the process and wanted to learn how to make more bath products. I had no idea how to make bath products, but we decided to research it and buy a few supplies so she could try some recipes. Once she had experimented for a while, she decided she wanted to make bath bombs, which are hard-packed balls that dissolve and become fizzy when wet. This is a complicated formula, especially for a seven-year-old. She failed many times before she was able to make a bath bomb. But each failure led to learning and eventually to success. By the time Rylan was in fourth grade, she had made her own label, distributed flyers at her school, and was selling her products. By taking a chance, she had learned something new and had grown and developed a skill. Parents must remember that confidence comes not just from success but also from experiencing challenges. Rylan's greatest success with her business came when she was able to donate a percentage of her profits to a humanitarian organization that digs wells to provide fresh water for people living in poverty. Through this experience, she learned not just that she could fail and then grow and learn from it, but also that her efforts could lead to positive change for others.

Character

Character is respect for societal and cultural norms or a sense of right and wrong. It is connected to conforming to expected moral standards of the culture in which one lives. The big question here is, which moral standards are children learning? Children need to be involved in conversations about right and wrong, not just labeling, but also having open discussions about why parents consider certain behaviors to be right or wrong. As caregivers and communities set forth their own standards and values, they will sometimes clash with those presented by the mass media. It is vital that parents give children the opportunity to hear the deep "why" behind their own standards, not just "do this, not that." Conversations about sexuality, agency, and character will follow. When talking with my own children about making choices about behaviors, I stress that the choices they make need to be in the context of who they are as a person and their vision for themselves as a person of strong character. If they do something that hurts someone else or take an action that uses or exploits another person, that does not reflect a strong character.

An example that might be helpful and applicable to middle school and high school children focuses on photo sharing on social media. Sharing photos of another person without their consent is wrong. Taking photos of someone who is not able to give consent because they are asleep or intoxicated is wrong. Why? Because it is not respecting the other person's agency or the right to make choices about his or her own body. A Steubenville, Ohio, sexual assault case was in the national news and on social media in 2012 and 2013.[36] Two boys were accused of sexually assaulting a girl who was under the influence of alcohol and unable to give consent for sexual acts. Multiple cameras captured photos of the sexual acts and of the victim and some were posted to social media sites.[37] This is one example that made the headlines, but this type of incident happens many times every day. In this digital age, these types of conversations are a must.

Conversation Starter

How might parents go about having this kind of conversation with children? With young children, you can talk about how we show our character by the way we treat people. Part of that is allowing others the right to say "no" about what happens with and to their bodies and the digital images of their bodies.

Here is a way you might approach this conversation with a young child. You might say, "What if you wanted to give a friend a hug, but the friend does not want to be hugged?" Listen to the child's thoughts on how he or she might respond. Ask: "Have you ever been in a situation where someone wanted to hug you and you didn't want that? What happened? If the person forced a hug, how did you feel?" After helping them think about the situation from the other person's perspective, ask them, "So, thinking of it that way, what would you do when your friend said they didn't want a hug?" Give the child the guidance to consider the other person's perspective and then problem solve a solution. Offer some examples such as, "Maybe you can ask for a hand squeeze instead" or, if the other person does not want any physical contact at all, then "You can give them a smile." The idea is to give young children the chance to think about the fact that both they and other people have the right to say what happens with their own body.

If your adolescent is old enough, share cases such as that in Steubenville with her and have her think about how she might respond if she were a bystander. Depending on your child's age and maturity level, you may choose to share more or fewer details of the case. A basic question about the issue of taking photographs or videos of others would be "Is it ever right to take pictures of someone without their consent?" Share examples of times when you have taken a picture of them as a surprise. Is that okay? When is it not okay, and how are those situations different? What about sharing pictures of someone without their consent? If one of their friends took a picture of them when they did not want it taken, would they want it to be shared? How would they feel if the friend shared it on social media or with other friends?

With your older middle school and high school students, you need to address the issue of the right to make decisions about one's own body. Adolescence is a time when understanding the right to say "no" about what happens to your body is extremely important. In the Steubenville case, expert Katie Hanna, the executive director of the Ohio Alliance to End Sexual Violence, said during the trial that it appeared that the bystanders and the boys involved in the case did not understand that what was happening was wrong or illegal. Hanna is quoted as saying, "People think that it [rape] is a violent act, using a weapon, perpetrated by a stranger. But that's not the reality of most sexual assaults."[38] Adolescents must be taught that a person always has the right to determine what happens to his or her body, and when consent is not possible for any reason, then it must be assumed that the person is not consenting to the act.

Parents can promote this idea by discussing cases in the local or national news and depictions in media of sexual behaviors. Parents may be uncomfortable bringing up such issues and worry that they may expose their child to sexual behaviors too early. But you should remember that if your children are going to parties or watching teen-focused movies or television, it is quite likely they are already being exposed to this issue, and without your feedback. You must be proactive in discussing issues of character involved in respecting the agency of other people in regard to sexual behaviors and the right and wrong way to show respect and care to others. Allowing children the chance to discuss and understand the family and community values and standards will bring them one step closer to becoming agents of change in the world around them.

Connection

Connection refers to those positive relationships with people and institutions that impact the child's life. This book explores many different connections that impact a child's development. These include family, the feeling of connection that a child has with the culture of celebrity, and the communities with whom a child is engaged.

Caring

Caring or compassion is defined as having empathy for others.[39] One very important aspect of media literacy is the ability to understand the worldview of the author of a piece of media, one's own worldview, and the ethics involved in producing and sharing media. Considering the ways that media impact others is an important aspect of aiding a child in thinking about the perspective of another.

MEDIA AND THRIVING

How might sexualized media and marketing impact a child's ability to thrive? First, let's consider some general research about media effects and then explore more directly the impact on the five C's involved in thriving. Media aimed at female adolescents have prevailing themes of "making oneself over" in order to get the attention of boys.[40] In a 2011 study, Wallis evaluated music videos for gender display by men and women. In 253 30-second segments, she found that significant gender displays reinforced the idea of women as submissive sexual objects, while men were depicted as aggressive. One aspect that was especially interesting in this study was the difference between the way male and female lead singers were presented. The overwhelming majority of the behaviors displayed by the female singers were sexual and their dress was provocative. The male singers displayed little sexual behavior and their dress was neutral. These findings emphasize the fact that in the entertainment industry, women are expected to and frequently do use their sexuality as a component of their performance, while male entertainers do not tend to do this nearly as often.[41]

In a study conducted by Towbin et al., 26 Disney films were analyzed for portrayals of stereotypes about gender, race, and age. In this study, the authors found that the majority of the films presented males as using their physicality rather than their words to express emotions or not being able to express their emotions and not being in control of their sexuality and behavior when a beautiful female was around, and overweight males had negative characteristics such as being stupid or villains. Females were also presented in stereotypical ways in these Disney films. They were depicted as having their appearance more highly valued than their intellect, being helpless and needing protection, and having the goal of being a homemaker and wife, and overweight females had negative characteristics, such as being ugly and cruel.[42] I will discuss these themes more thoroughly in later chapters, but what makes these stereotypes so insidious is the fact that Disney is considered by many parents a "safe" brand. In light of this, Disney movies are often purchased for the home and are viewed many, many times by children. The continual viewing of stereotypical representations of both males and females cannot help but have an impact on the way children develop their own ideas about what it means to be a man or a woman.

At the same time, there has been an increase in the sexual content in television shows. In one study the data showed that both sexual content and the number of scenes involving sex have increased significantly.[43] Another study found that 80 percent of popular television shows aimed at teenagers contained sexual content.[44] Television programming popular with adolescents varies in the amount of sexual content presented depending on the genre of the show.[45] For example, reality television shows that teens watched, such as *American Idol* and *Fear Factor*, had less sexual content than dramas. Animated shows (e.g., *American Dad*, *Family Guy*), comedies (e.g., *Sex in the City*, *Friends*), and dramas (e.g., *Desperate Housewives*, *Grey's Anatomy*) had more explicit sexual content. Dramas tended to have more messages about the risks and responsibility involved in sexual behaviors.[46] Along with the increased depiction of female value linked to sexual attractiveness, this trend sends the message that female power and value are found within their sexuality, with other qualities generally excluded or relegated to less importance.

Studies examining the effects of viewing sexualized media have shown that media can have negative effects, such as increasing the intention to engage in sexual intercourse, expectations about sex and peer engagement in sexual activities, permissive attitudes about sexual behaviors, and the timing of sexual intercourse.[47] But research has also shown that media messages about safe sexual practices can impact adolescent sexual behavior in a positive way.[48]

So how might the messages that children and adolescents receive from the media affect the five C's? How might it change the way they see themselves and judge their value and worth? Let's look at each area of thriving from the perspective of media messages.

Competence and Confidence

Suppose for a moment that as a parent someone says to you, "Hi, you don't know me, but I'd like to spend several hours with your child, without you present, and share these images with them." The images they begin to flash before you are filled with women in various states of undress, gyrating suggestively to music, harassed by males about their sexual attractiveness, and consistently depicted as more of a "decorative object" than a person who is actively engaged in relationships and what is happening in the story. What would you say to this person? Would you allow it? Of course not! But that is exactly the kind of images that children see everyday when they watch television, play computer games, listen to music, watch music videos, or read magazines.

Competence is about how well you do things that you think are important. For girls who see media messages that stress the importance of physical appearance, this can be devastating. Especially in the pre-adolescent and early adolescent years, girls' bodies are changing dramatically. Many of the idealized bodies that girls are seeing in media are not people of their age, and most are not even real. Remember the airbrushing, the computer manipulation, the lighting, the professional hair and makeup that are involved in constructing images of beauty? With this unrealistic and idealized standard, even the most physically attractive young girl will not measure up. If she views intelligence, kindness, warmth, and sincerity as her most important traits, then she may be able to maintain her view of herself as competent. But if she has adopted the view presented by sexualized media that her physical attractiveness is the most valuable thing about her, she is going to believe that she does not measure up to expectations. For many girls, this leads to feeling less confident, more angry, and more dissatisfied with their weight and appearance.[49]

The impact of sexualized media on boys has been demonstrated in studies conducted by Elizabeth Daniels. These studies explored boys' responses to female athletes who were either engaging in their sport or featured in sexualized poses.[50] I asked the author of these studies what overall lessons her research had taught her about how sexualized images impact boys. She said:

In my research examining how teen boys responded to media images of female athletes, I found that when the media depicts females as athletes in action poses, boys treat them as athletes by focusing on the athlete's physical competence and some boys even get involved in a play-by-play analysis of what the athlete is doing in the photo. In contrast, when the media depicts female athletes as sex objects, boys treat them as sex objects by focusing on their physical appearance and sexiness in the same way they respond to other sexualized images of women. By portraying female athletes as athletes in the media, there is an opportunity to show boys capable, strong, and accomplished women. However, sexualized media images of female athletes send the message that women are primarily sexual objects and what they do is not as important as how they look. These media depictions need to be challenged and replaced with more well-rounded portrayals of women to change the message aimed at boys that women's value lies in their bodies.[51]

The caring adults in a child's life must respond to these sexualized messages by presenting children with beliefs about competency that are in direct contrast to the messages they are receiving from sexualized media. Children should be encouraged to find their value in their kindness, strength of mind and purpose, intelligence, and sensitivity. A focus on strengths allows each child to explore her gifts and practice using them within the context of the communities in which she is a participant. As we provide children with these alternate views of value, we also help them to view competence in a different way. To be competent in standing up for what you believe in, in supporting your friends, and in achieving goals in different areas leads to positive outcomes. And when adolescents are at the stage when they are interested in exploring romance, we want them to understand that those relationships need to be based on respect and on understanding and valuing the other person as a whole.

Identity development is a major developmental challenge for adolescents. They begin experimenting with different roles, trying to figure out what their focus will be. Is drama my thing, or music? Do I want to focus on soccer or gymnastics? Early adolescents are especially interested in this kind of experimentation. As they are constructing identity, they need guidance in growing in their competence and confidence.

Character, Connection, and Caring

Sexualized media images and narratives provide us with information about what kinds of behaviors are being presented as socially acceptable to children.[52] From Britney Spears to Miley Cyrus, the message from a host of female stars that have grown up in the entertainment industry seems to be that, in order to present themselves as more mature, they must become sexualized. From the early 1990s to the present day, most of us could name a handful of young female singers and actors who have followed this pattern. Does this mean that all of these young women are engaging in risky sexual behaviors? Probably not, but what it does mean is that all of their fans, who tend to be even younger girls, are getting the message that it is valuable for a young girl to present herself as an object of male desire. As musician and actress Rashida Jones said in an article "The Pornification of Everything":

And then there's this: What else ties these pop stars together besides, perhaps, their entangled G-strings? Their millions of teen-girl fans. Even if adult Miley and Nicki have ownership of their bodies, do the girls imitating them have the same agency? Where do we draw the line between teaching them freedom of sexual expression and pride in who they are on the *inside*?[53]

These types of messages and models promote the idea that presenting oneself as a sexual object through the way you dress, move, or talk is a natural part of growing up.

If character can be defined as "conformity to a standard of right," then all of these messages set the tone for a different understanding of what is right than what parents, teachers, and professionals might want for children. Although adults may be teaching children to be respectful of their bodies and treat them with care and agency, sexualized messages suggest that female bodies are something to be used and exploited. In a class that I taught for a local youth agency, one early adolescent boy spoke about how girls whom he had known for years were now dressing in revealing clothes. He said: "It's confusing to me. I'm supposed to see these girls as my friends and treat them with respect, but the clothes they wear makes that really hard." What is going on here? Why does this boy, who has a relationship with these girls, struggle to continue to view them as friends? Daniels and Wartena's research suggests that perhaps boys are bringing the objectified view of women that they see in the media into their relationships with their peers and finding it a difficult course to navigate.[54] This is an important issue to consider when it comes to connection and caring. When boys learn to view women and girls as objects and girls learn to present themselves as objects in order to attain social power, everyone loses. It is natural to be attracted to the opposite sex, leading to relationships based on trust and mutual caring. But when we short-circuit the slow development of knowing and attraction with objectifying sexual images, that natural building of relationship gets off track. I asked Daniels how she believes sexualized media impact boys. She said:

Sexualized media trains boys to prioritize girls' physical appearance as the most important part of who they are and it teaches them to treat girls and women as sex objects. This is obviously problematic for girls and women because they are reduced to being valued for their sexual attractiveness instead of for who they are as people. It is also problematic for developing boys who are exposed to very unrealistic portrayals of women against which they might compare actual girls in their lives. In addition, through exposure to sexualized media, boys might feel pressured to engage in sexual behaviors before they are ready.[55]

The idea that physical attractiveness is highly important influences boys as well as girls. Many boys are feeling the pressure to become more muscular. Just as there is a "thin" ideal presented to girls, there is a "muscular" ideal presented to boys.[56] Smolak and Stein found that young adolescent boys who accepted media gender roles were more likely than others to engage in muscle-building activities.[57] If you watch entertainment aimed at adolescent and preadolescent boys, what you see is a depiction that is unrealistic in terms of muscularity. Think about the computer games that are popular with adolescents, such as the *Street Fighter* and the Batman franchises.[58] The male characters represented are extremely broad across the chest, muscular, and thin at the waist. Think about the "boys" in many recent films and television shows aimed at this age group. Most of the "boys" are actually portrayed by men who are in their 20s. For example, Zac Efron was already in his 20s when the second *High School Musical* movie was released, and Robert Pattinson was 22 years old when he played the perpetually 17-year-old Edward Cullen in the movie *Twilight*. Other male actors who are still in their teens often go to great lengths to reach a level of muscularity that is not normal for the average, healthy teen or preteen boy. In an interview, Taylor Lautner described how he achieved his muscular look for *New Moon*. He detailed a year-long period of working intensely with a trainer and dietician.[59] Of course the boys who see this movie most likely will not be thinking about the training and work that went into the actor's physical appearance. Instead, they will be comparing themselves to the actor and come up wanting.

It is important for parents and other caring adults to assure adolescents that their competence, confidence, character, and ability to build connection and caring is not rooted in either their sexual attractiveness or ability to be involved with others sexually, but rather in their identity as a whole. In later chapters I will discuss how to help children focus on their strengths, to view themselves as competent, confident, having a strong character, and able to build connection and develop caring relationships. Children and adolescents are not helpless victims. They have the ability to interact powerfully with the world around them and to choose their response to sexualized media.

IN THEIR VOICES

Byron McClure is a father and school psychologist who studies the convergence of psychology and hip-hop. He is currently pursuing his doctorate in school psychology while working full time in the schools and writes the blog Fligher Education: Where Hip-Hop, Entertainment, and Psychology Collide.

In my childhood, I recall sitting in the living room of my house with my brothers, anxiously waiting to watch the television show *The Mighty Morphin' Power Rangers*. The theme music began playing. Before I knew what was happening, I found myself standing on top of the couch, doing a flying scissors kick off of the sofa. My identical twin stood on the other couch furiously punching into the air, while my middle brother practiced his high kicks with almost perfect precision. My oldest brother sat by and smiled as he realized the excitement that this new television show brought to us. By the show's end, my brothers and I had learned an entire new repertoire of fighting moves that we could not wait to try on each other.

This example illustrates the influence that television shows had on us as children, even though we did not realize its initial impact. There is substantial research which demonstrates the impact that the media has on individuals, and oftentimes the influence is negative. Growing up in Prince George's County, Maryland, which is a predominantly African American county adjacent to the District of Columbia, hip-hop was not just a genre of music; it was a way of life. The culture of hip-hop shaped everything from the clothes we wore, to the music we listened to, even to the way we communicated with each other.

The culture and origins of hip-hop can be traced back to New York City beginning with artists such as DJ Kool Herc, The Furious Five, and transforming into movements led by African Bambaataa and others. Hip-hop gave a voice to disadvantaged communities and spoke of the atrocities and chaos that plagued many African American neighborhoods. This political movement in hip-hop during the late 1980s early 1990s was led by artists such as Run DMC, Public Enemy, Grandmaster Flash, and Melle Mel. Public Enemy spoke out loud and clear against racism and social injustice with songs such as "Fight the Power." Spike Lee served as a voice and gave classic visuals to the lives of African Americans through films such as *Do the Right Thing*, *School Daze*, *Crooklyn*, and *Malcolm X*. However, film and music took a drastic change for the worse with the movement of gangsta rap.

I recently conducted a seminar at Hampton University about the influence that media has on African Americans and we examined Byron Hurt's film *Hip-Hop: Beyond Beats and Rhymes*. This documentary addressed the oversexualization of African American women in hip-hop, the instant gratification and glorification of material possessions, and homosexuality and HIV in the black community. Many students voiced their concerns over the negative portrayals of blacks in the media.

One of the most important factors discussed was countering the negative portrayals of blacks in the media and the influence that family can have.

My family is the reason that my brothers and I could watch *Power Rangers* in the confines of our home and not confuse the fiction of the show with realities of the real world. My brothers and I knew that we could not go into public jumping off things and kicking people because that was not acceptable. I grew up with two loving parents in my house and my father was readily available to my brothers and me. Many of my friends in my community did not have father figures around nor positive role models, thus it was easier for them to get caught up in the instant gratification of material possessions often portrayed and glamorized in various media outlets such as BET and MTV. In the midst of all of the debating about the influence that media has on children, the most important thing to remember is that family, parents, and community ultimately shape a child's life.

3

The Case of the Missing Childhood

Sometimes it is easy, as we go along in our day-to-day lives, to begin to see things that we might have initially thought were bad as "no big deal." We get used to seeing sexualized images when we are exposed to them over and over again, and our initial revulsion fades to apathy. This is how many adults are with the sexualized images and stereotyped messages that are being fed to us by the media. We do not even notice them anymore.

One day I was discussing this topic with a colleague of mine and she said, "I have a video you have to see." She pulled up a video on YouTube that had been created by Dove's Campaign for Real Beauty. It was called *Onslaught*.[1] The video opens with the face of an angelic little girl, smiling innocently. Then, to the tune of a pumping rock rhythm, the close-up changes from the little girl's face to a quick succession of images pulled straight off the television, billboards, magazines, and other visual media showing women in underwear shaking their hips, others posing seductively and scantily clad, and products designed to make you look smaller, tighter, thinner, younger, and on and on. The video ends with the little girl walking away, and these words appear on the screen, "Talk to your daughter, before the beauty industry does."

I use this video in a lot of my public speaking to get the attention of parents and other adults about this topic. However, the first time I saw it, it sickened me for two reasons. First, I hate the thought of strong little girls being told they have to measure up to these unrealistic images. Second, I realized that I see those same visuals every single day, often without thinking a thing about them. I had become accustomed to these images of women being sexualized to such an extent that until I saw them through the eyes of a little girl, they did not strike me as particularly bad. I hate that. I do not want to be used to seeing women as objects only of men's desire, and I do not want that for other people either. The dehumanizing and objectifying of women by the media are unhealthy for everyone. The first step toward helping our children deal with this effectively is to become aware of the issues ourselves and recognize the problem.

This chapter will look at what the research says about how children and adolescents use media in order to expand our understanding of how specific corporations target them as consumers. The chapter will also explore some very adult themes of romance, sexuality, and gender stereotypes that are consistently woven throughout the products and shows that are developed for children and adolescents and discuss the implications of repeated exposure to them. The goal for this chapter is to provide an understanding of how the combination of increased accessibility to media through mobile devices, along with consistent exposure to age-inappropriate themes, is robbing children of their childhoods. As I begin to discuss media messages, I will continually return to the question of bioecological context and thriving.

TARGETING CHILDHOOD

In earlier chapters I presented statistics regarding children's media use and how it has grown exponentially as media have become both more accessible through mobile devices and more attractive due to the rise of advertainment. I also presented the ways that high exposure to sexualized media has been linked with body dissatisfaction, unsafe sexual behaviors, lower self-esteem, and general discontent. I explored some of the statistics about children and adolescents being targeted as consumers. This chapter will examine in some detail the marketing plans that companies put in place that target children and the impact of sexualized and stereotyped messages they often send.

It is well known that marketers consider children big business and spend millions of dollars every year targeting them. In 2000, a marketing executive was quoted as describing children as "a marketer's dream" due to the fact that they want to buy everything and do not consider the costs.[2] Even back in 1998, children were viewed by advertisers as important not just for their present-day influence on adult spending, but even more so for the future consumers they would become.[3] It was a truth acknowledged at that time that the most loyal consumers were those who were "nurtured" from young ages. A Disney executive was quoted as describing the Disney activities as working together to build brand recognition and loyalty, with the stores, television shows, theme parks, and products working as a continuous cycle that draws consumers into the brand of Disney.[4]

So has anything changed in the past few years? In 2000, Susan Linn founded the Campaign for a Commercial Free Childhood (CCFC) as a response to what she perceived as commercialization encroaching on childhood.[5] This group formed after concerned educators and professionals gathered in 1999 to discuss the growing marketing targeted at children. The CCFC works to educate parents and others about the dangers of commercialization and to pressure companies that are involved in promoting unhealthy consumerism. This group has spearheaded efforts that have impacted the marketing programs of corporations such as Disney, Hasbro, and Scholastic. CCFC has teamed with other advocacy groups, such as Eat Drink Politics, which advocates for public health and truth in advertising against such firms as McDonald's and PepsiCo. CCFC has also worked with groups such as the Brave Girls Alliance (BGA), a group of activists, professionals, and parents who have teamed up to ask media companies to take social responsibility to avoid sexualizing childhood. The BGA has developed campaigns asking for less sexualized and stereotyped media and marketing that targeted companies including LEGO, Mattel, and Disney.

Have these kinds of consumer advocacy groups had any impact on the way that marketers target children? Although there have been some victories, companies continue to market aggressively toward children, even extending their product aim downward from children to infants. In February 2011, the *New York Times* reported that the Walt Disney Company developed a new brand, Disney Baby.[6] To promote the brand, Disney representatives began visiting maternity wards to pitch their brand to new mothers. Although some new mothers may welcome any free product, especially from a well-known and trusted brand such as Disney, one has to wonder about the ethics of approaching consumers who are in such a vulnerable state. As anyone who has had a baby knows, the first few days after giving birth are a time when a new mother is usually getting very little sleep, recovering from delivery, and struggling to cope with the demands of a new baby. Is it ethically sound to go into someone's room and pitch products at this point? As someone who has had three children, I think I might have kicked those Disney representatives right out of my room! Not that I do not appreciate free products to sample, but getting a pitch for anything while you are in the hospital seems predatory. Do not think that this is all done just to give you something. For every marketing move that a company makes, they are hoping to reap the benefits from the consumer. Andy Mooney, chairman of Disney Consumer Products, was quoted in the *New York Times* as saying, "To get that mom thinking about her family's first park experience before her baby is even born is a home run."[7]

Although Mattel, the company that produces the Disney Princess and Barbie brands, reported declining sales in some areas in 2010, the Disney Princess and Barbie brands themselves reported continuing growth in sales through 2011.[8] In February 2011, the *Huffington Post* released a report discussing Disney's new promotion of the Cars brand, which they describe as particularly appealing to boys.[9] The Disney quarterly report for the last quarter of 2011 showed that the Cars brand had global annual sales of $2 billion,[10] while the 2013 fourth quarterly report in the area of consumer products demonstrated increased revenues of 9 percent to $3.6 billion, driven in large part by the success of Disney Junior, Monsters University, Mickey and Minnie, Iron Man, and Planes merchandise, many of which have targeted boys in their advertising.[11] Obviously, the point of this company is to make money, and that is fine. I do not object to a company promoting their products and providing consumers with freebies to encourage them to try new products. What I do object to is the targeting of consumers in the cradle or at vulnerable times in their lives. Of course, Disney and Mattel are not the only companies that do this, but they are very visible offenders.

One of the newer ways that marketers are targeting children and adolescents is through the Internet. As reported by the Media Awareness Network, the Internet is especially attractive to companies promoting their products because of its accessibility to young people, the fact that it is an unregulated medium, and the use of engaging and interactive ways of building brand loyalty.[12] For example, since 1979 the Federal Communications Commission has demanded that clear markers, such as a statement like "And now a word from our sponsors," must separate television commercials and programs in order to help children distinguish between advertisements and entertainment programming. But online advergames are not required to provide such markers, even though the immersive nature of these games makes it more difficult for children to tell if they are engaging with advertising or entertainment.[13] MediaSmarts 2012 report on "Young Canadians in a Wired World" reported that Canadian parents indicated they view companies that own the sites that their children visit as untrustworthy and focused on obtaining a child's personal information for profit. The 11- to 17-year-old children themselves reported that they do not trust the companies they interact with and are wary of having their words or shared pictures used for marketing purposes. Nevertheless, these children continued to use the Internet to play games, connect socially, and search out information.[14] Brands reach and influence children and adolescents through media such as advergames and social media marketing. In 2009, McDonald's and Burger King provided websites with 60 to 100 pages of advergames. McDonald's website attracted 365,000 unique young visitors on average each month in 2009.[15] Branded content on social media networks, such as Facebook, can take various forms. These include content shared directly from the brand, content that is reshared by people who the child is connected with through the site, and social marketing tools.[16] This means that the children themselves serve as brand ambassadors through the content they share with their social connections. Lipsman et al. suggest that the value of a fan of a product or brand can be assessed by the influence those fans exert upon their social media connections.[17]

Children often access the Internet without a parent's oversight. Although parents may be more aware of what advertisements a child is exposed to on television or radio, they are less likely to pay attention to the advertisements on the Internet. Research into advergames has found that many websites do not have any type of ad break, and those that did often were not highly visible or readable.[18] Combine this with the fact that parents are not usually aware of the impact of Internet marketing and the previously mentioned fact that children up to the age of 12 often do not even recognize online advertisements as such and you have a potent combination.

It astounds and disturbs me that oftentimes companies directly market music, movies, and games that are intended for adult audiences to children as young as 12 years old. In 2000, the Federal Trade Commission (FTC) published a report indicating that even when these industries have rated products as acceptable only for those over 17 years old, they continue to promote these products to children and early adolescents. In fact, the FTC report stated that "Companies in those [motion picture, music recording, and electronic game] industries routinely target children under 17 as the audience for movies, music, and games that their own rating or labeling systems say are inappropriate for children."[19]

The FTC found that many companies within these industries had developed marketing plans that clearly targeted the under-17 age group. As reported by the *Los Angeles Times*, the company Electronic Arts created an advertisement called "Your Mom Hates Dead Space 2" to promote a Mature-rated horror game. The advertisement consisted of video clips from focus groups of middle-aged women cringing and looking appalled while viewing the game.[20] Another example is

McDonald's Happy Meal toys. It is not unusual for toys for PG-13 movies to be included in Happy Meals, which are targeted at children in the 4- to 8-year-old age range with Mighty Kids Meals being described on the McDonald's website as for tweens aged 8 to 12.[21] In a 2010 lawsuit that the Center for Science in the Public Interest filed against McDonald's for using toys to market nutritionally questionable food and products directly to children, litigation director Stephen Gardner said "McDonald's use of toys undercuts parental authority and exploits young children's developmental immaturity—all this to induce children to prefer foods that may harm their health. It's a creepy and predatory practice."[22]

In 2013, the CCFC launched a campaign to "save the Tooth Fairy" from sexualization and commercialization after a group of former Disney, Hasbro, and Mattel executives began a pitch to license the Tooth Fairy name attached to a group of six scantily clad young female characters. In a press release, Susan Linn said:

The Real Tooth Fairies is an egregious attempt to commercialize an inevitable biological milestone, the celebration of which has always been the purview of family ritual. In Real Fairyland, branding replaces children's own creations with homogenized, corporate-constructed, sexualized images, constricting both imagination and cultural diversity.[23]

In 2014, a group of parent and advocacy groups filed a complaint against Facebook for violating the privacy of minors. Facebook claimed that if you agree to use their social network without working through the security preferences and intentionally opting out of having your images used in ads, then you have consented to have your information, including your images, used for advertising purposes. After a $20 million settlement was announced, CCFC refused to accept the settlement because the deal Facebook brokered with advocacy groups continued to violate the privacy of their minor-aged users. One mother, whose 16-year-old child was used in an advertisement, said, "They're turning her into an advertisement . . . there needs to be disclosure as well as explicit consent."[24]

One of the hot topics in the marketing field for the past several years has been that of neuromarketing. It has been noted in academic circles that there are many different definitions for neuromarketing, and that different companies offering a variety of services use the practice in itself in different ways.[25] A fairly clear definition that I would like to use in this book is that provided by Lee, Broderick, and Chamberlain, which described neuromarketing as "the application of neuroscientific methods to analyze and understand human behavior in relation to markets and marketing exchanges."[26] There are several ways that marketers have studied both children's and adult's reactions in order to focus their own marketing campaigns in more effective ways. For example, electroencephalogram studies have been used to explore reactions to television advertisements.[27] Others have used magnetoencephalograms to study how different types of advertisements impact recall.[28] Although marketers are using this technology, there are mixed feelings about neuromarketing from academics. Those who come from a business perspective tend to see neuromarketing in a more positive light,[29] but those from the field of neuroscience tend to be more concerned about the ethics of using brain imaging and new technology to target consumers.[30] In an article in the *New York Times* when it first became known that neuroscientists and marketers were teaming up to better understand the neurology of how consumers made purchasing decisions, there were some experts who thought it was a useful tool to understand how consumers think, while others worried about the ethics of influencing people using neuroscience.[31]

An article in the *Lancet* in 2004 noted that Donald Kennedy, the editor-in-chief of *Science* magazine, had expressed concern that brain imaging used for marketing purposes may infringe upon the personal privacy of consumers.[32] The ethical concerns in regard to neuromarketing can be broken into three categories.[33] The first is the protection of vulnerable parties in all aspects of the process, including research and selling. These authors suggest a published code of protections for those involved in this type of marketing research that is similar to those required for academic and medical research.

The second concern regards the exploitation of specific populations that are of interest to the market, such as children. In particular, it is of ethical concern when children are the target of "stealth marketing" techniques involving advergames and advertainment that may not be easily identified by the children as advertisements.

The third concern involves responsible public representation of what neuromarketing can and cannot achieve. Some consumers may become highly distrustful of marketing of any kind should they believe that neuromarketing has led to advertising that takes away consumer autonomy. And given quotes from A. K. Pradeep, the founder of NeuroFocus, a neuromarketing firm, it is not surprising that some consumers may become deeply wary of this practice. Pradeep has been quoted as saying that neuromarketing can "compute the deep subconscious response to stimuli."[34]

Critics such as Jeff Chester from the Center for Digital Democracy[35] and Allen Kanner[36] from the Campaign for a Commercial-Free Childhood have expressed concern about such marketing research and the resultant marketing directed at both children and adults. In the Thomas H. Wright lecture at Sarah Lawrence University in 2009 and in the film *Consuming Kids: The Commercialization of Childhood*, Susan Linn discusses current marketing practices. She says that the goal of marketing is to "insinuate their brand into the fabric of children's lives"[37] and notes "These days marketing is honed by child psychologists and brought to us by a ubiquitous and increasingly miniaturized technology and made possible by huge amounts of money."[38]

In 2010, the American Academy of Pediatrics (AAP) reaffirmed their suggestions that legislation provide significant restrictions on advertising to children, which would be appropriate given their study of both the harmfulness of the message and the inability of children and adolescents to understand the purpose of advertisements.[39] The AAP concluded that advertising significantly affects young people in the United States. They suggest that advertisements are not protected speech and can be restricted or even banned should they be linked to health risks. Recommendations include teaching media literacy skills to children so they can become critical consumers, educating pediatricians about the negative effects of advertising, empowering pediatricians to educate parents and communities about the negative effects of advertising and the positive effects of media literacy education, and working with both parents and public health groups to advocate for public policy that limits advertising during children's programming.

I hope that as adults we can use our own power of reasoning to stop and critique the messages that are being sent, even for the brands we trust. However, it is much more difficult for children to do this. Later in this book I will present some specific ways adults can prompt interesting and important discussions about how to evaluate the messages in media that children consume.

MEDIA AND MARKETING MESSAGES

Children are targeted as consumers by powerful market forces. The companies who want to sell to children use sophisticated methods to lure a child's interest and keep it focused on their products and programming. But what messages are being promoted, and are they damaging or innocent? I have already presented some of the ways that media negatively influence children and adolescents in the areas of body image, identity, and sexual behaviors. Let's delve a bit deeper into the themes that children and adolescents are exposed to through different types of media and marketing.

Television

Even children's television is not immune from offering romanticism and gender stereotypes to age groups for whom it may be inappropriate. For example, adolescents today grew up watching the popular Disney television shows *The Suite Life of Zack and Cody*, *The Wizards of Waverly Place*, and *Hannah Montana*. All of these shows featured frequent romanticism of children and young adolescents. In the 2006 "Kisses and Basketball" episode of *The Suite Life of Zack and Cody*, a romantic theme is introduced between Zack and his good female friend Max.[40] Considering the fact that the Disney Channel frequently cites its audience as 6- to 14-year-olds, one has to wonder why kissing needed to be introduced into the show. Is it not interesting enough to show a healthy, mutual friendship between Max and Zack? Max is an example of a girl who likes sports and develops friendships with boys. This could be a positive model of a nonromanticized relationship, but when the kiss and date are added into the equation, the show brings in romantic tension where none is necessary. In an episode in the first season titled "The Fairest of Them All," a child beauty pageant is held at the Tipton Hotel, where the show is located. Upon seeing one girl, the character of Cody seems smitten. His brother says, "You just met her!" to which Cody replies, "And yet, I know all I need to know about her." Zack then asks, "What's her name?" Guess what, Cody does not even know the name of his dream girl or anything about her other than how she looks.[41]

The Wizards of Waverly Place consistently depicted the main young female character, Alex, as not caring about grades but instead focusing on boys and her appearance. In an episode titled "I Almost Drowned in a Chocolate Fountain," Alex tells her best friend that her strategy for getting the attention of a boy involves being late to class so that the boy will notice her come in, forgetting her book so he will have to share his with her, passing notes to him so they will have to stay after class together, and failing a midterm because the boy was doing poorly in the class. When the boy she is interested in does ask her out, Alex says to her friend, "All those hours I didn't spend on studying totally paid off."[42]

Several more recent Disney shows have maintained this same concentration on romance. *Austin and Ally*, which premiered in 2011, focuses on the friendship and collaboration between Austin, a singer, and Ally, a songwriter. In the 2013 episode "Couples and Careers," Austin and Ally start dating and become unable to communicate clearly with each other.[43] Rather than retaining a great example of opposite sex teenage friendship, the show veers into romance.

In the 2012 *Jessie* episode called "Trashin' Fashion," two brothers, Luke and Ravi, try to outdo each other in order to get the attention of a model who is much older than either one of them. The boys talk about asking the model out on a date and "fighting for her favor," even though they have only just met her.[44]

A more recent Disney series, *Lab Rats*, which debuted in 2012, provides a different view of both boys and girls. Each of the characters is depicted as having their own unique strengths, which do not tend to be stereotypical. There is some romance, but it is age appropriate.

Aside from the obvious romantic themes in many feature-length films that are made for children, there is now a clear pattern emerging of romantic themes in children's television programming. Because many of these programs are targeting children who are younger than the actors themselves, there are children as young as six years old being bombarded by stories focused on romantic relationships.

In a content analysis of television programs for tween audiences, Gerding and Signorielli examined 49 episodes of 40 different television programs that appeared on the Disney Channel, Disney XD, Nickelodeon, and Turner Cartoon Network in 2011 that were aimed at the tween audience. These programs included some mentioned earlier, such as *Hannah Montana*, *The Suite Life of Zack and Cody*, and *The Wizards of Waverly Place*. The overall findings were that tween programs have more male than female characters, and females were more likely to be depicted as being attractive, while male characters were not.[45] This finding was especially important because of the emphasis on appearance and beauty as a primary value of being female. In fact, the authors note that these findings suggest "Males can be unattractive and still be a part of the story, but that, if you are female, it is unacceptable to be unattractive."[46] Female characters were shown to be concerned about their appearance and to receive attention for how they looked, while male characters were not concerned about their appearance and did not tend to receive comments about it. It was also noted that the male characters in action adventure programs were more than twice as likely to have muscular, attractive bodies than male characters in other types of programming.

Products

Both romance and gender stereotypes are evident in products marketed to young children. I have seen T-shirts in a child's size 5 at Walmart that say "I love boys, boys, boys, boys" on it, along with baby clothing that said things like "I'm a boob man" on a bib sold at the Hooters gift store. Gender stereotyping is also evident in children's clothing lines. LEGO Friends T-shirts for sale in the girls section at Walmart are adorned with the words "fun!" and "cute" and pictures of rainbows, flowers, hearts, puppies, and kittens, while LEGO Chimea T-shirts sold in the boys section say "Let's get wild" and feature a character holding weapons and wearing armor.

Researchers have claimed that toys and other products play an important role in a child's socialization and her view of herself and her place in society.[47] The gendered marketing of toys, with specific types and colors of toys being labeled by marketers as appropriate for one gender or the other, provides children with a template for understanding gender roles that are very stereotyped. Toys marketed to boys tend to promote an understanding of masculinity as being connected with physical action and aggression and one of femininity associated with nurturing, domesticity, and a focus on physical appearance.[48] The sexualization and stereotyping of children is found not only in television, movies, and products, but it is also an issue in popular music, music videos, and the Internet.

Music and Videos

Studies that examined music videos have found sexual imagery in 84 percent of these videos, with women usually being shown as sexual objects and 71 percent of women were scantily clad or wearing no clothing.[49] Music lyrics also often focus on sexual content, with it appearing more often in adolescents' musical choices than in their television, movie, or magazine choices.[50] Even in music lyrics by artists under the age of 18 who are heavily promoted to young people, there are questionable lyrics. Look at some of the lyrics by Justin Bieber in his song "First Dance," which states, "Girl I promise I'll be gentle, I know we gotta do it slowly." He then goes on to say that such a moment only happens "once in a lifetime" and references rocking back and forth. He also mentions that their parents will never know what they are doing.[51]

What is he talking about? Why would it matter if a girl's parents knew that she danced with someone at a school dance or if there were chaperones seeing them dance? The references to rocking back and forth and being gentle are clearly sexual. Justin Bieber has been heavily marketed to young people, and many of his fans are younger than eight years old. There was a famous YouTube video in which a three-year-old girl cries because she is such a devoted Bieber fan.[52]

Miley Cyrus is another singer who has been marketed to children in the past, and her lyrics and videos have become increasingly sexualized. In her song "Can't Be Tamed," she says, "Every guy everywhere just gives me mad attention, like I'm under inspection."[53] This song is clearly focusing on the female singer's body and the way she gets attention from men because of it. What is distressing about Miley Cyrus's move from child star to black leather, bustier-clad adult singer is that she continues to be marketed by Disney to children. On the Disney Channel website, Hannah Montana videos, games, and activities continue to be accessible, and there is a link to the video for the song "Party in the USA." Although the lyrics to this song are not particularly offensive, the fact that the then under 18-year-old Cyrus is flashing cleavage and gyrating her hips seductively makes it inappropriate for young children. Yet there it is on the Disney Channel website, along with games and printouts for children as young as five or six years old. If an artist wants to present a more "mature" side of herself as she ages, that is her prerogative. However, it is highly offensive for the Disney Corporation to specifically target young children with an artist who is clearly attempting to appeal to an older crowd. For Disney to continue to market this celebrity to young children once she has clearly moved into more adult fare shows a clear lack of concern for their young fan base.

Magazines

Along with television, products, and music videos, magazines have also been found to promote a focus on appearance and romance. I mentioned earlier how magazines often present sexualized imagery and the thin ideal and presented statistics that showed that consumption of these types of images tends to lead to body dissatisfaction for both girls and boys. A recent study examined the change across time in how girls have been depicted in the magazines *Seventeen* and *Girls' Life*.[54] The researchers found that the average number of sexualizing characteristics in *Seventeen* almost tripled over 30 years. *Girls' Life* was founded in the 1990s, so the researchers had fewer back issues to investigate. Even so, they found that sexualizing characteristics of the girls depicted increased more than 15 times from 1994 to 2011. The researchers noted that while there were some sexualized characteristics (e.g., low-cut tops, tight clothing, breast emphasis, high heels) depicted in the 1990s, the increase in sexualization of girls in these magazines began increasing drastically in the 2000s. These authors conclude that there is reason to be concerned about this change in depictions of girls for several reasons. First, it is likely that increased sexualization limits girls' views of who they are and who they can become, with a focus on their value being linked to their physical appearance above all else. Second, girls who adopt a sexualized ideal put themselves at risk for being viewed as less competent in general.

I decided to do my own investigation of magazines aimed at tween and teenage girls, reading a variety of both online and traditionally published magazines in order to identify themes that appeared. Not only was the thin ideal present, but there was also definitely a strong focus on appearance in most of the popular magazines. One of the more fashion-oriented magazines, *Teen Vogue*, featured makeover tools and style advice. They had a regular feature called "Beauty Crisis" that addressed common beauty concerns such as dark circles under the eyes and frizzy hair. Is it really necessary to label these as *crises*? Sharing advice with girls could be achieved without the hype of making a bad hair day into a crisis. Teenagers have enough drama in their lives due to hormonal changes and identity development. They do not need targeted publications promoting the idea that every little thing is a crisis.

One of the magazines that disturbed me most was *Seventeen*, which I remember reading as an adolescent. Their website was full of fitness advice with a focus on building the perfect body. This included not only articles about how teen and tween girls could find their perfect "fitness vacay" with a photo of a bikini-clad girl doing sit ups on the beach, but also recipes. Why does a 12-year-old need a recipe for a low-calorie salad? The recipe section was also full of drinks labeled "mocktails" and "teen-i's," an example of age compression, offering young girls something that is really out of their range of interest or experience. Another feature of this magazine was the "Hook-up Handbook" in which other teenage girls gave advice on "how to have the best hook-up ever."[55] Much of the advice was directed at how to arouse a boy, with several girls encouraging others to "tease" a boy to "keep him wanting more" or "make him wait for it." This was advice given by girls from 15 to 18 years of age to other girls.

The content of *Seventeen* was in sharp contrast to the kind of stories and columns that appear in the magazines *New Moon Girls* and *Discovery Girls*. These magazines are both dedicated to girls ages 8 and up, and the purpose of both is to help girls identify and honor their individual strengths and talents. *Boys' Life* is a magazine aimed at boys aged 7 to 14 years and has articles that focus on history, science, and outdoor activities. It is much more difficult to find positive magazines with messages about respecting oneself and seeing oneself as an agent for older adolescents. As we saw in the research on *Girls' Life*, even some magazines tailored to younger girls and with a presumed focus on things other than appearance can contain sexualized depictions. However, the online magazines *Rookie* and *Differences* both provide opportunities for adolescents to share their own thoughts with a large audience through articles, photographs, and videos. Some of my favorite features of these magazines are the way they support teenagers through issues that everyone struggles with in adolescence, such as feeling left out or worrying about the future. These magazines also empower teenagers to think of themselves as media makers and critics and provide them with a platform to share those creations and critiques.

HOW DOES THIS IMPACT THE FIVE C'S OF THRIVING?

One of the most important things to happen in childhood and adolescence is that children begin to figure out who they are, what they like, what they are good at, and who they want to become. Just when children are constructing their identities, they are likely to suffer loss of self-esteem and begin to doubt themselves if they perceive themselves as not measuring up to the idealized media images they are seeing. This can impact a child's view of his or her own competence as well as confidence. Adolescents may absorb ideas about what constitutes strong character as they see depictions of characters engaging in behaviors that objectify their sexuality and do not depict mutuality. A focus on appearance and romance that is not age appropriate does not allow connections to peers and caring relationships to develop at a natural pace.

In the past three chapters, I have shared information about how children develop, the ways that sexualized and stereotyped media and marketing can impact their development, and the interpersonal variables in children's lives that influence their response to sexualized and stereotyped media and allow them to thrive. In the next few chapters, I will explain these interpersonal variables in more detail to show what part they can play in helping children see through sexualized and stereotyped popular culture in order to become empowered, critical consumers and creators.

IN THEIR VOICES

Elizabeth Sweet is a sociologist whose primary research focuses on gender and children's toys. She earned her Ph.D. in sociology from the University of California–Davis in 2013 and she has continued her work there as a postdoctoral scholar. She is the mother of a 12-year-old daughter who inspires her research and activism on the topic of gender and children's culture.

In the 21st century, marketing has become an omnipresent feature of children's daily lives. In addition to overt and embedded advertisements on television and other media, licensed media franchises and branded marketing messages are also emblazoned onto many of the products children use in their daily lives—from toothbrushes to clothing to snack foods. Along with this constant exposure, the particular marketing messages that children encounter have been honed to appeal to them in insidious ways. For example, marketers have increasingly played upon gender stereotypes and exaggerated notions of gender difference, as well as sexuality, to appeal to children. In my research, I find that the gender-based marketing and stereotyping of children's toys is far more extreme today than it was at any time over the 20th century. Thus, not only have the messages become more prevalent, but they have also become more extreme and harmful. Unfortunately, in the United States, we currently lack the necessary regulations to ensure that companies aren't relying upon harmful messaging in order to boost sales to children.

I have witnessed firsthand the effects of sexualized media and marketing messages on my own daughter. As much as I tried to limit her contact with them through a careful monitoring of the media and products consumed in our home, marketing messages nevertheless crept in, especially as she became exposed to peer culture at school. So how can parents and educators help children to navigate this world of intensive marketing and harmful messages? First, it is important to limit young children's exposure to media, and hence marketing, as much as possible. This is especially true when children are very young and most vulnerable to marketing messages. Second, teaching media literacy skills that can help kids to spot and to decode marketing messages when they do encounter them is essential. I began this process with my own daughter when she was a baby. For example, if we were in a grocery store and she saw (and immediately wanted) a character-branded snack food, I would explain to her that the character on the box was a form of advertising and I would explain how the advertising messages were not accurate. While this felt like a futile endeavor with a toddler, over time my efforts to help her spot and understand all the myriad forms of marketing around her began to pay off. Eventually she began pointing out those marketing messages to me! After countless discussions over the years, today she has a good media literacy toolbox with which to deconstruct the plethora of marketing she encounters.

Finally, it is important that parents and children's advocates speak out against harmful media messages. In the early 1970s, parents and advocates brought their concerns about the effects of children's marketing to the media and into the political arena and, as a result, children's toy advertisements became notably more gender inclusive and children's marketing more tightly regulated. Sadly, those regulations have since been largely dismantled, but the need for them has only intensified. Thus, in addition to limiting media exposure and encouraging media literacy, we need to demand that companies be held responsible for the marketing messages they transmit.

4

The Culture of Celebrity

VIGNETTES: A TALE OF TWO CHILDREN

Anna is outgoing and finds it easy to build new social relationships. She tends to have a happy-go-lucky approach to life. Anna lives with her mother, who often watches television with her, and encourages her daughter to actively discuss media as they consume them. Anna finds it easy to talk with her mom about sex and sexual issues because the topic has been an open one between them for as long as she can remember. Anna's mom encourages her to think of her sexuality as part of who she is and something that will change and grow with her. When they consume media together, Anna and her mom talk about the decisions that the characters make, especially when it leads to sexual behaviors. Anna's parents are divorced, and she remains close to her father. She has an open, communicative relationship with him, and he talks with her about sexuality in the same way her mother does. Anna plays soccer and has for many years. She is on a team that focuses on cooperation and self-discipline. Hard work and commitment to ethical behavior are highly valued by the team. Anna identifies herself primarily as an athlete and solid student, making A's and B's in her classes.

Throughout her childhood, Anna has had the opportunity to build strong relationships with her peers and with caring adults. When Anna becomes romantically involved with someone, she will be able to use the sexual self-efficacy skills that she learned from her parents to set limits and make decisions about her sexual behaviors. She graduated from high school with a strong academic record and was able to attend the college of her choice. Anna is confident in her ability to make important decisions and to be an agent in her relationships. She is going to college, full of excitement about what the future holds.

Isaac lives with his parents and two siblings, one who is older than he and one who is younger. He tends to be anxious in social situations and does not make friends easily. Isaac tends to take a guarded approach to life, often feeling that people are not trustworthy. He consumes most media alone on the television and computer that he has in his room or on his smartphone, which he carries all the time. Isaac is frequently seen with ear buds in his ears, even at school or when eating dinner with his family. Isaac's family does not talk about sex, except when his parents tell him and his siblings that they should not have sex before they get married. Isaac does not belong to any extracurricular groups, but hangs out after school with a group of adolescents who live in his neighborhood. There is little adult supervision of this group as they play computer games, watch television, movies, and videos on the Internet, and listen to music. Isaac is academically gifted and tends to do well in school without much effort, but his lack of social skills and withdrawn behavior make it difficult to connect with his peers and teachers.

Throughout his childhood, Isaac did not participate in extracurricular or community groups and thus did not build connections with peers or adults outside of school. As he moved into adolescence, his parents were busy with work commitments and often left Isaac at home with no supervision, where he consumed many hours of media alone or with neighborhood friends. Isaac's family did not talk about sex, so when he had questions, he tended to try to find the answers through media or by talking with his peers. The media that Isaac and his friends watched, such as reality television, depicted a lot of young people engaging in casual sexual encounters. As Isaac got older, he began to engage in many casual sexual encounters with people he hardly knew. He contracted a sexually transmitted infection, and in his senior year of high school a girl who he had sex with told him that she was pregnant. Depressed and feeling disconnected from his school and peers, Isaac dropped out of high school.

As children grow up, a variety of forces combine to influence the way they learn to see the world. From a bioecological perspective, we understand that not only the microsystems of the home and family influence a child's view of the world, but also the exosystems and macrosystems in which they live. These systems include the mass media.

Mass media influence how people in a society view gender roles as well as sexuality and what is seen as attractive, desired, and appropriate for both males and females. In fact, media may be the most influential sources for learning which behaviors are socially appropriate[1] and are an important source of information about the social world outside of a child's microsystems of home, school, and community.[2]

MEDIA AND PERCEPTION OF REALITY

Anna and Isaac both consume an average amount of media for their age group, which is about eight hours per day.[3] They both listen to top-40 music, watch drama programs aimed at their age group, such as *Teen Wolf* and *Pretty Little Liars*, and watch romantically themed reality television, such as *The Bachelor* and *The Bachelorette* and old episodes of *Jersey Shore*. How might these media impact Anna's and Isaac's attitudes and behaviors?

This chapter will explore (1) how media influences the perception of reality, (2) the power of the culture of celebrity, (3) the effects that media can have on identity development in children and adolescents, and (4) the interpersonal variables in children's lives that determine how they respond to these media messages.

How do the media that Anna and Isaac consume impact the way they think about the world around them? For more than 30 years, George Gerbner, a professor of communication, led the Cultural Indicators Project, a research group that studied the effects of television viewing on the viewer's perception of reality. Gerbner examined the consequences of living with and learning from television. His findings led to the "Cultivation Theory," the argument that media consumption does, in fact, make "specific and measurable contributions to viewers' conceptions of reality."[4] Gerbner proposed that the amount of television a person watched influenced how much his or her perception of reality was tied to television content. He found that heavy viewers believed life experiences depicted in media were more common than they really were, even if the viewer's own experience contradicts those narratives. For example, people who view a lot of violence on television tend to believe that violence is more prevalent than it really is. Teens who view a lot of sexualized media tend to believe that more of their peers are sexually active than they really are. The power of television to influence a person's perception of reality, whether it supports his or her own experiences or not, speaks to the importance of investigating the content of the media messages viewed by adolescents.

How did consuming popular media influence Anna and Isaac in their perception of reality? When children are repeatedly exposed to themes and images, they begin to assimilate these into their own view of the world.[5] Although Gerbner's research focused on television, his findings are applicable to all media. Mass media influence how heavy users of media perceive gender roles, sexuality, attractiveness, desirability, and appropriate behavior.

MEDIA, PERCEPTION OF REALITY, AND SEXUALITY

How do media representations of sexuality impact a viewer's perceptions? Media messages tend to highlight the importance of fame, using one's sexuality to achieve and retain fame and attention, and casual sexual encounters. The advent of reality television, diary-like blogs, and YouTube video sharing has heightened our collective interest in the everyday lives of others, in particular the lives of celebrities. The ability and interest in the personal lives of celebrities has made celebrity sexuality big business. Media marketers respond to the high interest in the personal and sex lives of celebrities by encouraging the sexualization of well-known figures at younger and younger ages, leading increasingly younger children to identify with them. Some celebrities, such as Kim Kardashian, Justin Bieber, and Snooki, have attained their fame via Internet platforms and reality television, while others did so through playing characters who used such platforms, as depicted in the popular Nickelodeon program *iCarly*, which ran from 2007 to 2012 and was a popular childhood program for today's adolescents.

THE SEARCH FOR FAME

A recent theme that has emerged in popular television programming for tweens and teens is the search for fame. In both reality shows such as *American Idol* and in scripted programs like *Hannah Montana*, *True Jackson*, or *iCarly*, there has been a historical change in the portrayed value of fame. A content analysis of television shows from 1967 to 2011 demonstrated that beginning in 2007, fame began to take on an ever more important role in programming targeting children between 8 and 11 years old. Up until 2006, fame had a very low value in programs for tweens, but in 2007 things started to change. Now the value of achieving fame is depicted as the most important thing in programs that target 10- to 12-year-olds.[6]

HOW MEDIA SHAPES IDENTITY

As children and adolescents are developing their own identities, they are searching for successful role models with whom to compare themselves and whom they can emulate. As described by social comparison theory, people compare themselves to others and strive to achieve social rewards, such as attention and popularity, through imitating those who have achieved higher social status. The increase in the value of fame as depicted on television programming appears to be having an effect on children's future aspirations and view of self. For example, 10- to 12-year-olds now tend to value becoming famous above all else.[7] Researchers suggest that there may be a connection between children's consumption of fame-oriented television shows and their placing value on becoming famous. Participating in online social networking environments that allow the gathering of "friends" and "followers" may make the concept of fame seem accessible and highly valuable to tweens and teenagers.

There are several interpersonal reasons that children and adolescents may be particularly vulnerable to the culture of celebrity and the high value of fame. From a bioecological viewpoint, we need to consider the child herself and the characteristics that she brings to the interaction, including force, demand, and resource characteristics. For example, a high need for belonging and anxiety about social relations has been associated with a high desire for fame.[8] But forces within the child's microsystem are also at play. Research has found that individuals who report an intense desire for fame tend to perceive that fame is also highly valued by their family and friends.[9]

Media psychology researcher David C. Giles claims that one of the most important psychological influences of media for adolescents is the forming of what he calls "parasocial" relationships with celebrities.[10] As adolescents are forming their own identities, their use of celebrities as comparison figures leads them to look to the celebrity for guidance on values, attitudes, and behaviors.[11] There is considerable research supporting the idea that adolescents are susceptible to comparing themselves to celebrities and being influenced by celebrities.[12] At this stage of their development, adolescents are exploring and developing their own identities as emerging adults. When children are able to build competence, confidence, connection, character, and caring during this period, they develop a healthy understanding of who they are and what they can accomplish in life. What messages are celebrities sending about which behaviors one needs to be competent in, what makes one valuable, how to form connections and caring relationships, and what constitutes strong character? Quite often the messages promoted by mass media may not be healthy.

One example of this that was discussed earlier is the change in public persona of female celebrities as they move from childhood to adulthood. When an adolescent's favorite child star begins to signify her own move toward adulthood through increased sexual exposure, the message to children is that hypersexualized dress and behavior is an acceptable and normal way for females to identify their maturity.

Thinking back to Miley Cyrus, let me share a personal example. My children grew up watching Miley Cyrus on Disney's *Hannah Montana*. In 2013, child star Miley Cyrus performed on Music Television's Video Music Awards (VMA) with singer Robin Thicke. Thicke sang his hit song "Blurred Lines," which has been dubbed a rape anthem by critics[13] due to lyrics such as "But you're a good girl . . . must wanna get nasty."[14] During the song, Cyrus wore a nude-colored plastic bikini and performed a dance move called "twerking," which is dancing in a "sexually provocative manner involving thrusting hip movements and a low, squatting stance."[15] Since the VMA's target audience is 12- to 34-year-olds, adolescents are a large part of their viewing audience.[16] Adolescents like my 14- and 12-year-old daughters grew up watching Cyrus and identifying with her and were now being presented with a sexualized version of "growing up." Following the idea of the five C's of PYD, this emerging pattern of younger and younger females being sexualized provides girls with a negative pattern of superficial means of achieving these constructs. Competence and confidence become entwined with achieving attention and fame and using one's sexuality as a way to do so. Character appears to be focused on how much public attention one can attain.

PROMOTING THE CULTURE OF CELEBRITY

Increasingly, the trend of the women and girls being sexualized in media has affected the way that female celebrities promote themselves. In a study by Lambiase, content analysis was used to evaluate the websites of both male and female celebrities in terms of sexual dress.[17] That study found that female celebrities had a much higher percentage of sexualized dress than male celebrities. Lambiase proposes that celebrities use these strategies of a sexualized visual culture to increase their fame and garner public attention. However, the websites of those celebrities below 18 years old did not show heavily sexualized imagery. In the years since Lambiase's study, that has changed.

Considering the fact that sexualized images of women are being presented to adolescents and children at younger ages, Susan Lewis, an associate professor of journalism and mass communication, and I conducted a study comparing the official websites of two celebrities, one male and one female, under the age of 18. Our goal was to determine whether the female celebrity was represented with more sexualized images than the male celebrity. It was predicted that the female celebrity's website would contain more sexualized images than the male celebrity's website, both in terms of dress and posture. The results demonstrated that there was a significant difference in terms of both dress and posture between the male and female celebrities' websites. The female celebrity's website had significantly more photographs depicting her in sexually suggestive clothing and in a submissive posture than did the male celebrity's website.[18]

This is concerning because the increased exposure of celebrities through the growing popularity of the Internet, gossip sites, and mobile smartphone devices has inundated children and adolescents with sexualized, stereotyped images. This not only promotes sexualization and stereotypes, but it also disrupts the normal gradual emergence of sexuality in young people. Developmentally, it is appropriate for young adolescents to begin thinking about romance and their own sexual desires. Sexuality is a wonderful part of who we are, and it grows and emerges as we age so that it is naturally displayed in different ways from the time someone is 5 to 15 to 25. It is not natural for young girls to evolve overnight from being depicted as innocent children to cleavage-flaunting sexual objects. In the past 15 to 20 years, we have seen a change in the way young girls are presented in the media, and this has influenced children's understanding of sexuality.

The idea that fame is in itself an accomplishment, without any kind of talent, has been driven by the advent of reality television and the growth of celebrity gossip sites that focus on showing celebrities in everyday life situations. This genre has encouraged people to seek "being known" for its own sake, rather than exploring and growing in a craft or art. The apex of this type of fame can be found in reality television stars who are famous simply for being well known. The culture of celebrity has encouraged all of us to believe that any attention is good attention. This self-aggrandizing culture is one built on nothing but the shallow, vapid longing for recognition. As children and adolescents develop in the five C's of thriving, their involvement with the culture of celebrity can impact their views of competence.

The influence a celebrity really has on an adolescent's feelings, attitudes, and behaviors seems to be mitigated by how attached that particular young person is to the culture of celebrity and their reasons for pursuing information about celebrities. Researchers have proposed a very useful way of understanding where a young fan is in terms of his or her ability to be influenced by celebrities. In this framework, there are three levels of celebrity worship or attitude toward a celebrity.[19]

The first level is *entertainment-social*, which is described as a low level of celebrity worship. These types of fans enjoy hearing about and talking with friends about what a favorite celebrity has done.[20] We might think of this as the casual fan, and many children and adolescents fall into this category. They are interested in what their favorite celebrities are doing and tend to discuss them with friends, but that is about as far as their perceived relationship with the celebrity goes. Research has linked this type of attitude toward celebrity to extraversion and excitement seeking.[21] In the vignettes at the start of this chapter, as Anna interacted with media, she tended to have this type of attitude toward celebrities. She enjoyed engaging with media and learning about celebrities, but she did not highly identify with them.

The second level of fandom is called *intense-personal*, which involves more intense and obsessional thinking about a celebrity and compulsive seeking of information.[22] These are the fans who not only cover their rooms with images of their favorite celebrities, but also spend a fair amount of time thinking about and trying to learn more about them. These fans begin to identify themselves with the celebrity, wanting to dress and behave in similar ways. This type of celebrity worship has been linked with high levels of anxiety, hostility, depression, self-consciousness, impulsivity, and vulnerability.[23] As a person who tends to be more socially anxious and withdrawn, Isaac from this chapter's vignettes falls into this category of fandom. As Isaac became more engaged with media, he tended to want to emulate the performers that he connected with in dress, attitudes, and behavior.

The last and most extreme form of celebrity worship is called *borderline-pathological*. This type of attitude toward celebrity involves being willing to spend large amounts of money to obtain celebrity items or to go to great extremes to be near the celebrity.[24] This type of celebrity worship has been associated with difficulties in mental well-being, such as anxiety and depression[25] as well as with poor body image[26] and disordered eating.[27] Girls who strongly identify with media models tend to exhibit less satisfaction with their appearance and have lower body image.[28]

The implications of this are clear; young people who are more likely to develop strong parasocial relationships with celebrities put themselves at risk if the star they choose to emulate is following an unhealthy pattern of behavior. Oftentimes it has been said that a particular female celebrity herself is not really that sexualized, that it is only her way of promoting her "brand." Although that distinction may be important to the celebrity herself, it hardly matters at all to the young fan who is in the process of developing her own identity. The same is true for the hip-hop musician who promotes misogynist viewpoints through the lyrics of his songs and the images in his videos. Whether this man behaves in the same way in his private life has no impact on his influence on young fans. On the contrary, the public face of an adolescent's favorite celebrity is what he or she sees as the "real" person, and that is who the adolescent will identify with and emulate. To promote a sexualized version of oneself, which is targeted directly at emerging human beings, is highly irresponsible, especially when we consider that many celebrities are very heavily marketed directly to young people using tools and schemes that were designed to increase the fan's identification with the entertainer.

The creators of mass media use specific tools to attempt to draw in the viewer and encourage him or her to identify with performers. Such techniques include looking directly at the camera, speaking in conversational tones to the camera in monologues or asides that appear to require audience participation, and interacting in a casual way with others that suggests day-to-day engagement.[29] Celebrities also use common themes in a young person's life or even direct comparison to lead a fan to see them as relatable. For example, the soundtrack for *Hannah Montana*, a popular Disney show that ran from 2006 to 2011, claims, "I'm a lucky girl whose dreams came true, but underneath it all I'm just like you."[30] This "just like you" theme can also be found in Justin Bieber's *Never Say Never* movie with a focus on Bieber's rise to fame through posting his songs on YouTube. Several people in the film say things along the lines of "he was just a normal person and his dreams came true."[31] Through direct comparisons such as these or the more subtle techniques used in reality television such as having the celebrity discuss their thoughts and feelings with the camera as if it were the audience member, young fans are intentionally drawn into a parasocial relationship with the celebrity. Both Miley Cyrus and Justin Bieber are good examples of stars who have very specifically used the tools of the trade to elicit identification from their fans.

This blurring of the lines between reality and programming has been emotionally confusing from the very advent of this medium. With the introduction of reality television, the line has become even fuzzier for viewers. As Jennifer Pozner argues in her book *Reality Bites Back: The Troubling Truth about Guilty Pleasure TV*, although these shows claim to be unscripted, they are in fact manipulated so as to share the messages that the producers and the advertisers that are funding the majority of the production cost want to share.[32] Reality television has come to dominate primetime programming because it is inexpensive to make, requiring neither unionized writers nor actors. Pozner suggests that with sky-high advertising fees, networks can basically have advertisers pay for the production of reality television shows, thus reaping the benefits without the costs of producing quality television.

Reality television is especially adept at drawing viewers in, and it also powerfully influences sexual attitudes and behaviors in adolescents. Research has demonstrated that watching romantically and sexually themed television programs such as *The Bachelor*, *The Bachelorette*, *Jersey Shore*, and similar programming is related to permissive sexual attitudes.[33]

In a three-year study, researchers explored the effects of viewing romantically themed reality television on 498 adolescents. Their findings show that viewing shows such as *The Bachelor*, *Jersey Shore*, and other romantically themed programs changed peer-related sexual norms and the frequency of talking about sex with peers in adolescent girls. It also impacts the perception of the level of sexual experience in peers for adolescent boys.[34] The researchers believed that these increases in higher levels of communication about sex with peers and an overestimation of peer sexual activity are risky for teenagers, because adolescents who talk about sex more with their peers tend to be involved in more risky sexual behaviors. In the same way, adolescents who tend to seek sexual information from peers they assume to be more experienced have an increased chance of having sexual intercourse.

In a more recent study of the effects of watching romantically themed reality television, it was found that on *Jersey Shore* a sexual instance occurred one time per minute and the frequency of sexual instances were significantly higher on *Jersey Shore* than on other popular primetime television programs.[35] In their study of 246 undergraduate freshmen, researchers found that watching *Jersey Shore*, rather than television viewing in general, was likely to be connected to more permissive sexual attitudes. This was true of both the young men and young women in the study. Students who tended to wishfully identify with the cast members and those who had developed parasocial relationships with the cast members tended to have more permissive sexual attitudes. This has been found in other studies as well.[36] Young people who want to emulate reality television personalities may alter their sexual attitudes to reflect the permissive, casual sexual attitudes that are portrayed on the sexually and romantically oriented shows in this genre.

A young person's identification with a media figure can also provide him or her with positive models for sexual behavior. For example, one study looked at the ways that identification with media characters could impact a person's ability and willingness to have important sexual conversations with prospective partners.[37] Young people who identified more closely with a character who engaged in conversations with a potential partner about sexual topics (e.g., contraceptive use, sexually transmitted infections) were more likely to engage in similar discussions. The more the viewers identified with the character, the more likely they were to have their sexual self-efficacy increased by watching the program. Higher levels of identification with the character lead to greater self-efficacy, because it allowed the viewer to imagine him- or herself in a similar situation. This is an important finding, because a lack of self-efficacy in having sexual conversations often leads to avoidance of these conversations, which can impact an adolescent's sexual health and safety.

Although both Anna and Isaac in this chapter's vignettes watched romantic and dating-focused reality television, they had different responses to it. With opportunities to talk with her mother about sex, Anna did not feel the need to get information about sexuality and sexual relationships from these programs. Her outgoing personality and strong social skills allowed her to maintain a healthy relationship with the celebrities she admired. This allowed her to make decisions about her sexual behaviors based on her own concepts of competence, confidence, character, and caring rather than looking to celebrities for guidance in these areas. Isaac, on the other hand, did not have familial guidance about sexuality. His anxious and withdrawn social behaviors made it more difficult to connect with peers and easier to wishfully identify with confident, successful reality television stars. He tended to form his ideas of competence, confidence, character, and caring by looking for social guidance from reality television. This led him to copy the behaviors he was seeing on television and engage in casual sexual interactions.

For healthy development, both boys and girls need to be encouraged to view their sexuality and romantic interests as emerging gradually in a natural and personal way. Children and adolescents need support from their families and communities to develop confidence, competence, connection, and caring as their sexuality emerges rather than feeling as if their sexual development must meet the standards set by popular culture.

CONVERSATION STARTERS

Parents and professionals can use specific strategies to promote conversations about fame, parasocial relationships, and sexuality as depicted in popular media. Here are some ideas for addressing these specific areas.

Fame

The search for fame has become an increasingly important theme in children's media. It is important to discuss this theme with children beginning around age 10. As families watch a program such as *American Idol* or *The Voice*, parents might help their children process the messages about fame by asking questions such as, "How do you think being on this show might change a person's life? How might that person's life be better? How might it be worse?" Give the child an opportunity to think about both the benefits and challenges of fame. Ask the child to think about why people pursue an art. Is it to become famous or is it to develop their talent and share it with others? What is the difference between those two ideas? The point behind your questions is to prompt the child to consider fame within the context of other important aspects of life, such as developing competence and confidence in one's areas of passion, building connected, caring relationships, and becoming involved in a supportive community.

Parasocial Relationships

Adults should observe the types of relationships that children are forming with celebrities. If a child has entertainment-social relationships with celebrities, then parents and caregivers need not worry. However, if a child has formed intense-personal or borderline-pathological relationships, it is time to intervene. Children appear to form these unhealthy types of relationships with celebrities when they are having difficulties in their own social lives and are unsatisfied with their real-world relationships. These children are likely feeling disconnected and lack community. It is important for them to be supported in building stronger connections and provided with opportunities to connect with others with whom they share common interests. Parents and professionals need to help these children identify their interests and find a supportive community in which to explore it. You might ask your child, "What are you interested in learning how to do or learning more about?" Identify opportunities in the community, including arts, sports, community service, and so forth so that the child has a wide range of options to choose from. Allow the child the chance to try out a few interests before settling on one. The child may even decide to participate in more than one community, which will help him or her develop confidence and competence along with caring connections.

Sexual Relationships

Adolescents need support in processing the ways they see sexual relationships depicted in popular culture. Parents and caregivers need to consume media with their child in order to prompt conversation about the ways that sexual behaviors are depicted. For example, when watching a show such as *The Bachelor*, a parent might ask, "Do you think all of these women really care about this man? How would you feel if you were a woman in that situation? What about the man?" Then you might ask, "What do you think about kissing a guy who is 'dating' so many other women? Do you think the women feel pressure to get involved physically with him before they might be ready? Why or why not?" Provide the adolescent with the chance to think through the outcome of casual sexual encounters by asking, "How might you feel six weeks later if you had been one of those people and had been physically involved with the bachelor? Would you feel used, hurt, or sad? How do you make choices in your life about when to get involved with someone physically? How can you be sure that you are making the best choice for yourself?" Give the adolescent some suggestions for questions they might ask themselves, such as: (1) Will I be satisfied with this choice tomorrow, in a week, and in a month? (2) Am I making this choice free of outside pressure? Is it what I really want to happen? Let them know that if they feel unsure about a sexual behavior, that means they need to stop and rethink the situation, giving themselves time to be sure they are making a choice with agency.

Being involved with the culture of celebrity can have an impact on the way children feel about themselves and the choices they make. A child who has strong, caring connections, confidence in his or her ability to make choices about sexual behaviors, and competence in asking the right questions before engaging in sexual behaviors will be able to engage with celebrity culture in a healthy way.

IN THEIR VOICES

Andrew Boone is a 17-year-old blogger, media fan, and active social media user.

In the past three years, social networking has become an important part of my life: I manage a Facebook profile, a Twitter account (or two, or three), an Instagram page, and a personal blog on Tumblr. These sites have all been very positive outlets for me in connecting with people I know and meeting new people with whom I have mutual connections. As my online presence has increased, I've noticed an increase in real-world recognition by quasi-strangers—Twitter users who followed me after seeing a joke of mine retweeted, or perhaps someone who enjoyed a blog post of mine—and I do not doubt whatsoever that this is an experience shared by a large portion of my peers. Being publicly recognized for my Tweets, which I dedicate lots of effort to writing and perfecting, gives me a dopamine rush that I can immediately connect with the macrocosm of the world of celebrity culture.

With the advent of almost universal social media use among teenagers, local online celebrities have emerged. I humbly confess to having made confident judgments of people I only know of online, only to have been (sometimes, very pleasantly) shocked when they are nothing like I expected. These people are often referred to as being "Insta-famous" (having a large local following on Instagram that overshadows one's real-life fame) and are thus revered and even sometimes emulated by others.

The pursuit of online fame and recognition is alluring because of how much less effort it requires than does being well liked in real life. Friends commonly exchange "shout-outs" in order for multiple users to benefit from each other's respective following. High follower counts are usually associated with general success, as are the numbers of likes, retweets, or favorites on posts. There is also a considerable number of users on Twitter and Vine, such as @LOHANTHONY, Nash Grier, and Cameron Dallas, who, to my knowledge, are famous simply for being famous online; one might call them amateur Kardashians.

Brett Easton Ellis quoted a friend on his podcast of March 10, 2014, as saying that "any young artist that goes on Tumblr doesn't want to create actual art; they either want to *steal* the art, or they want to *be* the art." He connects this phenomenon to a victimization narrative into which many members of what he calls "Generation Wuss" have written themselves. Perhaps, "Generation Wuss" isn't necessarily the right name for a generation, but rather the name for the "Isaacs" of the world: those who are unable to express their opinions, emotions, and sexuality to their family members and therefore take to the blogs to express themselves.

Social media has leveled the playing field; this generation is slowly but surely becoming less dependent on "professional famous people" for their dosage of meaningless vapidity. For better or worse, or perhaps both, teens are becoming their own celebrities.

5

The Family Matters

Thinking back to Bronfenbrenner's bioecological theory of child development, it is clear that as children develop, they begin to understand the world and their place in it not only from their parents' perspective, but also from the information and messages they receive from exosystems and macrosystems such as media and culture. This chapter explores the way sexualized media particularly influence children as well as the parallel ways parents influence children in those same areas. I will then discuss strategies parents can use to minimize sexualized media's impact on children and adolescents and share narratives that promote healthy messages about sexuality.

Parents and media have some commonalities in the things that they communicate to children. Both have a distinctive worldview that colors the way they see and thus interpret the world around them. A worldview is simply the lens through which we view the world, the assumptions that we make about truth, value, and humanity. Parents, knowingly or not, will teach their children how to look at and think about the world around them. Parents will be communicating their worldview about gender and sexuality with their children in both direct and indirect ways.

In the same way, the people who develop media and marketing campaigns have their own worldviews. Their perspective will color the programs and products they develop. On top of that, these campaigns are promoting consumption. The point behind them is to sell something, so of course they will work to make consumers feel they need it, whether it is a beauty product or the latest toy. Both parents and media will present children with worldviews about what it means to be a boy or girl, what makes one valuable as a human being, and how to gain social power.

When we consider the billions of dollars in marketing and research that parents are up against, it is clear that if parents want their child to learn about healthy sexuality, they must be intentional. Parents have the opportunity to be a huge influence in how their child processes all of these messages. Research has established that family is a key component in how children and adolescents learn to understand their sexuality.[1] As I mentioned earlier, the way a parent approaches media sets the tone for their child's approach. There are two paths that parents tend to take: one is the path of seeing themselves and their children as active media consumers and critics while the other is that of passive consumption. The problem with the second path is that media messages are being carefully crafted and presented and they influence both our consumption and potentially our worldview.

Whenever authors of a book or script for a television show or movie create a piece of media, they are sharing their own worldview, whether blatantly or subtly. For example, in many of the early Disney cartoons, female value and goodness are linked to being physically attractive, nurturing, and romantic. In movies like *Snow White* and *Sleeping Beauty*, females are not part of the action, but instead sit passively waiting to be rescued. In recent Disney television shows, one sees a consistent dichotomy of the smart, sassy girl compared to the goofy, bumbling boy. These themes are reliable enough to be picked up on by the children who consume these media. If children are consistently consuming media that perpetuate a specific worldview about where an individual's value lies or what kinds of interests or traits one is expected to have based on gender, then those children will begin to be impacted by that worldview. This is important because worldview is about our own understanding of who we are and what makes us valuable.

PARENTAL INFLUENCE

Parents and Media

Research has shown that parents play a large part in their children's developing attitudes about themselves as well as in the way they respond to sexualized media. This means that parents and caregivers are not powerless, not just pawns in the game played by media, destined to respond in the way marketers would like. Parents and other trusted adults can help children move from individuals who passively accept images and narratives presented by media to individuals who actively create their own views and then work to influence the views of those around them. To begin the journey in helping children become active media consumers, adults first have to know that they are important in the process.

A study by Nielsen showed that teens' favorite television shows, websites, and genre preferences across media are almost exactly the same as those of their parents. Children tend to choose to watch the shows their parents watch, look at the websites they visit, and so forth.[2] This is important to keep in mind, because it shows that parents do influence the kinds of media their children consume.

Research that has examined the way parents engage their children with media has also provided some important information about how parents influence the effects of media on children. Nathanson defines three ways that parents mediate their child's engagement with media.[3] These include *restrictive mediation*, which involves setting up rules about what content can be consumed and limits to the amount of content a child can consume. *Coviewing* involves the parent and child consuming media together but not discussing the content. In *active mediation*, the parent and child consume media together and discuss the content.

Of course, some parents choose not to mediate and allow their children to consume media alone. However, it is important to know that research has shown that parental mediation of television is linked with children's attitudes and behaviors. When a parent understands the importance of actively engaging their child while consuming media, this strategy can aid the child in developing a plan for responding to sexualized media messages. A study conducted in 2008 that looked at the long- and short-term effects of parental mediation of media found that those adolescents who reported greater quality of (1) mother–child communication, (2) greater parental disapproval of sex, (3) greater parental discussion of television content, and (4) more limits on television viewing were less likely to initiate oral sex and vaginal intercourse than others.[4] Both active mediation and restrictive mediation are associated with an adolescent's ability to view media with a more critical eye and with media's ability to influence his or her sexual behaviors.[5]

On the other hand, the passive coviewing of sexualized media seemed to send children the signal that the parent who was watching agreed with the sexualized representation. This makes it clear that parents need to be actively involved with the media that their child is consuming. Even when not present at the time a child consumes a particular piece of media, a parent can still help the child process the

media later. For example, my teenage daughter and I both read the
John Green young adult novel *The Fault in Our Stars*. She then went to
see the movie with a group of friends, and afterward she and I sat
down and talked about the movie together. Even though I was not
with her at the time, we were still able to talk about what meanings she
drew from the film and compare the film to the book. This allowed me
as the parent to have a voice in how she responded to the film.

Research has shown that children who have supportive, involved
parents are less likely to personally accept media portrayals of women
as sexual objects.[6] Parents who actively discuss sexual content and
messages with their children are able to influence their child's understanding of media messages.[7] These findings are important because
they suggest that parents can have a significant impact on how their
child interacts with the media. Not only that, but parental involvement
in engaging media together with their child affects the way that sexualized media impact the child. For parents who may be feeling overwhelmed by the impact sexualized media has on children,
understanding that they themselves can mitigate their child's response
is vital. This knowledge empowers the parent to actively engage their
child while consuming media, providing the opportunity for critical
analysis of the content.

Parents, Sex, and Positive Youth Development

In the vignettes presented in Chapter 4, Anna was provided the opportunity for open conversation about sexuality with her parents.
During these conversations, Anna's parents focused on helping her see
herself as an agent in her sexual decisions who makes her own choices
about her behaviors. They made it clear that she should never engage
in sexual behaviors with someone out of pressure or guilt, and neither
should she pressure another to engage in sexual behaviors with her.
Consent and mutuality were emphasized. Isaac, on the other hand,
was left without guidance regarding sexual behaviors. Because his
parents were uncomfortable talking about sexuality, their only communication with him was, "You should not have sex before marriage."
Without a context for understanding his parents' values or a way to
obtain support from them about making healthy sexual decisions,
Isaac looked to his peers and the mass media for guidance, and both
promoted casual sexual encounters.

How do families like Anna's and Isaac's equip their children to
thrive in the area of sexual development? How do they aid them in
building the skills needed to effectively respond to sexualized media?
These are critical questions to ponder. We must begin to consider

sexual development from a positive and healthy perspective. When we take this approach, families can nurture children and adolescents and promote healthy sexual development. A look at the components of PYD applied to sexuality will help answer that question.

Connection

The connection that parents build with their child is a primary relationship that impacts a child's development. Parents play an important role in a child's developing body image, self-concept, and understanding of sexuality. Honest communication between adolescents and parents is an important part of building that connection.[8] From body satisfaction to unhealthy weight control behaviors, parents help their children learn to think about their bodies and habits in a healthy way.[9] Children are impacted by both direct parent feedback on the importance of appearance[10] and by a parent's own body esteem and the way that is expressed in front of the children.[11] Interestingly, a study that examined body weight dissatisfaction among adolescents in 24 different countries found that boys and girls who reported difficulty in communicating with parents had more body dissatisfaction, especially the father in the case of the boys.[12] These studies suggest that parents can contribute to a healthy body image by fostering open and warm communication in general, refraining from negative body comments about themselves and others, and promoting the idea that appearance is not what defines a person's value by focusing on other characteristics, such as a person's determination, kindness, and character.

Aside from body image, parents can impact the way their children think about sexuality and sexual behaviors. In particular, close relationships with mothers tend to be associated with a decreased chance that a child will be involved in risky sexual behavior.[13] This may be because in many families, mothers tend to be the parent who most often discusses sexual issues with the children. Studies have shown that children and adolescents want to learn about sexual matters from their parents.[14] Those adolescents who are closer to their parents and more satisfied with their relationships with them tend to be less anxious in discussing sex with their parents than other adolescents.[15] Several studies have found that both as an adolescent and later as an adult, people whose parents chose not to talk with them about sex clearly saw this silence as a negative aspect of their development, in terms of both their emotional and physical safety while growing up.[16]

The Sexuality Education Initiative was launched in 2008 and has continuously gathered data from adolescents participating in the program. Surveys of the adolescents in the program have demonstrated that teenagers want to talk with their parents about sexuality, but they find it difficult for both themselves and their parents.[17]

Parents play an important role in preventing early sexual activity and risk taking by talking with their child about sex, explaining the negative outcomes associated with risky behaviors and ways to protect oneself, and communicating disapproval of risky sexual behaviors.[18] In several studies, adolescents have said that they place a very high value on open communication with their parents. These children clearly see honest communication as a hallmark of a good relationship with their parents.[19] A closer relationship with parents has also been linked to less risky sexual behavior.[20]

A review of over 400 research articles indicated that the connection that parents form with children impacts sexual behaviors in that teens who feel connected to their parents are less likely to initiate sex at an early age and engage in healthier sexual practices, such as using contraceptives and having fewer partners.[21] This points to the importance of parental communication about sexual behaviors and sexuality in general as well as the provision of information about the negative outcomes of engaging in risky sexual behaviors.

Building warm and open communication is key to providing a child with the important information about sexual behaviors needed to successfully negotiate this highly sexualized media landscape. Children from families who spend more time actively doing things with one another and who have parents with whom they have fewer hostile interactions tend to engage in less risk-taking behavior.[22] Family closeness also tends to limit girls' sexual risk taking to a greater extent than boys.[23] It seems that for girls, seeing their family as closely connected emotionally is a bigger deterrent to taking risks sexually, while for boys setting limits is more important. For Anna, it was important for her parents to build a supportive, warm, and connected environment in their family. For Isaac, that would also be important, but he would have been well served by having his parents provide him with clear and consistent limits on his behavior, such as a regular curfew and more supervision.

Children are being bombarded by sexual imagery and messages about the importance of their sexuality. When we avoid talking with them about those messages and how they feel about them, we leave them open to interpreting these messages on their own. One study found that girls who see their relationship with their parents as negative and feel there are barriers in communicating with their parents about sexual topics were especially vulnerable to become engaged in early sexual activity.[24] Parents need to give advice about the emotional consequences of becoming intimately involved with someone at an early age, such as how to resist unwanted pressure and other emotional issues related to sexual behaviors. When parents avoid these types of conversations, the child is unprepared to handle pressures and confusion related to sexual desire.

The connection a child has with primary caregivers is an important resource for children and adolescents when it comes to engaging with and interpreting sexualized media. When parents understand their role in helping their child critically analyze sexualized media messages as well as providing a safe place of communication about self-concept, body image, and sexuality, they can mediate their child's response to sexualized media.

Competence

To become competent in critiquing media, navigating media messages about sexuality, and making decisions about sexual behaviors, children need parent involvement. In a study of college students, 67 percent indicated they believed parents should be a primary source of sexual education for their children. And yet, of those same students, only 15 percent said that their parents had been a primary source of information for them.[25] The students in this study said that one of the main barriers to parent–child communication about sexuality was embarrassment. In order to grow in their competence, children need to receive information about sexuality from their parents. Parents can alleviate embarrassment and become a key source of sexual information for their children in order to build their competence in this area. Parents can facilitate competence by building connections with their child, providing appropriate supervision, and openly communicating their sexual values to the child.[26]

Adolescents tend to rely heavily not just on their parents and friends, but also on the mass media as a source of sexual information.[27] Thus, it is important for parents to provide children with media literacy skills so they can effectively judge the sexual information they receive from mass media. Media literacy skills involve learning to ask those key questions we looked at before: who is the creator, who is the audience, what is the worldview being promoted, and what message is being sent. As parents provide children and adolescents with the opportunity to ask these questions around specific pieces of media that address romance and sexuality, the child will grow in his or her ability to be a critical consumer.

Confidence

Sexual self-efficacy is an important issue for parents to consider. As discussed earlier, self-efficacy is an individual's beliefs about his or her ability to perform a particular behavior in a given situation.[28] When we talk about sexual self-efficacy, we are talking about a person's confidence and perceived control and ability to choose to engage or not engage in sexual behaviors.[29] This includes specific confidence in areas such as contraceptive use, resistance to unwanted sexual advances, and asking for help when needed. Self-efficacy in these areas is linked to sexual behaviors, with those adolescents who have higher levels of sexual self-efficacy engaging in fewer risky behaviors.[30]

Parents can help their child gain sexual self-efficacy by providing him or her with information about common sexual behaviors, decisions, and situations. Resistance self-efficacy is key when it comes to sexual behaviors. Parents must talk with their children about how to express their own desires in a physical relationship, say "no" to unwanted advances, avoid situations that might lead to danger, and ask for help when needed.

Interestingly, the research suggests that parents tend to take very different tracks in talking about sexuality with their sons versus their daughters. Parents tend to talk more openly with their daughters about sex and sexuality.[31] It has been found that parents covered 40 percent fewer specific topics in regard to sexuality with their sons than they did with their daughters, and in some cases boys had a greater need for interventions to build self-efficacy than girls did.[32] Boys like Isaac are missing out on developing sexual self-efficacy and learning about developmental emotional issues related to sexuality. When parents refuse to talk with their sons about the emotional components of sexuality and only tell them "Don't have sex," they do not provide boys with the framework to understand how any kind of physical intimacy is connected to their and their partner's emotions and understanding of themselves as individual agents. Both girls and boys need to learn to see their sexuality and sexual behaviors in the context of their identity as a whole. They need to be given the opportunity to talk with their parents and other trusted adults about healthy sexuality, decision making, and setting boundaries. Framing sexuality as a part of one's self rather than some kind of separate thing to be afraid of allows children and adolescents to think about their behaviors in a more coherent framework.

STRATEGIES FOR SUCCESS

Talking about Sex and Sexuality with Children

It will not always be easy or comfortable for parents to talk with children and adolescents about sensitive issues, no matter how prepared they may be. Parents must accept upfront that some conversations may be uncomfortable. When tempted to avoid an issue because it makes them anxious, caregivers must remember that their child's questions will not go away just because the parent does not answer them. Children will find a way to satisfy their curiosity, but they will likely look to their peers or media for the information their parents did not provide.

One of the main reasons parents may be uncomfortable talking with their children about sexuality is that the parent did not have positive role models in this area. Maybe their own parents or caregivers never talked with them about their bodies changing and developing sexual desire. Many parents are in a strange cycle of discomfort where they do not know how to address these issues because nobody ever took the time to address them when they were growing up. Many of my friends who are parents today say that their own parents never talked to them about sex. They remember how difficult it was as a teenager to try to understand what was happening to their bodies and their developing sexuality when nobody was sharing information with them. And yet, when it comes down to having that same discussion with their own children, their instinct is to shy away. It is imperative that parents be their child's first source of information about the topic of sexuality. When children see parents as an open, reliable source of information on this topic, they will continue to ask questions. With sexualized media providing unhealthy lessons about sexuality, it is important that children not turn to this type of media for their sexual information.

Collaborative Sexuality Education

I asked Dae Sheridan, a licensed psychotherapist, board-certified clinical sexologist, and professor of graduate human sexuality at the University of South Florida,[33] share some advice on how to educate children about sexuality from a healthy, collaborative perspective.[34] First, I will present some general advice and then move into some specific ways to talk with children about sexuality at different ages and stages. Sheridan and I have both had conversations with our university students about sexuality education. The majority of them reported having "the talk" in about fifth or sixth grade. Most of them agreed that this conversation did not suffice to give them what they needed to know in order to make good decisions for themselves as they matured. So what can parents do? Here is the advice that Sheridan shared with me.

First and foremost, strive to eliminate the concept of "the talk." Sexuality education is not a one-time speech about "the birds and the bees," but a series of age-appropriate teachings and ongoing conversations with our children throughout the different ages and stages of their physical, emotional and sexual development. I like to call this collaborative sexuality education.[35]

In my work with children and as a mother, the times I have been most uncomfortable with a sexuality conversation were when I was not expecting the question. I have felt frozen with shock and wondered if I should even answer. This is an experience that most parents have faced at one time or another, and one that is uncomfortable enough that it keeps parents like Isaac's from wanting to address sexual issues in the first place. Parents must be prepared to address whatever question or issue their child introduces. I recommend that parents give themselves a few minutes to get over the shock and then tell the child they are surprised to hear him or her mention that topic. They might say, "That's not something I expected you to ask, so I was a little surprised that you brought it up. Let's talk about it." This helps the parent guide the conversation into a discussion about that specific topic. It also allows the parent to give suggestions to the child about how he or she might protect him- or herself in the future from inappropriate content. Children should know that they can tell a peer they are not interested in hearing anymore or leave the room if needed, empowering them to respond effectively to situations that make them uncomfortable. I asked Sheridan if she had specific thoughts on how to respond to questions that children may ask about sex.

One of the greatest myths, misconceptions, and outright errors in thinking about human sexuality is that if we teach children *about* sex, they will go out and *have* sex. Quite the opposite is true. Many parents fear that giving information about sexual health equals giving children permission to have sex. However, research shows that parents who are more open in their discussions about sexuality have kids who are *less* likely to become sexually active at a young age.

What we know about sexuality education and positive outcomes leads to this, talk early and talk often. Parents might take issue with sex education in schools starting as early as kindergarten; however, if you look at the teen pregnancy statistics and current sexually transmitted infection (STI) rates, you will see that if we start talking to kids "around puberty" a large percentage of parents will have been too late. Every bit of research in the field informs us that children who have had adequate sexuality education and who have parents who are open and willing to dialogue about sex are more likely to wait to have sex. Also, we know that those who do choose to have sex are more likely to use condoms or other types of birth control to protect themselves against unwanted pregnancies and sexually transmitted infections.[36]

CONVERSATION STARTERS

Conversations about sexuality are not about having one talk and being done with the topic. Instead, think of conversations about sexuality as an ongoing process of your child's development. Here are some specific tips from Sheridan for talking about sexuality with children of different ages.

Toddlers

Always discuss body parts with proper names. Nicknames can confuse and create issues down the line with shame, body image, self-esteem, and healthy sexuality. When we reference "down there" we send a message that our genitals and their functions are not something to be discussed. There needs to be a healthy working vocabulary about all of our parts. We celebrate potty training, so use that as a launching point to continue to discuss keeping one's private parts safe and healthy. Teach them basic anatomy, empower them to understand and take ownership and have agency over their bodies.

This is a good time to explain that their private parts are their own and that no one is to touch them other than trusted adults who are helping with hygiene or toilet care, or a doctor performing an exam with parents' and child's permission. Reiterate to children that they should not keep secrets from Mom and Dad and no one should ever ask them to do so.[37]

This is an age when many children will begin to touch their genitals experimentally and realize that it is pleasurable. Self-touch makes some parents nervous. I asked Sheridan for her thoughts on the best way to handle self-touch.

Recognize that children have no sexual frame of reference as we adults do, so when they stroke their genitals, or attempt to self-stimulate, this is perfectly normal and they have just found another wonderful part of their very own bodies. Avoid punishing them or saying things like, "that's dirty!" As a clinical sexologist, I see both men and women for varying degrees of relationship issues and sexual dysfunction. When I ask my clients to recall their first memories surrounding sex, an overwhelming percentage of them remember the exact moment they were caught masturbating and it was not a positive experience. Whether it was a pointed comment such as "good girls don't do that" or a slap on the hand with a disapproving look, or the extreme of being physically abused, an intense exchange with their parents bred shame and set a derogatory tone regarding their sexuality.[38]

Preschoolers

At this age, Sheridan recommends making sure you talk with your child about private parts being private. She says, "That means that you don't show them to anyone or let anyone else touch them and there are certain things we just do not do at the dinner table or at school."[39] This is also a good age to be sure that your child knows how to respond if someone does try to touch him or her in a way that is not appropriate. Be sure that your child knows what is appropriate and what is not. You can call these "good touch and bad touch" and role play ways for your child to say "No, don't touch me!" Also help them identify safe adults in each environment (home, preschool, neighborhood, etc.) whom they can go to if they need help. When children have a specific phrase to use and have identified adults whom they can seek help from in different environments, they are more likely to do so when needed.

One of the best pieces of advice on this topic comes form Joycelyn Elders, former surgeon general under the Bill Clinton administration. Elders said "Parents need to let go of the idea that ignorance maintains innocence and begin teaching age-appropriate facts to children. Informed children know 1) what sexual abuse and harassment are, 2) what normal physical closeness with others is, 3) what should be reported and to whom. Rather than tell children that touching themselves is forbidden, parents may gently explain that this is best done in private."[40]

Early Elementary (Grades K-2)

At this age, children will begin to form lasting friendships and be involved everyday with many different children. This is a great time to begin to talk about personal space. We have already discussed using the concept of a hug as a beginning point for talking about having a right to your own space and being able to decide what happens to your body. Early elementary school–aged children are able to understand this concept and begin to apply it more broadly. Children become very aware of gender and gender role stereotypes at this age. Sheridan recommends that parents discuss the many ways to be a boy or girl. For example, on my blog I share stories of men and women who have jobs that do not fit stereotypical visions of masculinity and femininity. I have featured such people as a male kindergarten teacher and a female biochemist. Providing examples of men and women who do not fit in to stereotypical roles can give your child a broader vision for roles that men and women can ultimately assume.

Late Elementary (Grades 3–5)

Regarding this age group, Sheridan says:

This is the age where the questions may come fast and furious, or may trickle out as schoolmates gossip about babies and body parts. Don't unleash everything you know all at once. Continue to answer simple questions with simple answers. Have this be a two-way conversation and keep it to your child's level. Ask them what they already know when they ask a question instead of just answering. Clear, informative anatomy lessons about reproductive parts and functions with the help of age appropriate books and materials can help both of you move through this time with ease.[41]

She recommends that as children ask questions or topics come up in conversation, parents begin to introduce information about abstinence, birth control, and risky sexual behavior, being clear about potential negative consequences of engaging in sexual behaviors, such as unintended pregnancy and sexually transmitted infections. It is also important to remember to share positive messages about sexuality in the context of emotions, intimacy, and well-being. Children at the upper end of this age group may begin to want to have boyfriends or girlfriends, so this is a good time to begin to have conversations about coercion and manipulation. For example, what if someone asks your child to go out, but he or she does not want to? How will your child handle that situation? Will he or she feel pressured to comply so as not to hurt someone's feelings? What if your child wants to go out with someone who is not interested in him or her? How will your child handle that rejection? Discussing and role playing these situations with your child will help him or her to feel empowered to handle social situations that might be stressful.

Middle School (Grades 6–8)

If they have not already, children at this stage will begin to see changes in their bodies. Whenever you notice your child's body beginning to change, it is imperative that you educate them about what is happening. Sheridan says:

Celebrate this next stage of development and describe the very cool science behind hormones and pubertal changes. Be clear that everybody and every body is different! Discuss how the timing of puberty and adolescent development varies and will happen at the right time for your child. Discuss positive body image and point out and discuss cookie-cutter, unrealistic portrayals of airbrushed perfection represented by advertisers and the media. Encourage your child to be "Body Image Warriors," recognizing that their worth, value, and self-efficacy has much more to do with what is inside rather than outward appearance.[42]

Some adolescents in middle school will begin to be involved in physical relationships and engage in sexual behaviors such as oral sex and intercourse. Any parent with a child in this age group must be prepared to talk with them about sexual behaviors. I asked Sheridan if she had some specific advice for talking about sexual behaviors with children of this age. Her recommendations were:

Teach not only reproductive and mechanical aspects of varied sexual behaviors and sexual intercourse, but relational and pleasurable ones as well. Demonizing or omitting information about sexual pleasure simply robs your child of his or her fullest potential for healthy sexual development.

Discuss abstinence as the only 100 percent way to avoid pregnancy and sexually transmitted infections, however, introduce information about hormonal and barrier birth control options, including condoms. Provide information about sexually transmitted infections, both bacterial and viral. Do not use scared straight techniques, but rather give clear, accurate information, and real statistics about how common STIs are in the teenage population and beyond.

Reiterate the family's value system and set standards for the who, what, when, where, why, and how of sexual behavior. Talk about sex being a positive and wonderful thing in the context of self-love and respect for self and others at the right age and circumstance.[43]

As the mother of adolescent girls, the advice that Sheridan gives rings true for me. As my girls entered middle school, our conversations gradually changed from body changes to sexual behaviors in general to much more specific scenarios about how to make a decision about what behaviors you want to engage in, with whom, and how to protect yourself from negative consequences. The scenarios we have discussed include taking and sharing digital "selfies," accessing pornography online, and specific sexual behaviors inside and outside of relationships. This age group is beginning to be very involved with social media, so parents need to discuss safety and legal and ethical issues that go along with posting and sharing information or pictures. Sheridan says, "Educate, trust, but verify. Let your children know that technology usage is a privilege, not a right, and that all use is subject to transparency and inspection."[44]

What I have found is that when parents spend time listening to and consuming media with their adolescent, these types of conversations emerge naturally from something that is going on with peers or in the media. For example, when one of my daughters was in seventh grade, a friend told her that she was afraid she might be pregnant. This friend had been sexually active without using any type of protection. When my daughter told me about this, we were able to talk about how, if you were going to be sexually active, it is vitally important to protect oneself from pregnancy and STIs. I answered her questions and we role played how she might be able to talk with her friend about ways that friend could protect herself in the future. To be honest, I would rather not have had to have this conversation with my 13-year-old daughter.

But, the fact is, our adolescents will talk with their friends about these issues, and it is our job as parents to help them learn how to process such scenarios and how to best respond to keep themselves healthy and safe.

In order to help our children thrive, we need to provide them with connection and guidance on how to develop caring relationships. As they become more deeply involved in romantic relationships, this age group needs opportunities to practice life skills such as decision-making skills and communication strategies. These kinds of conversations allow them the chance to do that in a safe, secure environment. Discuss and model what healthy relationships and communication look like. You can even use media depictions to start those conversations.

Besides sexualized narratives, media also provide thoughtful, healthy messages about decision making around sexual behaviors. For example, the movie *Valentine's Day* portrays a couple who are seniors in high school. Both are virgins, and they have decided they want to have sex with each other in order to build a closer bond. They plan and prepare and make sure they have considered how to protect themselves from unwanted consequences such as sexually transmitted diseases and pregnancy. In the end, the girl decides she is not ready to have sex after all. They talk about how she is feeling and why and are able to continue their relationship in a way that makes them both comfortable. This is a great example to discuss with teens. It provides parents a chance to talk about situations their children or their friends may encounter. Here is an example of how you might discuss this with your adolescent.

CONVERSATION STARTER

Many adolescents will have friends who are sexually active to some degree, even if they themselves are not. Using media to prompt conversations about sexual behaviors may be more comfortable than just asking the questions outright. These types of scenes provide a good conversation starter with adolescents about the way couples mutually negotiate what they want in a physical relationship.

The parent may say, "What did you think about the reason this couple decided to have sex?" Listen to what your adolescent has to say, then follow up with something like, "Do you think that trying to build their bond makes sense when they are about to graduate and go to different colleges? Why might that sound like a good idea to them? Why might it not be a good idea?" Explore with your teen the idea that sexual intimacy does build emotional bonds, but that closeness is likely to be painful when a couple then separates. Ask: "Are there other ways to build a relationship besides having sex? What might those be? Why might it not be a good idea to build emotional intimacy with someone, even if you care about him or her?" This gives your teen the chance to explore the idea of emotional intimacy and the positive and negative consequences of close romantic relationships in adolescence. Although it is normal and natural for teens to want to have close relationships, they need to be aware of the ways that physical and emotional intimacy may be connected to both positive and negative feelings.

Follow this line of questioning to prompt your teen to explore the different ways to think about the actions of the couple in *Valentine's Day*. For example: "What did you think about the girl deciding that she didn't want to have sex? How hard do you think that was? If you were in a situation where someone wanted you to be more physically involved with them than you wanted to be, what would you do?" Then ask: "What did you think about how the boy handled it when his girlfriend said she had changed her mind? Do you think he was angry? How did he eventually deal with his own feelings?" This type of conversation gives adolescents the chance to plan and practice ways to respond to uncomfortable situations with the guidance and feedback of a trusted adult. It is important that parents have these types of conversations with both their sons and daughters. Both may end up in situations where they are either initiating physical intimacy or are the recipient of physical activity that they do not welcome. Both boys and girls need to be prepared to handle either situation with thoughtfulness and grace.

In the television show *Pretty Little Liars* there are repeated themes of sexuality that might be discussed. In one incidence early in the series, the character Hannah attempts to initiate sex with her boyfriend, but he rebuffs her because he says he is not ready to have sex. In another storyline, a main character named Emily initiates passionate kissing with her boyfriend, and then later says no when he tries to press physical affection on her. Her boyfriend refuses to stop until someone else intervenes. This type of media depiction can be a great chance to ask adolescents, "What might you do if someone was pressuring you to try something you didn't feel ready for?" and "What would you do if you wanted to do something physical in a relationship and the other person didn't? How would you feel? How would you handle those feelings while also respecting the other person?" All of these are great examples of media that depict adolescent sexuality in a realistic way, sometimes with positive and respectful interactions and other times with more contentious interactions.

Give your child specific examples from both real life and media of positive, reciprocal ways that people show affirmation, kindness, love, affection, appreciation, and attention toward one another and also examples of ways that are inappropriate. For example, middle school is a time when many adolescents will touch one another in the hallway. Oftentimes, this happens without the consent of the person being touched. Talk with your child about why nonconsensual touch is not okay, even if it does not appear to be hurting anyone. Role play with them how they might handle it if someone touches them without their consent, and what they might do if a friend engages in nonconsensual touching. Sheridan recommends having conversations with children at this age about risky behaviors. She says: "Remember that information does not equal permission. Talking about sexuality is a gateway conversation. If children know that their parents are open to talking with them about sex, they are more likely to talk to their parents about peer pressure, cigarettes, drugs, alcohol, bullying, curfews, friendships. Children think, 'If I can talk to my parents about that, I can talk to them about anything.'"[45]

High School

Parents must notice what is happening in their child's world. Most parents lead full lives, and it is easy to lose touch with what is important to a child. Providing opportunities for the child to talk while the parent listens and asks questions about their interests, hobbies, and thoughts will help the parent stay connected and aware of what is happening in their child's life. Parents need to pay attention to the trends for adolescents. For example, a trend for adolescent girls in past years has been reading the *Twilight* book series and watching the movies or watching the television series *Pretty Little Liars*. If all of her friends are involved with this series, a child may want to be as well. Parents need to find out what the stories are about, read or watch them, ask a trusted friend who has read or watched them, or check out websites devoted to helping parents with media choices, such as Common Sense Media. In other words, parents must inform themselves. Rather than immediately saying "yes" or "no" to any given trend, when parents take the time to explore the trend, they are able to engage with their child in a more knowledgeable manner. As an adolescent, a child is learning to reason and make choices. Parents can help their adolescents problem solve by giving their reasons for decisions and talking the issue through calmly and openly.

As discussed earlier in this chapter, being approachable is key to having children who ask questions. Sheridan says that at this age, it is especially important for our children to know that we as parents are not perfect and do not know everything. She says:

We as parents also need to give ourselves permission to say: "I don't know." Don't shy away from difficult topics in order to save face. Tell your kid: "This is a little embarrassing for me; I really don't know! But it's important because you are important, so let's figure it out together!" Parents need to educate themselves. Find relevant resources, books, articles, websites, and mobile apps that continue to reiterate the messages you have shared with your child to date. This is the stage when you need to begin to discuss sexual fantasy, desires, increased hormones, and the biological drives/neurochemistry of crushes and romantic love. Remind adolescents that their underdeveloped prefrontal cortexes will try to play tricks on them at this point in their lives, and that they need to be especially intentional about considering long-term consequences.[46]

Parents of adolescents need to remember that children at this age may not be having intercourse, but they may be engaging in other types of sexual behaviors. It is important to talk with them about these as well. I asked Sheridan what kinds of sexual behaviors parents need to discuss with their adolescents. She said: "Clarify that any type of foreplay or 'outercourse' can lead to either positive or negative outcomes, dependent upon the circumstance. Be clear that any shared sexual behavior is indeed sexual behavior and there can be both physical and emotional risks."[47] For example, oral sex can lead to the spread of STIs, and many adolescents do not know this. They tend to think of oral sex as "safe."

Adolescents need to be inundated with information about the importance of consent. As we have discussed earlier, the issue of consent tends to be blurry for children at this age when alcohol or drugs are involved. Have frank conversations with your adolescents about the fact that drug and alcohol use can decrease inhibitions, but that once someone is clearly unable to make informed decisions, then everyone should consider that person unable to give consent. Sheridan recommends using role play or very specific scenarios as a way to talk about controversial and difficult situations that may require increased assertiveness.

CONVERSATION STARTER

Earlier I discussed a sexual assault case that revolved around high school boys who had sexual relations with a girl who was heavily under the influence of alcohol. Although it may be difficult, parents need to talk about these very specific cases with their adolescents and ask questions like: "Do you think this girl gave consent? Why or why not? If you were the initiator in a similar situation, what would you do to make sure you obtained consent? At what point do you know that the other person is not able to consent to sexual behavior?"

Talk with your adolescents about their responsibilities as a by-stander. "What would you do if you were at a party and saw someone having sexual relations with a person who was passed out?" Brainstorm possible solutions, such as finding the nearest adult, calling a parent, directly intervening, gathering a group to intervene, or calling the police. All of these are possible solutions that might be best in given situations. Providing your adolescent with the chance to think and talk through these difficult situations will leave them better prepared to respond if the chance arises.

Family discussions about sexuality are vital. I asked Sheridan if she had any final thoughts on talking with children about sexuality.

Remember that this is a series of discussions throughout childhood, adolescence, and young adulthood. When you are open to having the dialogue, discussions will come more easily. If you have been talking about your value system, your family's moral code, your hopes and dreams for your children, your expectations of them, your availability as a parent, then you will not have to fear that information equals permission. You will have had conversations that other parents dread and you and your child will be the better for it. Your rewards for taking these steps will be apparent as you see your children moving through their adolescence and young adulthood with greater confidence and ease.[48]

Although sexualized media images can have an effect on self-concept, body image, and sexual behaviors, it is clear that parenting practices also influence children in these areas. When parents promote warm and open relationships and provide their children with healthy, realistic ways of viewing their bodies and sexual practices, they are able to help their children learn to engage in healthy and effective behaviors. Family has a great deal of power to engage a child with positive practices and healthy media messages in order to build strong and healthy perspectives on body image and sexuality.

IN THEIR VOICES

Clare is a seven-year-old girl whose parents make strong efforts to send a counter-culture message about what makes her valuable as a girl. I asked Clare, "What do your parents teach you about what makes you important and special? How is that different from what you see on TV and movies?" This is what she shared with me.

My parents say that I'm special, because, well . . . well not because I'm beautiful, well some of the reason is! But in movies you're special because you're beautiful. What makes you special isn't how you look. It's how you . . . how do I put this? It's how you *act* to other people. It's all about who you *are*.

Heidi Morris is an assistant professor of family studies at Abilene Christian University and the mother of two sons. She teaches human sexuality classes and works with families in establishing effective conversations about sexuality.

As both a mom to three young boys and a professional within the field of human development and family studies, I find that the subject of sex is an important topic to address within the context of child development. Unfortunately, however, families and some professionals often shy away from the teaching of healthy sexual development. Perhaps this "hush-like" tone is a result of our own uneasiness surrounding the topic or even a by-product of a larger cultural awkwardness. Yet, the result of the silence often means that our children will clearly hear the booming voice of the media and larger society concerning sexual values and practices. Our silence leaves them vulnerable to messages that can be detrimental to healthy sexual development.

My personal desire is to see more families and professionals unite to break the silence and begin educating our young people about healthy sexual development. It is a developmental perspective of teaching that begins in infancy and evolves through the stages of a child's development. It is relationally centered and carries with it a desire and aim to help young people gather correct information about sex, combat negative messages from the media and society about sex, and grow into healthy and well-informed adults concerning sexual development. In raising children, we strive to teach and prepare them for life tasks such as tying their shoes and crossing the road safely. Isn't the task of teaching them about healthy sexual development equally, if not more, important?

When it comes to approaching the subject of sex with children, here a few recommendations to keep in mind along the way:

1. Prepare your mind for a broad approach of teaching, instead of a one-time conversation about the "birds and the bees." (And besides, let's keep the teaching in the realm of the human species and not confuse kids with what birds and bees do. Leave that for biology class.) From helping a young toddler understand the names for the body parts, to personal hygiene and dress in middle childhood, all the way to more intimate aspects of sexual development in the teen years, there are many topics of conversation that fit within this window, not just the topic of intercourse. Your child needs you to be a part of each of these sexual developmental milestones.

2. Think relationally. You are wanting to build rapport, trust, and comfort with your child as you guide and teach them about the broad array of topics within their growing sexual development. Seek to nurture this relationship by honoring questions they have with correct and truthful answers, and applaud them for being curious and trusting you to ask. With this relational mindset, your child will be left with the impression that you are approachable and a trusted and reliable source in their lives. What parent doesn't want that?

3. Pace with your child. As they ask questions, give them what they need and don't go beyond. Too much information too soon, is too much information. The time will come to share more.

4. Speak up if your child is not. Some children are very curious and will come to you with questions. However, other children may not approach the subject. When teachable moments present themselves, use those times to guide and teach. Or, bring up important topics as life presents them. For example, the transition to middle school can mean that a child is exposed to slang and provocative language. Perhaps this is a time to help prepare your child for what they may hear from their peers and encourage them to come to you to ask questions and get clarity.

5. Remember you are not a perfect parent and you don't have to be. We all make mistakes along the way and we can't be all things for our children. We do the best we can. I encourage you to seek support from others as you go along this journey with your child.

6. Your child needs you. You are the best advocate for your child's healthy sexual development. Even when you may feel ill-equipped at times, your love and support of your child means a lot and nothing can replace the important role you have in their lives. Nothing.

Paul is the father of three children and regularly volunteers with his church's youth group. He has a master's of arts in Christian ministry and a master's of marriage and family therapy and currently works at a nonprofit devoted to helping those who are unemployed and underemployed gain the confidence and skills necessary for gainful employment.

Being a parent is the most challenging job I have ever had. Mostly because there are no simple rules to follow; instead, there are relationships to be built and little people to help form. One of the challenges has been realizing what my children are seeing on TV and in movies.

Although we have never let our kids watch things that were violent or overtly sexual, my wife and I have both remarked at how sexualized the storylines are; even in the seemingly innocent shows. Not only are the clothes worn by the female characters revealing, the dialogue is often extremely suggestive. This is even true of the so-called "kid" cartoons.

As our kids have grown older and have begun watching television shows targeted at older audiences, I have struggled with my role as a father. Normally, I see a few minutes of the show and then go to another room. There have been very few conversations. I have expressed my displeasure with the sexualized storylines after the fact. This is something I am starting to change. I am becoming more intentional about either watching shows with my children or talking about the shows with them shortly after they watch them. I want to know how they are processing the messages they are seeing.

I have two sons, aged 15 and 11, and a daughter, aged 13. I have always been cautious of how my daughter is treated. I have said I do not want her to let anyone mistreat her. I have spent a lot of time with her thinking and talking about how she is treated. But I have spent less time with my sons on how they should treat girls. By watching the shows with my children, I am gaining more opportunities to ask what they think about the shows and what they observe in real life.

The greatest thing I have learned through being more intentional with my children is this: they want to talk about it. They are willing to ask questions. They may hold back in some areas, but they really want to talk about the proper way to treat people. They want to stand up for themselves and for their friends. And luckily for me, they want to learn from me.

6

Boy versus Girl

Childhood today has become segregated into pink and blue boxes. From products to entertainment to clothing, parents and children are bombarded with the message that gender should determine a child's interests and activities. Even before the birth of their child, many parents in the United States are overwhelmed with the pink princess vision of girlhood and the blue aggressor vision of boyhood. The problem with this is that it promotes very rigid, stereotyped ideas about what it means to be a boy or a girl. When a child does not fit in to the pink or the blue box easily, he or she can feel as if there were something wrong with them. The environment in which the child is living and growing will send specific messages about what it means to be a boy or a girl, and whether or not the child needs to fit in to the pink or the blue box. The bioecological model tells us that children are responsive to cues from the systems that surround them in the microsystem, exosystem, and macrosystem about expected behaviors, interests, and appearance. When children fail to meet these expectations, they are likely to question their own competence in achieving that which appears to be important and to struggle with developing confidence in themselves.

In the bioecological model, one of the demand characteristics of a person is their gender. Remember that demand characteristics are those things about a person that demand a response from the environment. The mass media target children in very different ways based on their gender. Although both boys and girls receive specific messages about what is and is not appropriate for them, the messages are quite different. Boys are prescribed a very narrow view of masculinity that focuses on competition and aggression and physical muscularity, with little room for emotionality. The vision of femininity that is promoted to girls is one of a passive nurturer or a sassy princess who loves to shop and is primarily interested in romance. Neither of these portrayals is complex nor varied enough to provide children with an accurate idea of what it means to be a boy or girl.

This chapter explores the difference between biological sex and gender in order to clarify the cultural influence on gender expectations and the ways that media messages influence a child's perception of gender roles and stereotypes. It will examine the ways that media and marketing promote sexualized, stereotyped, narrow versions of masculinity and femininity in products and programs aimed at children and adolescents. In considering the effects of these stereotypes, I will delve into the research on stereotype threat and the very real effects that stereotypes have on behaviors, feelings, and academic performance. Lastly, I will share some strategies that can be used to reduce stereotype threat in a child's environment along with ideas for minimizing the influence of media stereotypes on children.

SEX AND GENDER

Sometimes people use the words *sex* and *gender* interchangeably. But the two are different constructs. When we talk about someone's sex, we are talking about biology. This refers to a person's anatomy and chromosomes. Gender, on the other hand, has to do with identifying how a person who is male or female is supposed to behave within the context in which they live. Gender expectations are relevant to appearance, personality traits, behaviors, and academic achievement. We see in the media the promotion of gender stereotypes, which are widely held beliefs about characteristics that are appropriate for each gender.

Children themselves go through developmental stages of understanding gender and gender identity and phases of rigidity and flexibility in their own expression of gender and in their acceptance of the ways that others express their gender.[1] Around the age of two years, children begin to identify themselves with one gender or the other and begin to label others by gender as well.[2] By the age of three or four years, gender stereotypes have become very strong and rigid. Between the ages of three and six years, children see gender stereotypes as rules and will not easily accept those who do not meet them. Most of the stereotypes that children of this age are attentive to are those that focus on appearance or activities and interests. For example, a four-year-old will be aware of the fact that certain toys and colors have been designated as "for" boys or girls and will not want to violate that expectation nor will he or she condone the violation of such by a peer.[3] The microsystem of the peer group and the setting in which they mix provide children with clear indications of which behaviors and interests are important for boys and girls to master in order to achieve competence. Children who defy gender expectations at this age will likely receive negative feedback from their peers. Because children function in a social context, this feedback matters. The more their peers pressure them to fit gendered stereotypes, the more likely they will be to accept those stereotypes as true reflections of what it means to be a girl or boy.

MEDIA AND GENDER

Earlier I introduced you to Gerbner's Cultivation Theory[4] and how it shows that media can alter our perception of reality.[5] Ward[6] and others[7] apply this same idea to adolescents' ideas about sexuality and gender stereotypes. As children build their understanding of gender, media are part of their macroculture and will play a part in that formation. Portrayals of what it means to be male or female will shape the child's perception of normative behavior, interests, and abilities for each gender. Children and adolescents who consistently see females being depicted as sexualized objects will learn to internalize that idea. Even if they do not see the women in their lives being treated in an objectified manner, cultivation theory suggests that those who are heavy media consumers and particularly connected to certain shows or characters will likely begin to adopt the gender stereotypes and sexualized views that are presented. Even adults seem to believe that girls and boys can and will only be attracted to very narrowly prescribed interests. Why have adults come to believe so strongly that children can only like this or that according to their gender?

The problem seems to be a pervasive view in our culture that presents masculinity and femininity in very narrow and inflexible ways. We see this in media and marketing directed toward children now too. Unlike the 1970s and 1980s, marketing has become more highly segmented.[8] Because that idea has also been heavily promoted by media and marketing, a cycle has been set in place in which marketers, companies, and consumers continuously feed and buy into the idea that to be a girl means to be nurturing, caring, appearance oriented, and passive, while to be a boy means to be active, loud, and aggressive. Neither gender is well served by these limiting stereotypes.

Gender stereotypes are pervasive throughout the media. In a content analysis of gender roles in media in 21 separate studies, three trends emerged.[9] These trends were that women are underrepresented across multiple media platforms, that when women do appear in media they are often sexualized or in subordinate roles, and that gender stereotypes persist. Another study examined gender portrayals in the top-grossing G-rated films from 1990 to 2005.[10] The authors found that males outnumbered females 2.57 to 1. They also found the frequent portrayal of traditional roles and responsibilities for both genders. Studies have documented a pattern of stereotypes in media depictions of males. From the aggressive, emotionally unavailable superhero to the funny but ineffective slacker[11] to the withdrawn and stoic male,[12] boys are presented with particular patterns of acceptable male behavior that often preclude vulnerability and emotional involvement. Media targeting adolescent boys promote a muscular ideal, aggression, and lack of emotionality.[13] We also see stereotypical representations of both males and females in popular media for children such as the Disney princess line of movies. Even though the later movies do tend to show more flexibility in gender stereotypes, even the most recent ones continue to portray some gender stereotypes.[14]

Beliefs and behaviors can be changed by exposure to media,[15] and stereotypical messages can impact children's developing ideas about gender.[16] There is a connection between children's exposure to sexualized media environments and viewing women as sex objects and men as sexual aggressors.[17] When a girl or boy repeatedly sees males and females displayed in very confined roles, it is sure to impact his or her own view of how to behave, what his or her dreams should be, and who he or she might become.

MEDIA, GENDER, AND IDENTITY

When I present this information about children and media through social media or in face-to-face seminars, someone usually mentions the idea that children and adolescents understand that media do not depict reality. Adults tend to think that children and adolescents understand media in the same ways they do. And yet, Cultivation Theory tells us that even adults may have their perception of reality changed based on depictions they see in media.

As I mentioned in the discussion of the culture of celebrity, adolescents are particularly vulnerable to using celebrities and media depictions as social models.[18] From a bioecological perspective, media act as a force within the exoculture that shapes and defines a child's idea of acceptable appearance and behavior for his or her gender. In order to interpret where he or she falls on the continuum of acceptability, the child will compare her- or himself to social models presented as ideal.

The mass media in their many forms have been identified as particularly potent purveyors of ideal gendered behavior and appearance.[19] People who identify more strongly with media characters and celebrities and who have already developed concerns about their own appearance are more likely to be impacted negatively by sexualized and stereotyped media images.[20] Stephen Want frames this concept nicely by saying "strong commitment to sociocultural attitudes regarding appearance is likely to lead to appearance dissatisfaction, which then creates the potential for both concerns to operate simultaneously when women view media portrayals."[21]

As children grow, they begin to understand stereotypes in a more complex way. By the time they are about seven, children expand their ideas of gender to include personality traits and academic achievement areas as well as physical characteristics. For example, Powlishta found that adults tended to describe more desirable traits such as leadership skills, ambition, self-confidence, and independence as masculine and less desirable traits such as being emotional, needing approval, getting feelings hurt easily, and passivity as feminine traits.[22]

In early elementary school, children also begin to designate certain academic subjects as masculine or feminine. For example, language and performing arts tend to be more strongly associated with females, while mathematics and sciences are more strongly associated with males. Interestingly, stereotypes also impact the way children rate their own abilities in an area. For example, a girl with high math ability is more likely to rate her abilities lower than a boy with the same math ability would.[23]

Between the ages of 6 and 10, children begin to have more flexibility in their thinking about gender stereotypes.[24] Whereas a four-year-old might argue that a girl cannot and should not play football or that a boy cannot and should not have long hair, a 10-year-old will understand that being male or female does not necessarily correlate with all male or female traits. This ability to see that all gender stereotypes are not necessarily applicable to all people is called *stereotype flexibility*. When children begin to achieve this flexibility, they are able to understand the world from a wider perspective. As children age, they tend to become more flexible in their understanding of gender. Gender stereotype flexibility is a benefit to children because it allows them more freedom to develop relationships with playmates of the opposite gender and to view their own prospects from a wider perspective. Children who indicate more gender stereotype flexibility are more likely to play with opposite sex playmates, engage in opposite sex activities, and endorse interest in careers that are not stereotypically considered for their own gender.[25]

PUTTING CHILDREN INTO PINK AND BLUE BOXES

Gender stereotype flexibility may not be easy for children to achieve when they are getting consistent messages that promote stereotypes. If you watch Saturday morning commercials or other advertisements directed at children, you will see a very gendered approach to marketing.[26] Even in toy stores, toys are clearly delineated into blue and pink sections. Want to guess what is in each section? The pink/girl section is full of dollhouses, baby dolls and baby care products, Barbie dolls, and play cleaning products. The blue/boy section is full of cars and other forms of transportation, sports equipment, and action figures. There are clear lines drawn in advertisements directed toward children between which toys are "for" boys or girls. Packed into these advertisements are consistent messages about behaviors, interests, and activities that are appropriate for girls and boys. That is not the type of message that allows a child to see gender roles and characteristics as flexible.

Television commercials for children overwhelmingly present gender stereotypes, with pastel colors, cooperation, and indoor play associated primarily with girls and competition and outdoor play associated with boys.[27] In a study conducted by Johnson and Young, researchers examined the themes of gendered voice and words present in children's television commercials.[28] Clear gender patterns were found in the types of verbs that were used in commercials featuring the different genders. Action, competition, and destruction words, such as break, flip, hit, smash, transform, and construct, were used most often in advertisements that featured boys and boy-targeted products. Verbs that focused on limited activity, feelings, and nurturing, such as look, see, wait, cuddle, and caring, were used most often in advertisements that featured girls and girl-targeted products. Another pattern that was found involved the use of verbs of agency or control. These words were found more often in boy-oriented advertisements than girl-oriented advertisements, with a ratio of over four to one. This study also examined the ways that boys and girls spoke in advertisements aimed at children. In advertisements that were oriented toward both girls and boys, boys spoke more and girls often spoke only in response to the actions or statements of boys. When we consider the use of the word "power" and related words, 21 percent of boy-oriented advertisements used the words "power" or "powerful," but in all of the girl-oriented advertisements, there was only one incident of the word "power" being used, and it was in the context of identifying the maker of a Barbie car (Power Wheels). Johnson and Young conclude, "Toy makers and their advertisers either make no effort to associate or may consciously avoid associating girl-toys with power or their potential to transfer power to their users."[29]

That is a very compelling statement. But might we expect to find something different in the advertising and packaging of toys that both boys and girls like to play with, like LEGO, Lincoln Logs, and other building and craft-making equipment? But, these toys are often in the boy aisle. When those products are in the girl section, they are marketed in a distinctly different way. For example, consider the new LEGO Friends line of toys.

In 2012 LEGO released their Friends line, which was heavily marketed as "LEGO for girls." LEGO stated that they had done exhaustive consumer research trying to understand what had kept girls from playing with their product before and what would make LEGO more attractive to girls. I wonder if perhaps girls do not see LEGO as appealing because since 2005 the company has been targeting boys in their advertising. In fact, in a statement in *Bloomberg Businessweek*, a LEGO spokesperson discussed the fact that LEGO had begun focusing primarily on boys in the early to mid-2000s.[30] It is not surprising then that when a company develops heavily gendered advertisements, packaging, and products, eventually children of the opposite gender will turn away from their products. In this case, girls seemed to be getting the clear message from LEGO that their products were for boys, and thus girls were not interested in purchasing them. In fact, the stereotypes represented in advertising and packaging seem to permeate the toy market.

Children are internalizing these stereotypes and the message that certain products and activities are gender specific. A study in 2009 examined the accessibility of gender stereotypes and found that girls and boys tended to describe girls as nice, liking to play with dolls, and as having their value linked with appearance.[31] This focus on appearance seemed to be particularly strong for girls in fourth and fifth grades when compared to younger children, with an average of half of the girls of that age describing appearance as an important component of a girl's identity. The traits most often associated with boys included being active, athletic, and aggressive. We see in the research literature that children identify with activities they see someone of their own gender engaging in.[32] So, when advertisers consistently depict their products being played with mostly by only one gender, children of the opposite gender will not see that toy as accessible to them. When commercials show toys being manipulated by only one gender, children are likely to identify that toy as "for" the gender of the child shown in the commercial. Even in educational software, you see over and over that boys are represented as aggressive, active, and competitive, while girls are dependent and passive.[33] When children repeatedly see these gender stereotypes, they begin to believe them.

On the other hand, when both boys and girls are depicted as playing with the same toy in a commercial, children are more likely to later identify that toy as being "for boys and girls."[34] In fact, advertising research has suggested that instead of developing two different sets of advertisements for boys and girls, advertisers can more effectively appeal to preadolescent boys and girls by choosing themes that either focus on agency or community. Preadolescent boys and girls are both interested in the idea of promoting agency through acting independently and in building community and relationships. By the age of eight, girls actually begin to show more favorable attitudes toward advertisements that promote agency.[35] However, when children are exposed to high levels of gender salience, meaning clear demarcations of being in one group as opposed to another, they tend to demonstrate increased gender stereotypes, have less positive feelings about opposite-sex peers, and not play with them as much.[36]

THE TRUTH ABOUT STEREOTYPES

How much truth is there in gender stereotypes? Is the female brain designed so differently from the male brain that it just cannot attain the same level of mastery in math and science? Are males built for aggression and competition, unable to nurture? Are females born to shop? In popular media, we often hear the phrase "hard wired" to describe gender differences. Are girls and boys in fact hard wired differently? If parents and teachers read books such as *Why Gender Matters* by Leonard Sax,[37] they may become convinced that girls and boys are fundamentally different and that it is imperative for parents and teachers to know this. And yet, as early as 2005, Janet Shibley Hyde was using meta-analytic research to develop her "Gender Similarities Hypothesis."[38] Hyde inspected the effect sizes of 124 peer-reviewed studies that examined gender differences in a range of areas from cognitive and motor areas to personality and psychological variables. What Hyde found was that 78 percent of gender differences that have been studied are not significant. Only one area was found to have large significant gender differences and that was motor performance (especially throwing velocity), where differences increase with age. Hyde concludes that the data demonstrate that males and females are similar on most psychological variables.

What about biological differences? For example, Sax claims that sex differences are biologically programmed and have an impact on how children respond to parenting and education.[39] Lise Eliot views these "biological" differences in a very different way.[40] As a neuroscientist, her specialty area is brain plasticity, meaning how the brain changes depending on environment and experience. Her belief is that the brains of each sex are more similar than they are different, lending biological support to Hyde's psychological theory of similarities. In the public debate about gender stereotypes being promoted by children's media and marketing, we hear an interesting argument coming from those who do not believe there is anything wrong with companies promoting stereotypes. The argument is similar to Sax's perspective. It goes something like this: Girls and boys are biologically different and have different inborn preferences. There is nothing wrong with recognizing and promoting these preferences, in fact, companies should do this to provide access to both girls and boys.[41] However, Eliot points out that there are only three small early sex differences that appear to be biological. This means they are promoted by either prenatal hormone exposure or sex-specific gene expression. These early developmental differences are (1) the fact that baby boys are a bit more physically active than baby girls, (2) toddler girls tend to talk earlier than boys, and (3) boys appear more spatially aware. These are incremental differences for the most part, and the large differences that emerge as children get older seem to be driven by nurture rather than nature. In fact, there are very few real significant differences identified by neuroscience between the ways girl and boy brains function.[42] She says, "Our actual ability differences are quite small . . . there is more overlap in the academic and . . . social-emotional abilities of the genders than there are differences."[43] A child's ability and interests develop in the context of the systems in which he or she lives and functions. These systems, whether it is the microsystem of the home or school or the exosystem of media, provide the child with guidance and feedback about what behaviors and interests are appropriate for the child, individually and in reference to his or her gender. Within these systems, the ways and frequency in which parents talk to their child, the toys and activities the child is exposed to, the media messages, peer groups, and communities of which the child is a part all influence the things a child learns about what it means to be a boy or a girl.

When we look closely at the evidence, it does not appear to be true that boys and girls are "hard wired" differently. Instead, many of the behavioral differences that appear in boys and girls seem to be connected to the kinds of behaviors, interests, and activities that are promoted by the micro- and macrosystems of the environment in which the child is living. Experience seems to play a key role in gender differences when it comes to the behaviors and interests of boys and girls. Experience is mitigated not only by the types of stereotypes a person accepts him- or herself, but also by the types of stereotypes that person believes others hold about him or her. When our beliefs about the stereotypes that others hold about us influence our behavior in a negative way, we are exhibiting stereotype threat effect.

Stereotype Threat

Have you ever walked into a room and become immediately aware that something about you makes you stand out in the crowd, makes you different, or might lead others to believe certain things to be true about you before you have even met? Maybe it is your gender, your race, your height, or your weight. There are certain parts of our identity that we may not actively consider, but often these are used by others to identify us as being a part of a particular group. When we become aware that those parts of our identity are being used by others to understand us, we tend to become self-conscious about what people may think they know about us.

There are stereotypes, both good and bad characteristics, that are attributed to us because of different parts of our identities. This is not to say that we believe those things about ourselves. In fact, very often we know them to be untrue, but we are aware that others are thinking that they understand something to be true about us. For example, tall people are often considered to be leaders, while short people are not generally seen as leaders. As a tall or short person, when you enter a group, you know that you are going to have to either confirm or break that stereotype about your height. You know that it is likely that the people in the group have formed ideas about who you are based on that characteristic.

This chapter has focused on how marketers tend to set up their marketing to target children by gender, and much of the marketing promotes gender stereotypes. One stereotype in the culture of the United States at large is that girls and women are not as good at math, science, and engineering as are boys and men. Gendered marketing directed at children advances the stereotypes that girls are more concerned with beauty and relationships than they are with achievement. Unfortunately, we even see products marketed to girls that say things like "Allergic to Algebra" or "I'm too pretty to do math."

But those are just silly products and advertisements, right? How could they make any difference in what a child really believes about him- or herself and his or her abilities? From a bioecological perspective, we develop our identities based on what we know about who we are in the context in which we live as a person of our race, gender, social class, region, mental health status, and so forth. These are called *identity contingencies*.[44] These are those things about who we are that we think will lead others to believe certain things about us.

What is interesting about identity contingencies is that they are based on our social identity, not what we think of ourselves but what we believe others think about us. Many of these contingencies are based on stereotypes. We ourselves do not have to believe or accept the stereotype to be forced to deal with the contingencies; it is enough for others to believe it. Or, in the case of stereotype threat, it is enough for us to even be aware that someone else might believe a certain stereotype about us.

The research on stereotype threat comes out of the work of Claude M. Steele, a social psychologist and the dean for the Graduate School of Education at Stanford University and professor emeritus in the Department of Psychology at Stanford.[45] The work that Steele and his colleagues have done has established that when a stereotype exists about our social identity and we are aware of it, that awareness alone can lead to changes in our academic performance, behaviors, and success. One great example in Steele's research involves women and math. He and his research team wanted to figure out what was behind the lack of women in math and science careers. Was it, as some have proposed, that women are just biologically not as good at math as men or were there other forces at work? What Steele and his colleagues found was that when they gave high-achieving math students of both sexes difficult math problems, the women tended to do worse simply because, as Steele believed, they were functioning under the pressure of worry that they would confirm the stereotype that women are not good at math. This worry sapped some of the intellectual energy that they needed to actually do the math problems and thus inhibited their performance. On the other hand, when the researchers conducted the study in the same way but told the women beforehand that on this particular test men and women scored evenly, the women performed at the same level as the men! When the women were free from the concern that they might confirm a negative stereotype about their sex, they were able to concentrate fully on solving the difficult problem.[46]

Our culture is sending both boys and girls ridiculously mixed messages. We tell boys "You must be strong, self-assured, muscular, and sexually attractive, but never have emotions about whether or not you meet those standards." We tell girls "You can be anything, but you better be beautiful, young, and thin while doing it." What does this say to children? That no matter how smart they are, no matter how creative, no matter how kind, what really matters at the end of the day is how they look and how much social power they achieve through being attractive.

A TALE OF TWO RESPONSES TO STEREOTYPE

From the vignettes presented in Chapter 4, as Isaac went through puberty, he was consuming reality television and computer games that depicted muscular males who had multiple sexual partners and expressed little emotion. When he felt insecure about his own body in comparison, he felt unable to talk with anyone about his concerns. Because he lacked social support from his family, he worried about his appearance and ability to attain competence in attracting girls, which seemed like the most important thing to him. His way of alleviating that worry was to continue to seek out casual sexual relationships.

As Anna was going through puberty, she also faced concerns about her appearance. As a muscular athlete, she did not meet the thin ideal. She was able to talk about her feelings with her mother and father, who assured her that her body was healthy and strong. The social support that she got from her teammates and her coach focused on fitness and strength rather than thinness, and this helped alleviate the pressure she felt to fit the thin ideal. Because Anna received counter-messages from her family, peers, and team about what it meant to be competent, she was able to be confident in herself.

In order for boys and girls to thrive, we must provide them with messages about what it means to be competent as both men and women that focus on developing strengths and character. Rather than focusing on appearance, social power, and aggression, we must help boys and girls both learn to focus on gaining confidence in their ability to achieve in areas in which they excel. We must help them learn to think about developing character and understanding how to treat others in ways that show kindness, compassion, and respect.

As adults, we must be teaching all children that they are more than their physical appearance. Their competence, confidence, and character come from internal qualities that can be developed like their talents, their intelligence, and their kindness. Adults must start pushing back on these stereotyped ideas that teach girls to value their appearance above anything and that place boys in the position of being competitive, aggressive, and emotionally detached.

CONVERSATION STARTERS

Media literacy interventions that build a child's ability to critically analyze media content have also been shown to prevent the internalization of unhealthy messages.[47] Here are some specific strategies parents and professionals can use to prompt conversation about gender.

When talking with children, adults should keep fat and appearance talk to a minimum. They should avoid criticizing their own bodies, the child's body, or other people's bodies. Instead, adults should talk about health and fun when discussing exercise and fitness. Keeping the focus on moving the body and eating healthy foods allows children to build an understanding of health that is not primarily about appearance.

Parents can also let children hear them promote the idea that people are valuable for who they are on the inside. When adults honestly express their admiration for people's talents and good qualities, children will learn to value those things as well. For example, if someone your child knows well has lost weight, instead of commenting on the weight loss or appearance, try to make comments about traits that you value, such as persistence. In general, let your child know when you admire something about a person such as kindness, compassion, or determination.

Parents and professionals can openly address stereotypes and appearance-related messages that children are receiving. Asking "What do you think about that?" when children are faced with stereotypes and sexualization provides them with the opportunity to explore their own feelings regarding these issues. Parents can also engage media with their child, and when appearance-related messages come up, point them out and discuss them.

In one study with elementary-aged children, the researchers found that using active mediation to contradict gender stereotypes and to point out nonstereotyped incidents lead children to be less positive about stereotyped portrayals and to endorse stereotyped attitudes less often.[48] These authors suggest that parents and other adults keep three things in mind when using active mediation to contradict gender stereotypes in the media. First, it is important for the contradictory message to be sent as the child views the stereotyped portrayal. This can only happen if adults are actively engaging their child with media. So, when a parent is watching television with their child and they see a girl portrayed as loving to shop or being bad at math, they can point it out and contradict it. Second, point out portrayals that run against stereotypes. For example, if there is a portrayal of a boy or man expressing his feelings openly and well, children need to have that brought to their attention. Lastly, to effectively provide a contradictory message, the adult will likely need to repeat that message several times in order to build a strong counter to the stereotype.

Adults can also work as activists to push companies to provide healthier messages. When consumers refuse to spend money on products that promote narrow, gendered ideas of value, companies will begin to pay closer attention to providing healthier messages. To get change from industry, consumers must put their money where their mouths are. For example, American Apparel is a clothing company that markets strongly to teenagers and young adults. I have made it clear to my teen daughters that we will not purchase any of their items due to the fact that they often sexualize the women in their advertisements. In order to help my daughters understand what I mean, I show them the advertisements in question and we talk about them. In one advertisement for a shirt, the male model is wearing a dress shirt with slacks while the female model is wearing the shirt open with nothing else except underwear. I asked my daughters, "What do you think about how the two models are depicted?" and we were able to have a conversation about how advertising in a way that objectifies one gender is not something that we want to support.

Adults also need to think about how to mitigate stereotype threat in general. It has been suggested that mothers' gender stereotypes may play a key role in moderating how girls perform academically under stereotype threat. In a study with children in kindergarten through second grade, researchers had children listen to a story that either had a stereotypical portrayal of a girl or no animated characters. The girls were then asked to perform difficult math tasks. Before the study, children and parents had both completed surveys indicating whether or not they endorsed gender stereotypes. What the researchers found was that when gender was salient, most girls performed more poorly on math tasks. However, this was only true for girls with mothers who did not reject the stereotypical idea that males are better at math. Girls with mothers who strongly rejected the gender stereotype that males were better at math did not show a decrease in performance under stereotype threat.[49]

In order to mitigate stereotype threat, Steele suggests that adults provide an environment that demands high levels of achievement while making it clear that the authority in the situation believes that the child has the potential to succeed.[50] Too often parents and other adults seem to have different levels of expectation for children based on gender. They might subtly be sending the message that their expectations for performance in different academic or social areas are dependent on gender. Another strategy is to provide information that normalizes struggles. For example, if a boy is struggling with difficult reading or a girl is struggling with difficult math, give the child the opportunity to talk with fellow students of both sexes about the work. Once the child sees that the task itself is difficult for everyone, he or she will have a more realistic understanding of the task as leading to the struggle rather than thinking that he or she may be having trouble due to stereotypes.[51]

Researchers have suggested that providing children with same-sex role models who have achieved success in a counter-stereotyped field may serve to undermine the adoption of gender stereotypes about abilities and career fields.[52] As stated in the documentary *Miss Representation*, "If you can't see it, you can't be it."[53] This idea is borne out in research as well, with both college-aged men and women indicating that one of their primary reasons for choosing their field of study was that they perceived themselves to be similar to those already in the field.[54] Providing children with opportunities to see adults who are making choices in their behaviors, careers, and interests that contradict gender stereotypes opens their eyes to a new way of thinking.

Caring adults need to keep sharing a different message with their children. We need to let children know that they have a set of talents that is all their own. If the world does not get to see that because they are hiding it behind a facade of pseudo-masculinity or femininity, then everyone loses out.

IN THEIR VOICES

Crystal Smith is a freelance writer and parent of two boys. Through her book The Achilles Effect *and its accompanying blog, she seeks to raise awareness and generate discussion about the influence of popular culture on boys' understanding of gender and masculinity.*

"We're rescuing a girl? Is she hot?" These words were spoken by an animated male character in a video clip for the Ninjago line of LEGO toys. Sadly, the sexism expressed in this clip is not uncommon in children's pop culture. I could cite many more examples of this kind of sentiment and produce countless pictures of sexualized female characters from television programs, films, and books aimed at boys in the primary grades.

The highly sexualized fictional females that boys see from a young age lay the groundwork for their future attitudes toward girls, especially if these attitudes are reinforced by peers and ignored in the home environment. Current pop culture stereotypes teach boys to value girls' looks more than their capabilities and accomplishments, while also creating a beauty ideal based on wasp-waists, large breasts, doe eyes, and long, flowing hair.

In addition to sexualized images, there are others that place females in a position of relative inferiority to males while emphasizing their looks over any other qualities they might possess: females are depicted in domestic settings far more than males and rarely afforded the opportunity to be a hero. They also worry over their appearance far more than male characters.

It is in part because of pop culture images that girls are marked by boys as sexual at an early age, independent of the girls' behavior. As a report by Toronto's Sick Kids Hospital notes, if such views of girls are allowed to escalate, they can result in sexual harassment at school, a form of social aggression that occurs at the age of 10 or earlier.

I feel that too little attention is paid to the impact of gender stereotypes on boys. Although initially inspired by negative portrayals of females, I became equally concerned by the traditional depictions of masculinity in children's popular culture, which emphasize physical strength, stoicism, and male dominance over females. It is my goal to raise awareness of the ways boys are affected by male and female gender stereotypes and give parents of boys the confidence to challenge traditional gender roles.

Living in Atlanta, Georgia, Kara Norman is the founder of Empower Her, Inc., an empowerment agency for women and girls that focuses on providing events, resources, and programs for women and girls. She is also the co-founder of the girls mentoring program G.E.M.S. & Jewels, promoting self-esteem, self-awareness, and self-worth within the lives of young girls and teens. Kara is a wife and mother of two girls ages 10 and 16.

I have worked to empower girls and women for the past six years through my community-based organization G.E.M.S. & Jewels Empowerment Group for Girls and my newly formed nonprofit Empower Her, Inc. As a mom of two girls, ages 16 and 10, I have worked tirelessly not only helping girls in my community but also trying to raise my daughters to be strong and confident.

Until recently I thought I was doing a great job as a mom. You would think that as a leader I would get it right, that my daughters would not struggle with the many things that girls are facing in this day and age. I was totally wrong! My youngest daughter asked me recently if she needed to go on a diet after a conversation with a friend. The friend asked her what she weighed. Having gone to the doctor recently, my daughter noticed her weight and reported it back to her classmate. The girl told her that she weighed too much and told her the appropriate weight for her age. My daughter came home deeply troubled by her friend's advice and suggestions. She is in the fourth grade! How does this girl know what an average fourth-grader should weigh and why is she polling girls in her class?

I was saddened that the ideal body image message that we are bombarded with via television, magazine, movies, music, and social media had trickled down to my youngest daughter. I have held countless self-esteem workshops and enrichment events with my daughters in attendance. I have drilled into them that feeling beautiful comes from the inside out and that we come in all shapes and sizes, yet my daughters are not immune to the messages that they are being sent.

I have also faced challenges with my teen daughter. She told me that in middle school she was approached and threatened by boys, trying to get her to take off her clothes via video chat. She told me of other instances when boys who she knew well and trusted asked her to send them sexy pictures or take off her clothes while on FaceTime. I was completely shocked. In our culture, boys and girls are fed messages through music and videos that girls and women are sexual objects. I think this is especially true in my African American community. Dancing on stripper poles is normal, dressing in a sexual way is the norm, and being sexy is the most important thing about being a girl or woman. The wrong message is being sent to our girls and boys on so many levels! My heart is heavy for our society and my community.

As a leader I am now reevaluating my empowerment approach. I feel that creating awareness for parents and girls is very important. If we are not aware of the messages that are being sent and the effect it is having on our society, then we cannot make changes.

Watching great documentaries like *Sexy Baby*, *Miss Representation*, and *America the Beautiful* are great ways to get the conversation started as well as reading books like this. Unplugging and paying attention to what our daughters are watching and listening to is also important. Telling your child that they should not watch or listen to certain things is not enough. Instead, sit down with your children while they are watching or listening to things that they like. If you feel that the media is sending the wrong messages, casually discuss the behavior or inappropriate things that you see. With my daughters, I make suggestions and discuss where a person's value comes from and that we should have certain morals and standards.

I find now that my youngest daughter will ask questions like "Why can't a girl be president?" or "Why is she only chasing boys on this show?" I also feel it is important to expose my daughters and the girls in my program to different things that break the gender role mold and helps them take the focus off of the importance of being sexy and onto their talents and skills. I took my daughters to an air show recently and they met a female pilot. Both my daughters admitted that they had never thought about women flying or the fact that they could be pilots. Getting children involved in volunteer work and community service also keeps their focus on more positive things. We certainly have an uphill battle to fight, but awareness is key to creating change.

7

It Takes a Village

From volunteer organization to sports teams to religious groups, many children have communities in their lives that promote specific value systems and aid them in thriving. I refer to these as connected communities. These groups tend to encourage the children within them to view their value as arising from internal characteristics and talents rather than physical appearance and sexual attractiveness. The key concept that provides these connected communities with a different perspective from sexualized media is the promotion of wellness factors such as the development of individual assets, engaged living, and peer and community support for these positive behaviors and attitudes. Rather than promoting and glorifying harmful concepts such as the thin ideal, objectification, and risky sexual behaviors, connected communities provide children and adolescents with support for living a life that is dedicated to achievement, service, and connectedness.

A nightly viewing of any number of reality television shows such as *The Bachelor* or *Jersey Shore* might provide adolescents with models of people fighting with one another, having casual sexual encounters, and manipulating situations to achieve their individual goals. Connected communities, on the other hand, provide adolescents with opportunities to see real people who are passionate about connecting with others, serving their communities, and growing as individuals and members of a team.

This chapter explores the protective influence that such communities can have on children and adolescents as they navigate sexualized media. This occurs due to specific steps that these communities take in the way they communicate about the individual value of each member. Connected communities become a powerful force in providing children with open communication and important ways of understanding identity and sexuality. Using both positive youth development and general positive psychology theory as a backdrop, this chapter explores the wellness factors that aid children and adolescents in successfully navigating the challenges presented by sexualized and stereotyped media. In previous chapters I explained the negative effects of such media on children and adolescents, and three areas of threat stood out: self-concept, body image, and risky sexual behaviors. Given that fact, this chapter delves into those same themes in relation to connected communities, investigating the ways these communities influence those three risk areas. Lastly, I will discuss strategies for promoting wellness and engaged living using systems consistent with connectedness.

FLOURISHING

Positive psychology is a fairly new branch of psychology that focuses on studying positive emotions, emotional strength development, and healthy emotional living. The main tenant of positive psychology is that of well-being and flourishing, which, according to Martin Seligman, is built upon five constructs that make up his PERMA theory:

- Positive emotion
- Engagement
- Relationships
- Meaning
- Accomplishment[1]

Seligman sees these five concepts as the fundamental components of human well-being, which he terms *flourishing*. Connected communities promote flourishing for children and adolescents. Social relationships are vitally important during this time period, and engagement with a connected community allows adolescents to do the work of forming their identities within a supportive setting of like-minded peers and adults.

To understand flourishing, we must understand the ways people seek well-being. Schueller and Seligman say that people tend to use three different avenues to seek well-being: pleasure, engagement, and meaning.[2] Pleasure may be easily understood as positive emotions.

But what about engagement and meaning, what exactly are they? In positive psychology, engagement is the pursuit of activities that are absorbing. Csikszentmihalyi discusses the state of "flow" that emerges when we are fully absorbed in something.[3] That state of hyperengagement leaves us feeling good. Think of the way you feel after you engage in an activity that really absorbs you, such as yoga, jogging, painting, reading, or gardening. That sense of well-being that fills you when you have been completely absorbed with something is engagement.

The other key area of well-being is finding meaning in one's life. Steger, Kashdan, and Oishi define meaning as what occurs when an individual experiences his or her life as purposeful, significant, and understandable.[4] People find meaning in approaching life as being about more than just their individuality. They focus on positive social causes and relationships or connecting to a higher purpose. To have meaning, individuals must feel that what they are doing in their lives matters to others, that their lives are about more than just their individual happiness. Schueller and Seligman say that activities that increase engagement and meaning, rather than those that simply give pleasure, seem to have the most influence on well-being.[5] These two aspects of well-being are particularly important because they build social and psychological resources and promote relationships with others.

The study of well-being has also focused on exploring the differences between the psychological outcomes of pursuing meaningful activities to foster one's full potential as a human being and pursuing pleasure for its own sake. Sexualized media promote the pursuit of pleasure and consumption. Television shows and movies that portray frequent sexual hook-ups, sexual pleasure as an end to itself, and the pursuit of romance and beauty endorse the idea that pleasure is something to be pursued. No deeper meanings are attached to these pursuits; rather experiencing pleasure is a hallmark of the life that is promoted by sexualized media.

So what do we know about the pursuit of pleasure compared to the pursuit of meaningful activities that also foster engagement, relationships, meaning, and accomplishment? Can the seeking of pleasure alone lead to psychological well-being? Research shows that engagement and meaning are significantly related to well-being, whereas pleasure is negatively related to objective well-being, including things like education, achievement, and the absence of mental disorders.[6] Engagement and meaning contribute more to well-being than pleasure, because they help people build resources that are valuable. Seeking pleasure provides a short-term reward but does not provide further skill or resource development. For example, when an adolescent volunteers as a mentor for a younger child, she is building her skills in interacting with others, her empathy, and her experience. When an adolescent gets drunk, she may experience pleasant feelings, but she is not building any long-term resources.

These differences can be best understood by considering eudaimonic theory. *Eudaimonic theory* suggests that well-being is achieved as people engage in meaningful activities that lead them to achieve their potential. The idea behind eudaimonic theory is ancient, growing out of ideas proposed by Aristotle.[7] Steger, Kashdan, and Oishi contrast this approach to life with a hedonic approach, which they define as seeking well-being through maximizing pleasure and minimizing pain.[8] In their study of university students, these authors found that young adults who engaged in more eudaimonic activities tended to have higher levels of well-being than students who engaged in more hedonic activities. This is an important distinction to make, because connected communities provide an eudaimonic approach to life, while sexualized media promote a hedonic approach to life. Spend a few minutes watching *Jersey Shore* and you will get an eyeful of hedonic behavior. The characters spend their time drinking, having sex or seeking sex, and fighting with one another. Rather than building relationships or resources, the characters in sexualized media tend to engage in pleasure-seeking for its own sake, with little concern for building connections.

ASSETS AND CHALLENGES TO FLOURISHING

Connected communities are unique from others in which a child may be involved because they serve as an asset to well-being. They encourage the eudaimonic approach to seek meaning and achievement in life rather than seek pleasure for its own sake. Some communities clearly serve as assets toward developing healthy behavior patterns that lead to well-being, while others tend to put challenges in the child's way of achieving well-being.

So which assets can contribute to healthy behaviors? Specifically, which kinds of community assets can aid a child in avoiding risky sexual behaviors and developing a healthy self-concept and body image? Research suggests that peer role models are key assets, and that these are often found in connected communities such as volunteer organizations, churches, sports teams, and other extracurricular programs. These communities tend to foster achievement and future aspirations and can lead to avoidance of risky sexual behaviors.[9] Participation in extracurricular activities can lead a child toward flourishing and protect against involvement in harmful behaviors that have been linked to consumption of sexualized media, such as disordered eating and risky sexual behaviors. Involvement in connected communities builds skills and develops positive social networks that provide a focus on engagement, relationship building, finding meaning in one's activities, and accomplishment.

Different types of extracurricular activities can develop different assets.[10] In a study of the effects of different types of extracurricular activities on self-esteem, Kort-Butler and Hagewen found that those adolescents who participated in some kind of school-based extracurricular activity had higher self-esteem than those who did not.[11] They also found that adolescents who were involved in several different types of extracurricular activities, such as sports and clubs (language clubs, academic clubs, student council, band or orchestra, etc.), had healthier self-concepts than those students who were only involved in one type of extracurricular activity. The authors believe that this is because different types of activities help children develop different skill sets and extensive social networks. I have seen this with my own daughters. When my oldest daughter went to high school, she expanded her extracurricular activities from just playing in the orchestra to also being involved in cross-country and track. Just the addition of one activity greatly expanded her social circle and allowed her to build relationships with people whom she had not known before. It also gave her the opportunity to build competence in a completely different area and increase her overall confidence.

Communities also influence sexual behaviors. It has been well documented that peer attitudes about sexual behaviors influence both healthy and risky behaviors in adolescents.[12] Using a brief HIV/STI prevention intervention with African American adolescents, researchers found that even a short-term program that raised awareness among a preexisting friendship group led to changes in both the group's social norm expectations about sexuality and in their sexual behaviors.[13] This simple intervention that focused on raising awareness about risk behaviors led to different group expectations about sexual behaviors, influencing adolescents to make healthier choices. In a larger study with Latino adolescents, researchers found that when there was a perception by teenagers that their peers believed in and supported safe sex practices, such as the use of a condom during intercourse, the teen practiced safer sexual behaviors.[14]

TYPES OF COMMUNITIES

Participation in extracurricular activities such as sports, church, visual and performing arts, and academic clubs tends to provide children and adolescents with positive peer relationships, practice in an activity that is engaging and meaningful, and a sense of accomplishment as the child and team or group achieves goals. Different activities may have different impacts depending on the child's characteristics. For example, athletic participation is associated with higher levels of general self-esteem in boys, while participation in non-athletic clubs is linked to higher levels of general self-esteem in girls.[15] To understand these communities, we need to explore each and the ways that they influence children.

Sports

Sports participation is beneficial to both physical and emotional well-being. Physically, sports participation encourages the development of physical competence as well as agency. As a child learns to use his or her body to perform specific tasks and accomplishments, the child grows in ownership of his or her body. As a child achieves goals by using his or her body as an instrument, the child learns to see his or her body as his or her own.

In a study that examined sports participation and both psychological and physical well-being, researchers wondered how girls' participation in sports contributed to their physical and psychological well-being later in life. They wanted to know what exactly was happening as the girls participated in sports that led to better outcomes. What they found was that girls who were involved in sports tended to think of themselves as physically competent and to view their bodies as instruments.[16] This perspective leads to having more positive feelings about one's body. Although girls receive many cultural messages about the importance of the way their bodies look, sports participation allows them to master and own their bodies for their own uses. Sports gives girls the chance to build positive feelings about their bodies that has nothing to do with the way their bodies look, but is completely about being assertive, independent, and in control. Participating in sports is not about the development of physical competence alone, but about the ways this experience allows children to begin to view themselves as agents. This suggests that physical competence and seeing one's body as an instrument are fundamental contributors to the positive benefits of sports participation. Participation in sports as an adolescent has also been linked with more long-term subjective health and positive beliefs about oneself.[17]

Adolescent girls who are involved in any sport have more functional body images than girls who are not involved in sports at all.[18] That is likely due to the fact that involvement in sports increases a person's awareness of and satisfaction with the functional components of his or her own body. They learn to make their bodies do what they want them to do, gaining agency as they learn to see their bodies as purposeful tools to accomplish a goal. Even when compared to physically active girls who did not play sports, the girls who did play sports tended to value and invest in their bodies as functional.

Although this functional view of the body may not completely replace the thin ideal promoted by the media, it likely allows adolescents to develop a more complex perspective on body shape and size.[19] Rather than just seeing their bodies as objects to be desired by men, girls who participate in sports tend to think of their bodies as instruments by which they can accomplish meaningful goals through sports. This further allows girls to step away from viewing their bodies as passive objects and to move into thinking about their physical competencies with pride and agency.

School

Because most children attend school for several hours a day, the community of school has the potential to have a strong effect on them. If a child experiences positive emotions at school, becomes engaged in some aspect of the school experience, forms relationships, finds meaning in his or her time at school, and experiences a sense of accomplishment, then the school community becomes a connected community that builds the child's sense of flourishing and promotes thriving.

As a professional educator who has worked in both public and private school settings, I have seen firsthand the ways that schools can positively influence children who are struggling. Some of the adolescents with whom I have worked have been virtually abandoned by their families. Sometimes the child's guardian is someone barely over 18 years old. Oftentimes those guardians are overwhelmed by poverty, lack of opportunity, and even substance use and abuse. For children such as these, the school may be one of the only communities to have an influence on their lives. It is vital that educators fully embrace their role of nurturing in the lives of the children who pass through their halls. When schools are purposefully focused on providing a nurturing environment to children, they then have the opportunity to be one of the few connected communities in the lives of some of their students.

In the context of sexualized media, schools can provide connectedness for students through providing an environment that allows children to flourish. What we see in a school that promotes flourishing is a place where children (1) experience positive emotions, (2) are engaged in learning, (3) build positive relationships, (4) find meaning in their work, and (5) experience a sense of accomplishment. In an ideal world, all schools would promote the flourishing of their students, and yet, we know that often they do not.

What gets in the way of flourishing? There are three aspects of school that can lead to flourishing or contribute to the lack of flourishing: academics, extracurricular activities, and personal relationships. I have already discussed the importance of extracurricular activities in emotional well-being, so here I will focus on the other two categories.

From an academic perspective, if a school is to become a connected community, it must be focused on providing students with an appropriate amount of challenge combined with support. For those students who struggle academically, support and strong teaching are key. If struggling students do not receive these, they are likely to feel negative emotions, lack of engagement and meaning with their academic work, and little sense of accomplishment. On the other hand, gifted and academically advanced students who are not challenged will also feel disconnected from their schools. So, schools have a special undertaking to provide each level of students with the right amount of support and challenge. This only comes with proper funding, teacher training and assistance, and a system that provides positive behavior supports. When students feel underchallenged or overchallenged academically, they tend to be less engaged. From a developmental standpoint, what we want to see is a consistent level of engagement where children are challenged appropriately but also provided with support to learn and grow in their skills and knowledge. When schools are able to strike this balance, the children who attend can flourish academically.

From a personal perspective, children need to feel that their school is a place where they are safe and accepted by both their peers and teachers. When they are able to connect emotionally with their peers and teachers, they can build positive relationships. In an interesting study on the academic lives of boys, Reichert and Kuriloff conducted surveys and interviews with school-aged boys to find out how the culture of their school impacted their identity.[20] What they found was that boys' sense of self was shaped by their ability to feel connected and supported by the school environment. When they did not feel that they were able to belong or meet the standard set for masculinity, the boys experienced a sense of anxiety. When the messages that boys are getting about masculinity line up with a rigid, narrow standard such as that set by stereotyped, sexualized media, many boys will struggle to fit in to that mold. These boys then feel anxious and are often subjected to ridicule and exclusion by their peers who are enforcing the stereotyped masculine ideal.

This also applies to girls, children of different races, sexual orientation, and so forth. Schools provide a microcosm of the world for the students in attendance. These students are either able to find acceptance and nurturing within that environment, or they feel forced to assume particular roles that may not be reflective of their true identities. To fully flourish and thrive, students need to see their school setting as a place where they can develop their identities in a positive, encouraging environment.

Aside from self-concept, it is clear that school settings can have an impact on adolescents' sexual behaviors. Schools have taken on the role of sex educator to some extent. As children move through elementary into secondary school, they will likely be provided with some form of sex education. Sex education can provide protection against risky sexual behavior through raising awareness and increasing knowledge. Schools also provide an environment that gives children a place to celebrate themselves in ways beyond the sexual. Not only do adolescents receive sex education in the school system, but their engagement with the school also impacts their behavioral choices. Formal sex education in the school setting has been proven to reduce sexual risk-taking behaviors and increase healthy sexual behaviors, such as delaying the first sexual experience and increasing the use of contraceptives.[21]

Interestingly, it is not sexually focused programs that have the most effect on risky sexual behaviors. Instead, school engagement, involvement in service learning programs at school, academic success, and career plans have all been shown to have an impact on adolescents' sexual behaviors. Research has found that adolescents who are more strongly connected to their schools are less likely to engage in risky sexual behavior and more likely to engage in health-promoting behaviors.[22] As Kirby says, "if schools can implement programs that keep youth in schools, make them feel more attached to school, help them succeed, and help them develop plans for higher education and future careers, they may delay their students' onset of sex, increase their contraceptive use, and decrease their pregnancy and childbearing."[23]

When schools foster positive emotions, engagement, relationships, meaning, and accomplishment, they become connected communities for their students and a primary place of flourishing and thriving for children and adolescents.

Religious Groups

From rules that regulate dress to those that prohibit alcohol use to regular meetings with one another, religious groups have developed customs that provide children and adolescents with a strong sense of belonging and identity. Religious groups often shape sexual attitudes and beliefs about sexual activities, which leads to a reduction in risky sexual behaviors in religious youth.[24]

Religious groups more than other community systems have developed rules about sexual behaviors. The question is, are these rules helpful? Do they promote healthy sexual development and avoidance of risky sexual behaviors? Or, do the rules simply fall into general "Do Not" categories, with little processing of the information? Is there silence in the pews when it comes to true discussion of healthy sexuality?

In a study conducted by the National Institute of Child Health and Human Development[25] and in follow-up studies using the same data,[26] researchers wanted to investigate the connection between adolescent religious beliefs and practices and their attitudes about sex. What appeared to actually impact risky sexual behaviors was the child's adoption of religious beliefs about the negative consequences of having sex. This was especially true for girls.

Another study examining the role of religiosity in risky sexual behaviors for African American adolescents found that the variables in an adolescent's life that were most directly associated with a decrease in risky behaviors for girls was the child's own religiosity and her tendency to associate with peers who were less sexually permissive. This is most salient for religious youth when they are taught to think of their sexuality with meaning rather than as simply for pleasure.[27] Adolescents who indicated that religion was important to them, attended religious services frequently, and endorsed religious attitudes were more likely to delay intercourse and to have fewer sexual partners.[28] This idea is consistent with the principles of flourishing and thriving. When adolescents begin to think of their sexuality in terms of building connections and finding meaning, they are less likely to simply engage in risky behaviors for the sake of seeking pleasure.

Some have suggested that the approach that religious parents take in talking about sex may play a role in how children's attitudes about sexuality are shaped. For example, Regenurus found that when it came to discussing birth control, parents who felt that their religion was very important to them, rather than just having a religious affiliation, were more likely to talk with their adolescents about sex and birth control.[29] Thus, it seems that what is at issue here is the parents' personal religiosity and spiritual commitment, rather than just church attendance. Other research has found that religious parents tend to monitor their daughters more closely than they do their sons, and that they discuss sex and sexual decision making more often with their daughters than with their sons.[30] These conversations, however, tended to remain focused around moral issues rather than straightforward advice on how to use birth control or how to avoid unwanted sexual encounters. Perhaps religious parents feel that talking with their child specifically about birth control or sexual situations may lead to more planned sexual behaviors, thus parents may avoid those conversations in preference for conversations about the morality of sexual behaviors.

It is clear that religious adolescents engage in fewer risky sexual behaviors. This seems to be especially important in terms of religiosity, or the strength of the individual child's own religious commitment, rather than just his or her religious affiliation.[31] However, it is important to point out that many of these young people are lacking information about safe sex practices. What religious young people do seem to be getting is a lot of opportunities to think about how their sexuality is tied to their unique identity and to think in terms of mutuality and relationships rather than objectification. This type of conversation is happening more with girls than with boys. When addressing sexuality, a community needs to provide all adolescents with conversations about agency, mutuality, and sexual pleasure while also broaching topics such as the emotional and physical consequences of risky behaviors and how to protect oneself from them.

When we consider the ways that connected communities aid children in thriving, it becomes clear just how important these assets are. In the vignettes in Chapter 4, Isaac obviously suffered from not having a connected community. As a gifted learner, he lost his motivation to achieve when he was left unchallenged in the school setting. A school community that noticed his talents and provided him with optimum challenge and support could have provided him with a place to build positive connections, engage with his work, peers, and adults, find meaning in his actions, and develop a sense of accomplishment. Without a connected community, he was unable to flourish. On the other hand, Anna built a connected community both through her sports team and through her school. Both settings provided her with a positive place to build connections, engage with things that she found meaningful, and accomplish her goals.

Connected communities can provide children and adolescents with the support and encouragement they need to develop healthy self-concepts, body images, and sexual behaviors. There are certain things that these communities need to do to ensure the development of confidence, competence, and connectedness. Below I will consider each community and the specific strategies that they might employ to achieve the maximum benefit for the children involved.

CONVERSATION STARTERS

Positivity

The foundational belief that lies at the heart of flourishing is the belief in the true value of each individual. In order for a child to feel positive emotion when participating in a community, his or her experiences must be positive. Each child in the community must be viewed as having unique strengths to contribute. This allows the adults in the community to look at a child individually and ask, "What does he or she have to offer this group?" rather than trying to force each child to fit in to a particular mold.

In a classroom setting, a teacher might observe how the children interact with one another and the curriculum. She might notice that one child is very focused on the academics, while another is more social and still another child might be creative. Each of these can be viewed as a strength that brings a positive dimension to the classroom. For that outspoken child who always wants to answer every question, instead of seeing her as an annoyance, think of her as a leader. Perhaps she could be helpful in working with another child who does not have as much confidence in academics. For that child who is always drawing instead of doing the assignment, think of him as creative instead of lazy.

This technique of *finding the strength* can be used in any group to allow the adults in charge to reset their own ways of thinking about the children in a group, thus allowing each child's strengths to shine through. When children experience this acceptance of their uniqueness, they will have positive emotions about that community.

Positive emotions flow from positivity. If adults in the community have negative feelings about being a part of it, they may squelch the general positive feeling of the group. It is important for communities to be intentional about promoting a culture that focuses on their meaning. Instead of focusing solely on winning, a sports team might focus on building skills and teamwork. Regardless of the outcome of a game, if the coach is able to provide constructive feedback to the players about the way that their skills are growing or the times they functioned as a team, the experience will be positive for the children involved.

Engagement

In order to engage children in their efforts in schools, teams, or any other organization, a community must offer them an appropriate level of challenge balanced with success. Challenge is highly connected to the idea of "flow," an optimal state of concentration on a task.[32] Howard and Rice-Crenshaw found that, in school settings, academic achievement is increased when students are provided with educational experiences that are consistent with their skill level and interests, thus inducing flow.[33] Experts who study academic engagement and its benefits to students recommend that schools attempt to offer linked, stimulating, and action-driven educational experiences that take into consideration different ability levels and interests of students.[34] Here are some strategies for engaging children in communities:

• The key to engaging children in any task is offering them a balance of challenge and success. Provide children the opportunity to work just above their ability level.

• Whether in academics, sports, or performing arts, adults can facilitate engagement by taking the individual child's ability level into consideration and then providing him or her with an experience that builds upon skills or knowledge that has already been mastered yet pushes the child to continue to grow with support from the adult involved. This kind of careful planning allows children to engage in activities and moves them toward flourishing.

Relationships

Relationships are vital to flourishing. Within connected communities, children have the opportunity to build relationships that are based on mutual respect and liking. Some strategies to foster this type of relationship are:

• Create communities that set expectations and environments that promote these qualities. For example, a sports team will endorse teamwork rather than teasing between its members. Coaches will model this behavior by providing support to each team member for his or her unique contribution, rather than pitting one member against the other. Whether in schools, extracurricular activities, or religious groups, relationships can be built based on respect for each person.

• Adults in communities can model positive relationship strategies for children by using positive words to build others up and effective discussion to handle conflict. For example, if two adults in the community disagree, they can model how to respectfully discuss differences of opinion. Key phrases to use include, "Can you explain what you mean?," "Help me understand your point of view," "From my experience . . . , what about your experience?," "Let me be sure that I understand what you are saying."

• Adults need to provide rules for behavior as well as feedback to children about the way they are conducting relationships. This means that adults need to be aware of their own interactions with children and one another. Rules might include listening respectfully to each person's perspective, restating what the other person said to be sure you understand their perspective, and allowing each person to share his or her thoughts.

- Positive relationships will be supportive, accepting, and collaborative. This does not mean that people within the community will always agree, but that when they disagree, they are able to do so in respectful and civil ways. Labeling others with name-calling, assuming negative intentions, and trying to force one's own perspective should be avoided. Instead, the best should be assumed about each person's intentions.

- Conversations should be open and nonjudgmental, with a focus on coming up with a solution that is acceptable to everyone. Key phrases to use include, "Let me make sure that I understand what you are saying," "I would like to share my thoughts now," and "How can we make this work for all of us?"

Meaning

Finding meaning in one's activities is important to flourishing. Connected communities promote the idea that what the child does there matters. I have already discussed how the simple seeking of pleasure cannot lead to long-term well-being. Instead, to ensure long-term well-being, communities aid children and adolescents in their search for meaning. What does this mean on a practical level? It means that communities provide students with guidance on how what they are doing within that community matters in the big scheme of things. Some ways to do this in different social settings include:

- Volunteer groups can easily point to the needs that are being met for the community or individual's life who is being served.

- Religious groups can discuss the higher calling of service based on their view of the nature of life and the purpose of living.

- Sports teams might focus on building strength and skill or learning to be a good team member.

- Schools can provide their students with a vision for themselves that goes beyond the individual course and focuses on using their knowledge to make the world a better place through their choice of profession.

All of these communities have the potential to provide children with a view of their work there as having deeper meaning. It is crucial for the adults involved in the community to formulate their own understanding of the higher meaning behind the things their community is doing. If playing sports is just about winning, it may lead to a sense of accomplishment, but it will not provide a child with the ability to see a deeper meaning in his or her efforts. Of course, all activities do not have a meaning beyond simply completing them. But for most of the communities discussed in this chapter, there are connections that can be drawn for the children involved to begin to see the place of their work in the grand scheme of things. This concept of meaning is central to the idea that children and adolescents can become world changers through their own activism and creation of media. When they are taught to look at the world as a place to which they can contribute meaningfully, sexualized media can be responded to with empowerment rather than victimization.

Accomplishment

The last key component of flourishing is the sense of accomplishment. Connected communities provide children with the opportunity to achieve. This may be easy in some cases, such as when a child wins a sporting or performing arts competition or receives an academic award. What about when a child is struggling to achieve in a given area? Are there ways to help that child come to a place of feeling a sense of accomplishment? I believe there are. Some ways to accomplish this are:

- The adults in the community must identify steps toward goals that need to be accomplished.
- A coach might mark the improvement of specific sports skills, praising the child and promoting a sense of accomplishment as he or she is developing.
- In a school setting, teachers can focus on providing encouragement each time a child masters a component of a skill leading to the larger skill set, allowing that child to achieve a sense of accomplishment in the process of developing.
- The idea is not to praise children for doing something that took no effort, but to provide them support as they move up a ladder of skills that will eventually lead to achievement. For children with learning disabilities, this can be crucial in keeping them motivated in the school setting.
- Each academic, sporting, or performance skill is made up of a subset of smaller skills. Focusing on those and encouraging the child's progress will provide the child with the sense of accomplishment he or she needs to continue to work on the larger skill development.
- Religious groups and volunteer groups can think of the work that the children in their groups do developmentally, allowing them to build their service skills or spiritual understanding one step at a time. Understanding the concept of providing feedback at each stage of development is crucial to encouraging motivation and continued effort.

Sexual Behaviors

All of these communities have the potential to provide children with guidance regarding sexual behaviors. How do communities do this in practice? Here are some specific strategies to remember:

- *Context*: Sexualized media often depict sexuality void of context. Children need to understand how we share physical affection with those whom we care about. We share hugs as a family because we love one another. People hold hands, kiss, hug, and share other physical behaviors as a way of expressing their affection. This begins to place physical affection in the context of relationships. As children grow and community members feel that it is time to talk about sexual intercourse, caregivers can talk about it as an extension of physical behaviors that two people who care about each other share. The goal is to allow children to see sexual behaviors as positive and natural ways of sharing and caring rather than as a way of having power over others or a way of gaining attention.

- *Mutuality*: Sexualized media depict female sexuality as an object for someone else's pleasure. Children need to understand sexuality as mutual. Talk to them about how people engage in physical and sexual activities with one another because they want to, not because it is expected or demanded. Both people involved in the behavior need to be equally desirous of the interaction.

- *Honesty*: When a child asks a question or shares something that was said to him or her by a peer or seen on media, listen and answer the child honestly. Children want the trusted adults in their lives to be a source of advice and information about sexuality, just as they are for other issues. If this feels uncomfortable or does not naturally fit in the goals of a specific community, that is okay. The adults can let the child know that they appreciate the child's trust and build a strong bridge of communication with the parents so that the issue can be discussed in more detail at home.

- *Acceptance*: Avoid shaming the child for asking questions or expressing sexual desires. Sexual feelings and questions are natural, and providing children with resources and guidance about whom they can talk to about them is an asset for a community. Believe me, most of these children are being drenched with sexualized images and narratives through media and marketing messages. They need to know where to go to ask questions and get good information.

Connected communities provide children and adolescents with an environment that allows them to achieve well-being. They are places of flourishing. They provide counter-messages to those of sexualized media and promote healthy self-concepts, body image, and sexual behaviors. It is important that adults work to establish connected communities in the lives of children in order to promote well-being and provide children with encouragement to begin to see themselves as people of power.

IN THEIR VOICES

Jacey Ferrara is a college athlete. She spent the majority of her youth playing soccer and deeply involved in her sports community. As a recent college graduate, Jacey hopes to work as a teacher and soccer coach.

I am a part of one of the first generations required to navigate a media happy world. In elementary school, it became popular to have a computer in one's home. In middle school, AOL instant messenger, or AIM, became popular, as well as MySpace. In high school, Facebook was discovered, and was all the rage, and still is for people in my age group. But, navigating this constantly connected world has been difficult.

I remember my middle school days . . . the awkward pictures, learning about body changes, trying to remember to wear deodorant, and changing in front of others for athletics! Add in some social and sexualized media, and bam, you have a recipe for disaster. Around the time I was the most vulnerable in my life, AIM came out, tempting me with chat rooms, and the thrill of anonymity. At the same time, MySpace was created, adding a whole different kind of drama. At this same time in my life, I also became deeply engaged in sports. Instead of being completely vulnerable and trying to live up to screen names like "blondebabe22" or to the numerous Victoria's Secret commercials popping up during an episode of *American Idol*, I was busy getting stronger, physically and mentally. I had a slight distraction that saved me in many ways from destruction.

In high school, Facebook came out, causing all sorts of insecurities to emerge. I saw only the "best" everyone had to offer: the best pictures, beautiful vacations, new and authentic clothing, big birthday bashes, fancy new cars, etc. Oh, the things this can do to a girl trying to find her place. Again, thankfully, I was involved. I was involved seriously with soccer, playing for both a select team and the school. And with desires to go to college, I knew I needed to be well rounded, and more than one-dimensional. I was involved in a volunteer organization at school called Heroes of Tomorrow and I attended weekly Fellowship of Christian Athletes meetings at my school, which connected me to other athletes.

I quickly learned through volunteering that my problem of not having a cool or beautiful picture to post on Facebook really wasn't a problem. I learned that there were a lot of other people wanting to pursue sports, too, that were willing to sacrifice things like partying, drinking, and engaging in risky behaviors. I also learned that I liked feeling strong and athletic. Many people that work out know that there is typically a decrease in fat and an increase in muscle mass if done consistently. However, when you stop working out, or in my case, take a break from sports during the winter or summer, the muscle mass decreases. I have frequently received comments during these breaks from people like, "Wow, you look so thin!" And, "Are you doing anything differently? You look great!"

What a tempting moment that could be for me . . . to latch onto the word "thin." Yet, there's this fighter in me. There's this part of me that longs and desires a challenge, and to be strengthened. I played college soccer for four years, and I still train hard. Why? My body is a vessel. It is not an object for pleasure. It has meaning. It has the ability to be strengthened and to be mentally and physically strong. It has the ability to jump, run, climb, carry weight, engage in conversations, help those in desperate situations, hug someone, etc. My body is amazing. I've learned that I don't need a Facebook picture to prove that. I don't need a cool screen name or to fit into a Victoria's Secret size 0 swim suit for pleasure. The greatest pleasure I've had is in training for something bigger than me, and doing it with people I love, and who love me.

8

Promoting Media Activism and Creation

The way children learn to engage with, interpret, and respond to media messages is mediated by interpersonal variables within their lives. The bioecological systems within a child's life, including his or her own unique characteristics as well as the microsystems of family, school, and community and the macrosystem of larger culture, provide a child with assets or challenges to effectively respond to sexualized and stereotyped media. With the help of caring adults, children can learn how to process media messages on their own terms. This chapter will explain how children can become empowered to critique and create media as consumer activists. I will present specific strategies for aiding children in becoming active media critics and using their creativity to make media that promote their own value systems and perspectives.

What is media, after all, but the creation of something that shares an individual's or group's worldview with others? When children begin to understand that each piece of media or marketing they consume has been crafted to promote a particular perspective, they can learn to identify that perspective and ask themselves how they feel about it. Do they agree or disagree with the worldview presented? Once children see themselves as media critics, they can also learn to think of themselves as media makers. With the ready accessibility of high-quality cameras, children and adolescents can create media with a laptop computer or smartphone. They can use sharing sites such as YouTube to share their creations with the world.

Large media corporations are no longer the only ones that can widely disseminate their viewpoint. Now, children and adolescents are capable of crafting their own stories and sharing their own worldviews widely.

Promoting the idea of children and adolescents as empowered consumers, activists, and creators is a strong stance that turns the usual victim mentality on its head. Rather than teaching children and the adults who care for them to see media and marketing as evil and scary, I want to teach them to see power in making informed choices. I will focus on thinking about ways to give children and caregivers the chance to become aware of what they are consuming, identify the worldview being presented, and decide what they think of it. Once children become comfortable with critiquing media, then they can begin to create media. As they work to develop their own ideas and express their own values and belief systems, children will become even more aware of the techniques that media makers use to connect with and persuade their audience.

Adolescents themselves are great advocates for their perspective because they are at a particular stage of development when their power to resist peer pressure is growing.[1] Many adolescents are hungry to make a difference in the world, to be world changers. By harnessing that energy and helping them to become critical media consumers, we can lend them a hand in learning to critically evaluate media and marketing campaigns. Using social media and word of mouth, adolescents and caring adults can work together to fight for their rights and advocate against companies that promote unhealthy behaviors and worldviews.

Media is influential. The beauty of artistic expression through various forms of media is that it can touch the audience right where they are. The reason that I push for media makers to construct media from a perspective of social responsibility is because I believe so strongly in its power to touch hearts and minds. Media makers work with media messages that move their audience, persuade them, make them believe, or make them laugh or cry. Media are beautiful and powerful forces. I call upon those who create and work in the media to believe in the beauty that they can create and to think of the influence they can wield.

Now that you have considered the different variables in a child's life that influence the ways he or she will respond to media, it is important to consider strategies for developing an effective response. The strategies that I will discuss below are designed to build awareness of media messages, facilitate critical conversations, and then to help you and your children begin to create your own media.

STRATEGIES

Write Your Own Once Upon a Time Story

This is a fun activity to do with children that helps them see that "once upon a time" does not have to be about a girl waiting to be saved, yearning for true love, and so forth. In fact, it is a fun activity for boys and girls! Say to the child, "A lot of fairytales start with 'Once upon a time.' Let's tell our own Once Upon a Time story, where we get to be the heroes!"

Challenge

Say: "These stories usually include a description of a challenge and how the hero overcame it. Think about what challenge you have faced that might be interesting." *Here the adult can give some examples, such as learning a certain sport or skill, being bullied, moving to a new school, going to camp for the first time, friendship troubles, anything that the child or adult has struggled with.*

Action

Say: "Heroes in fairytales take action to solve their problems. What actions did you take to solve your problems? Describe your thoughts as you were getting ready to act. Were you scared, worried, wondering if it would work?" *Help children work through the emotions they felt as they were getting ready to act to solve their problems. The point is that problem solving is not easy, and sometimes it involves overcoming our fears or worries. The fairytale stories we hear do not always focus on this, but discussing it with children will allow them to understand that negative emotions are a part of facing challenges, and it is okay to feel them. It also helps them begin to understand that negative emotions do not have to stop us from acting!*

Outcome

Say: "Fairytales often end with the words 'and they lived happily ever after.' Let's come up with a new phrase that fits how we see things moving in our own stories." *The old "happily ever after" phrase is, of course, not realistic. Brainstorm with the child to come up with one you both like. Give examples like "and they lived thoughtfully/strongly/bravely ever after" or "and they all kept working hard to . . ."*

This activity allows children, adolescents, and even adults to see themselves as the heroes of their own lives, to see the actions they have already taken to solve problems, and to encourage them to view themselves as active participants in the world around them. It can be a compelling way to learn to see one's own story in a different way.

Here's an example of a story that I did with my seven-year-old daughter, Allie.

Once upon a time, there was a little girl named Allie who wanted to play soccer. A lot of her friends were on a soccer team, and Allie wanted to play with them. But, she didn't know how. Allie's mom and dad asked if she wanted to sign up to play on the team, but Allie was worried that she wouldn't be good and her friends would laugh at her. Would it be hard to learn? What if she was bad at it? Would people make fun of her? Allie cried and worried and told her mom that she didn't know how to play. But after a while, she decided to give it a try. She signed up for soccer, and at first she wasn't very good. But she kept learning, going to practice, going to camps, and playing at school. Now Allie is a pretty good player, and she is working to get better. She doesn't worry about not being good enough anymore and she just has fun playing. And she'll keep working to become the best soccer player that she can be. The End.

Deconstruction Activity

Your child receives a gift that does not mesh with his or her own value system, your child is exposed to a television show or movie that you would rather he or she not see, your child chooses a product or program only for you to have second thoughts about its value. These scenarios have happened to most parents or caregivers at one time or another. It is a good thing to be critically aware of the meanings and implications of the media and products with which we interact. That recognition that a product may be more than "just a doll" and may be sending some messages that do not promote the caregiver's core values is the first step in becoming a critical media consumer. Because the mass media will provide varied experiences, from amazingly creative programming and products that espouse higher ideals to dumbed down mind candy, consumers must make informed choices about which products and programs to choose for themselves and the children in their lives. Some of these strategies have been adapted from ideas presented in the work of Renee Hobbs, a media literacy expert. Her book *Digital and Media Literacy: Connecting Culture and Classroom* provides an excellent guide to understanding the importance of digital and media literacy along with information and specific plans for using literacy activities in the classroom with varied curriculum.[2] Another great resource that provides a framework for these activities is the online Center for Media Literacy.[3]

This strategy will walk through specific steps in deconstructing a product's or program's key message. As an example, I will use the webisodes that promote Mattel's Monster High brand. This is a brand that has claimed to promote socially responsible ideas such as acceptance of diversity and prosocial behaviors. It is also popular with children, so it is one that caregivers may actually have to make a decision about.

The first step is to ask a few questions about the target audience:

- Who does this message come from?
- Who is the target audience according to the developer?
- Paying attention to what you see and hear, who seems to be the target audience to you?[4]

It is important to understand who the target audience is in order to determine if the product or program is appropriate for a specific child. Although the original Monster High press release says the brand's target audience is tweens and teens,[5] the actual Monster High dolls have a manufacturer recommended age of 6 to 12 years.[6] The Monster High clothes are sold at Kmart with sizes ranging from 4 to 6X for some products and 7 to 16 for others.[7] Popular online stores such as Target list Monster High dolls in the top choices for fashion dolls for five- to seven-year-olds.[8] So who is the target audience for Monster High? The products I see most often are the plastic dolls, plush dolls, clothing, and videos, all of which, when considered within the context I have described above, suggest that in general this brand is targeting children between 6 and 12 years of age. Only the upper end of that range could be considered a tween audience. And yet, upon watching the videos and looking at the plastic dolls, there are very mature themes and dress. What I see are girl dolls dressed in skimpy clothing and very high heels. What I hear are themes of dating, a search for popularity, and friendship problems. So, there seems to be some confusion about the target audience. We hear from the manufacturer that tweens and teens are the audience, and yet much of the product base is targeted downward.

Next we ask what message is clearly displayed through words, music, images, and stories? What about the unspoken messages? Are there impressions you get very clearly whether they are or are not spoken?

In the announcement that Monster High was joining with the Kind Campaign, a program that promotes prosocial behaviors in girls,[9] Mattel's vice president for marketing Global Girls Brands Lori Pantel was quoted as saying, "The Monster High brand uses the monster metaphor to show girls that it is ok to be different and that our unique differences should be celebrated. We see our partnership with Kind Campaign as a natural fit because their message of kindness and acceptance goes hand-in-hand with the Monster High brand's message to embrace our own and each other's imperfections."[10]

As a deconstruction exercise examining this brand, I wanted to see if this "embrace your differences" theme rang true as I watched the webisodes. What I found was that although every monster has a "freaky flaw," they are not consistently shown as being embraced for it. For example, several times Frankie, a stitched together Frankenstein-like girl, has her stitches come undone at unlikely moments. Rather than accepting her as is, her flaw often leads to others getting angry or frustrated with her.

What about embracing difference in terms of the way the monsters look? Just making the characters monsters might seem like a big step in the direction of accepting and celebrating something beyond the thin ideal and beauty standard. However, the Monster High characters continue to have the extremely small waists, long, thin legs, and curviness of the thin ideal. They do have different skin colors and some "monster" identifying characteristics, such as fangs on the werewolf and vampire characters and stitches on Frankie. The overall impression that I got was still the celebration of the conventional thin ideal of beauty. As a part of a qualitative research study examining prosocial themes in Monster High webisodes, a team of researchers conducted a content analysis of the themes across seven webisodes as well as the themes of viewer comments. Overwhelmingly, the viewer comments focused on the appearance of the characters. These comments were either critical of a character or praising the character's looks. Either way, viewers of Monster High webisodes who commented seemed to focus on appearance rather than prosocial behaviors.[11] A positive aspect in Monster High related to appearance was that the monsters have different skin tones and accents.

Lastly, we consider what values are presented. What positive and negative messages come through? How do these compare to your own value system?[12]

As a parent, as I watched the webisodes, looked at the products, and explored the website of Monster High, I did not see any groundbreaking value messages about embracing difference being expressed. In fact, I noted many incidents of cruelty, most of it directed by a girl toward another girl. These incidents ranged from cruel words such as, "Enter Frankie into the lowest rung of the popularity database" to cruel actions such as one group of girls dumping liquid on another group and even cyber bullying through a viral text campaign against a "friend."

In comparing the values presented by Monster High and my own, I think about what I am trying to teach my own children. I focus on teaching them that they need to learn to be people who make a difference in the world, who treat others with respect and respect themselves, who do their very best to achieve in the areas that are important to them, and who work to be good friends and avoid toxic friendships.

Looking at this list as a parent, my own values do not seem to mesh well with Monster High. For one thing, the issue of respect is a big one. Friends in the webisodes I watched were not being kind and respectful, even to one another, at times. There are some characters who are generally good and kind, such as Frankie; but Cleo, who is often cruel even to her friends, counterbalances her. Maybe the creators are trying to make a point about how to handle negative friendships? My research team wanted to see if these cruel scenes were preparation for an overall message of kindness and acceptance. We examined the ways that the webisodes dealt with conflict resolution. In our analysis, there were few consistent representations of realistic, positive depictions of handling friendship difficulties or bullying.

Because Mattel has promoted Monster High as encouraging prosocial behaviors, we compared the webisode themes to a television show for children in the same age range that has been awarded the George Foster Peabody Award for excellence in public service and received several Emmys and Emmy nominations. The Public Broadcasting Station's *Arthur* series has been widely recognized for promoting prosocial behaviors to a child audience. So we wondered how Monster High would compare. What we found was that both shows presented conflicts and friendship problems. What was different was the way that the conflicts were resolved. In the Monster High webisodes, conflict was resolved either by one character getting back at another through cruel behavior, by doing something elaborate and unrealistic to make up for a slight, or through a very simplified response. There were a few webisodes in which the conflict was resolved through a realistic explanation and apology. In the *Arthur* episodes, conflict was resolved through more complex social learning and development. It is possible that part of the issue for Monster High is the length of their webisodes, which are usually just over three minutes long, whereas *Arthur* tends to be about 11 to 12 minutes of programming. Perhaps if the Monster High webisodes were extended or the storylines were carried across webisodes, more complexity could be added in depicting realistic ways for children to accept diversity and develop prosocial behaviors.

In examining a product or program to determine if it is right for a family or class, parents and teachers also have to address the issue of the appearance of the characters. The Monster High characters are very sexualized, with skimpy clothing, very high heels, and a lot of makeup. In the end, as a parent, I decided that Monster High is not a brand I wanted to promote or have in my home. If my girls decided they were interested in this brand, I would walk them through these same questions. Using this activity will help you think more critically about the media and products you choose and make an informed choice.

Deconstruction II

There was a controversy in 2011 over Skechers marketing Shape Ups to young girls. A petition was circulated through the website change .org calling on Skechers to discontinue marketing these shoes to children. In response, the president of the company, Leonard Armato, defended the shoes as a way for young girls to get healthy, much akin to First Lady Michelle Obama's "Let's Move" campaign.[13] Parents and other caring adults can use this type of controversy to help children develop media literacy skills. This is a deconstruction exercise that can help consumers decide what they think about an issue. Here are the steps adults can go through with the children in their lives:

1. What words do you hear? What are the people in the advertisements, the songs, and the words on the screen saying? Jot down the words and put a checkmark by them if you hear them more than one time.
2. What are you seeing? What visual images are being used to sell the product? What activities are the people/cartoons/animals on screen doing?
3. What is the theme of the piece? What is the overall message that a child would walk away with? For an advertisement, come up with one sentence that starts with "If I buy _____, then I will _____."[14]

When I did this exercise with the Skechers Shape Ups' advertisements with some tween girls, this was what we came up with:

• What we heard were the words "look good" and "have fun." The advertisement mentions a girl having "height and bounce," but there is no real application in the sense of physical fitness. The words on the screen at the end say, "stay fit, have fun," but that is the only reference that we noticed to fitness. We viewed this advertisement several times as we were doing this activity.
• What we saw were images of girls singing on a stage, not moving much. All of the girls jump at one point, and the main character walks. There is not a lot of action, playing sports, running, and so forth. The girls in the commercials are not dressed for sports activities or even for active play. They are wearing short skirts and skinny jeans or leggings.
• I asked some 11-year-old girls about the main message of the advertisement. One said, "If I buy Skechers Shape-Ups, then I will be popular." I had not really

thought of that word, so I asked her to clarify. She went on to say, "After all, people are following her around and watching her at a concert." So, in her mind, and she is the target audience for these shoes, Skechers Shape Ups are about making you more popular. I asked, "How would they do that?" She said, "They don't say anything about the Shape Ups part, really. Are they supposed to make you taller?" If you have watched Shape Ups commercials aimed at women, you will know that they are supposed to make you look better by firming your legs and behind. I showed the girls a few of the Kim Kardashian television advertisements, and one said, "Eww, so they're saying if you wear these shoes your bum will look better and then everyone will like you? That's a disgusting message to send to kids!" So if a girl gets the popularity message and understands exactly what Shape Ups are designed for, then the message is: Get firmer legs and bottoms and you will be more popular. Was the Skechers Shape Ups advertisement saying to kids, "Get moving, and get active" or was it saying, "If you wear these shoes then you will have a firm behind and everyone will like you"?

I used another short video advertisement for Skechers Sporty Shorty shoes in a deconstruction activity with the same group of girls. This video featured girls wearing appropriate clothes for exercise. The girls in the advertisement engaged in fun, physical activities that children enjoy, such as jumping rope, running, and tumbling. After viewing these two commercials and deconstructing them, the girls felt that the Sporty Shorty video sent a more realistic and positive message to children than the Shape Ups advertisement.

Using this type of deconstruction exercise can be really helpful for understanding the messages that children are getting from media and for helping children understand those messages themselves. Rather than just singing along with the upbeat song, they will start evaluating the message that the company is sending. Deconstructing media messages allows children and adults alike to become more confident consumers and puts the power back in their hands, where it belongs.

MAKING MEDIA

It can be easy at times to feel overwhelmed by the sexualized and stereotyped media and marketing directed toward children and adolescents. But caregivers and children can become empowered not just to critique media and marketing messages, but also to create their own media. Using simple techniques and accessible tools, children and adolescents can make potent statements promoting their own value systems. This provides an opportunity for positive activism. When I use the term *positive activism*, I am not necessarily saying that all of the messages a media maker will send will be nice. Instead, I am using the term positively in reference to the fact that the media maker is adding something to the conversation. Rather than sitting back and being an armchair critic who feels powerless, I hope that these strategies will give caregivers, teachers, and children the tools to view themselves as people who have something important to share.

Photos: Make Your Own Advertisements

You can make your own advertisements using prints that you find in magazines and your own markers, stencils, or stickers or you can use photos on your computer. The idea is to compare what is out there to what you would like to see or to make an ironic and powerful statement about the overall message of the program or product. Some ideas for the advertisements include:

1. Make a negative advertisement positive. Is it the clothes or the words you find offensive? What are the changes that could be made to make the advertisement more positive?

2. Make an ironic advertisement commenting on the sexualized or stereotyped nature of the product or program. In one workshop I did with fifth graders, we looked at Candie's print advertisements, which are aimed at tween and teen girls. We noticed that the woman in the advertisement was typically very sexualized; wearing few clothes, and in submissive or sexy poses. Using a computer program, the girls wrote captions that they thought were appropriate as they considered the photo. In one advertisement, a girl wrote, "Fight teen pregnancy, one sexy advertisement at a time" to comment on the fact that while the Candie's Foundation promotes teen pregnancy prevention, the Candie's Clothing advertisements are highly sexualized and directed at young girls.

3. Use your faux advertisements to talk with the children in your life about what makes certain advertisements sexualized or stereotyped and what they would rather see. What kind of advertisements would you and they like to see? What would make you want to buy this product?

4. What makes you not like a certain product or program? What could be changed to make it acceptable to you? For example, I discussed the Monster High dolls with tween girls. We talked about what they did and did not like about them, and then what would make them like them more. For example, the skirts could be longer, the shoes could have lower heels, the body shape could be more realistic, and the characters could wear less makeup. In this exercise, you might want to use print offs or pictures of specific products and change them with markers, colors, or your computer programs.[15]

Videos and Remixes

Remix

Children and adolescents can use sites such as Creative Commons to make remixes or their own video camera to create a program or music video. Once a child develops a video, he or she can then share it on his or her own website or YouTube. Some great examples of these are Jonathan McIntosh's Rebellious Pixels remix titled "Buffy vs. Edward," which he describes as "transformative storytelling."[16] It is designed to question the different gender roles promoted through mainstream media. On the Rebellious Pixels website you can also find a remix application that allows users to remix their own gendered advertisements.[17]

Video Critique

Anita Sarkeesian of Feminist Frequency is a popular culture critic who produces regular video commentaries, pointing out particular themes that run through media and critiquing them. Her video critiques guide the viewer in deconstruction exercises similar to the ones discussed above. Have children think about the media messages that really bother them. What specifically disturbs them? Encourage adolescents to use that annoyance to spur creativity and develop a clear, concise message to share with others.

Video

Making a video satirizing mainstream media or calling out particular products or programming and then posting it publicly is a very effective way to get a message out. An example of this that adolescents may be aware of is the parodies created by Josh Chomik known by his YouTube name as The Computer Nerd01. Adolescents might also consider making a faux television clip or music video that satirizes a particular theme in mainstream media. For example, Ryan Higa produced a satirical music video questioning the idea of male emotional distance and what women might do if it was turned on its head.[18]

Children can also consider writing their own script or song or producing a documentary to share messages that are consistent with their own values. Jennifer Pozner created her own "Reality Rehab" show to point out the stereotypical stock characters that are manufactured and promoted by reality television.[19] Another example of this type of work was done by the founders of the Kind Campaign in the creation of their documentary *Finding Kind*. Lauren Parsekian and Molly Thompson were motivated to develop their documentary out of their own passion for helping girls learn to be kind to one another.[20]

The key behind all of these ideas is that we have the tools to create media that we want to see and to comment critically and publicly on products and programming that we do not like. Adults can use these ideas with the kids in their life to jumpstart active media critique in a fun way. Adolescents can use these ideas to make a public statement promoting their own values or questioning those promoted by particular programs or products. And, if a child is really interested in producing quality media, he or she can try to get it produced professionally. Look for workshops, contests, and other opportunities to share the work. Encourage children and adolescents to see themselves as active media users and creators.

ACTIVISM

The Great Sticky Note Campaign

This activity provides an easy way to make a public statement about products and advertising campaigns. There are several premade sticky notes that can be used, or children can make their own. For example, *New Moon Girls* online magazine has a "Girl-Caught" downloadable file that can be printed out on sticker paper. The stickers say, "This is GIRL-CAUGHT! It disrespects girls & women. STOP IT!" or "This is GIRL-CAUGHT! It RESPECTS girls & women. THANK YOU!"[21] Caregivers can also make their own sticky notes or stickers with their children. Research tells us that children and adolescents learn more from media literacy lessons when they are actively involved in creating something, not just analyzing it.[22] So, providing children with the chance to create a sticker that shares a message they want to send is a good move. Groups can brainstorm together and come up with a message and design that everyone likes. This can be as complicated or simple as the group wants it to be. Caregivers can buy some small sticky notes and use markers and scissors to create messages, or they can use a computer to create something more complex. Either way, both the caregiver and children will have fun and they will all become consumer activists, sharing their own viewpoints.

So what happens with the stickers in the Great Sticky Note Campaign? They can be used in a few different ways:

- The easiest and simplest is just to put the stickers on items in a store or advertisements that consumers see in public places. Make sure that the notes or stickers used will not ruin the product. The idea is not to cause destruction, but to make a point.
- To go a little further in sharing a message, *New Moon Girls* magazine suggests collecting a group of products, boxes, print advertisements, and so forth from one company that have caught the consumer's eye. Put sticky notes on all of the products or advertisements and mail it to the head of public relations or community relations or the president's office for that company. Consumers can include a note to let the company know what they do or do not like about the messages that are being sent to children.[23]

- Consumers can encourage friends to make notes too, and if there is a particular store or product that a group feels needs to get a message, they can make a point to get everyone sharing. For example, our local seasonal Halloween costume store sells some horribly inappropriate costumes for children. When October rolls around, several of us will go by and share our thoughts using sticky notes.

The Great Sticky Note Campaign is a simple way to share an important message, and it gets children and adolescents involved in promoting their own voices, rather than seeing themselves as passive consumers.

Speaking Up

Think about the story of my friend, Marcia, who called a national retailer out for the depiction of women as shallow and frivolous in their romantic relationships. With all of the other sexualized media messages that emphasize this same point, you have a damaging and dangerous pattern. Apparently, her voice was one of many that spoke out about that product. What is important about this story is that it is a perfect example of using activism to influence the larger systems that touch a child's life. When Marcia and the rest of us as individuals decide to take a stand and let our voices be heard, we have the power to change the larger systems around us that influence children. The merchandise in the store is there because people buy it and because nobody complains. When enough customers start complaining, the stores will remove the merchandise, because they do not want to offend their customers. They want consumers to continue to shop there, to keep buying things at that store. And the businesses know that if they continually offend the majority of their customers, they will not make a profit.

It is vital that caregivers begin to understand the part that sexualized media play in shaping a child's view of sexual behaviors, self-concept, and body image. Once parents, teachers, and other caring adults are aware, they can begin to plan a response, promote conversation with the child, and provide the child with guidance in learning to become an activist and media creator.

Through the examination of the culture of celebrity, family, gender, and community systems, you have gained insight into how these variables influence the way the child responds to sexualized media. Considering each variable will allow you to see both the challenges of each factor and some specific strategies that adults can employ to reduce the negative impacts of sexualized media.

This last chapter discussed approaches that promote active media critique and creation. The fundamental idea behind each of these activities has been to provide caregivers and children with active, thoughtful ways of understanding and responding to sexualized media. This method of thinking about sexualized media puts the power into the hands of the consumer and promotes a positive and active way of dealing with sexualized media. Instead of feeling overwhelmed by negative messages or just accepting them, active media consumers and makers are aware of the messages that are being sent, decide for themselves which to accept or reject, and get involved with promoting their own viewpoints. With this perspective, children and caregivers are armed with the tools to approach sexualized media with confidence, knowing that they have the skills necessary to understand and respond to it effectively.

IN THEIR VOICES

Amy Jussel is the founder of Shaping Youth, a nonprofit consortium dedicated to changing the direction of media influence toward a healthier worldview for kids. Shaping Youth uses counter-marketing and persuasion techniques to flip the messages of vapid values and toxic cues being marketed toward youth by deploying critical thinking skills and lifting the veil to reveal the agenda through hands-on media literacy games.

- "Is your butt *really* Juicy?" *(third-grade boy taunting a brand-wearing classmate)*
- "He said I had big boobs" *(fifth-grade Latina girl in tears, speaking Spanish/miming to a parent volunteer on the playground)*
- "Ew, she's got, like, a unibrow! Gross! Wax, already!" *(fifth-grade girl "smoking" pretzel sticks)*
- "OK, THAT is WAY scary-freaky!" *(fifth-grader about a very developed, large-chested fourth-grader)*
- "Do these jeans make me look fat?" *(second-grader, hands on hips viewing her own backside)*
- "Oh yeah? Well you have wet dreams!" "Do not!" "Do too!" *(fifth-grader bullying a peer)*
- "I'm too sexy for my shirt . . ." *(fourth-grade boy, in full chorus with sexy dance moves)*

Every week for three years as a parent noontime volunteer, I captured schoolyard conversations like this at the lunch table and on the play yard, documenting the trickle-down impact of media on kids, and launched ShapingYouth.org as an intervention to combat the copious quantities of junk food for the mind and body seeping into kids' psyches.

There are staggering financial and health care implications if we don't stop "body snatching" wee ones and dragging them into adulthood at ever-earlier ages. After all, body image links a child's emotional and physical health, and consumer-oriented media has grown into a virtual 24/7 presence with "always on" behavioral messaging that accentuates fears and nurtures obsessions. With "age compression," it used to be these sexualized messages impacted teens the most, but now it's also "tweens" (8–12 years) and even young kindergarteners are at high risk of exploitation, heavily bombarded with tactics to mine their insecurities for profit.

So what can we do? Spring-boarding off the national focus of childhood obesity and nutritional nightmares (external/physical health) and deep diving into the pool of early sexuality, objectification, body image and peer angst (internal/socio-emotional health), we set our goal on getting kids to develop critical thinking by turning the "what is the purpose, who created it and why, what attention techniques are being used, how does it make you feel" basics into playful games. In short, kids "spot the spin" and empower themselves by taking some of the heat out of manipulative messaging so they can use it as a powerful shield of self-knowledge to be "in the know" and take back control of their own wellness compass.

How do we specifically leverage the "problem" into the "solution"? By using the power of media, turned on itself. Based on some of the wildly successful reality shows and game style challenges, we use entertainment tactics to lift the veil and reveal the profit-driven, psychological agenda, so that *kids* get to the "aha" moment on their own and their eyes snap open to *see* that media and marketing are defining them before they can even define themselves.

For example, one game we loosely refer to as "Idolized" is about voting up healthier role models and squashing stereotypes in media messaging while using bubble gum flinging to "pop" the culture.

Kids identify iconic advertisements, snap judgments they make based on "looks," narrowcast roles in race, gender, body type, and beyond all gleaned from cartoons, videogames, and television shows. . . . Another game is a riff on *Survivor* about being "voted off the lunch table" as kids role play about cliques and tribes to "put yourself in their shoes" switching out scenarios with shout-outs and taunts ranging from "fat talk" and appearance cues to teasing about what kids are eating, wearing, watching, sounding, and even smelling like. . . . These are the microscopic nit-picky annoyances that wear kids down, setting them apart as "outliers" . . . and our game helps establish some solid anti-bullying life skills like "upstanding rather than by-standing" with pals, and with hands-on "who has had this happen to them?" line games to build empathy, trust, and a sense of compassion and community of shared experience which kids can relate to. The approach works because it's upbeat and demo-driven *not* heavy-handed "sage on the stage" preach and teach, so it refreshingly puts the onus on *kids* to connect the dots with informal learning that sticks.

Like marketers tactics, our "get 'em while they're young" strategy of behavioral influence is based on research showing increased success in shifting habits if intervention occurs before they're fully formed. At this age, youth are more receptive to adult "authority figures," like parent volunteers, playground mentors, teachers, etc. We back-flip damaging messages to shift behavior in a positive direction, using the same tactics and techniques that commercial media use to target kids. The messages, motivations, and "triggers" are all in good fun, media literacy with life skills served on the side.

Notes

INTRODUCTION

1. M. Gigi Durham, *The Lolita Effect: The Media Sexualization of Young Girls and What We Can Do About It* (New York: Overlook, 2008); Sharon Lamb and Lyn M. Brown, *Packaging Girlhood: Rescuing Our Daughters from Marketers' Schemes* (New York: St. Martin's, 2006); Diane E. Levin and Jean Kilbourne, *So Sexy So Soon: The New Sexualized Childhood and What Parents Can Do to Protect Their Kids* (New York: Ballantine Books, 2008).

2. Ibid.

3. Linda Papadopolous, "The Sexualisation of Young People Review." Report presented to the Home Secretary, London, 2010, 100; Reg Bailey, "Letting Children Be Children: Report of an Independent Review of the Commercialisation and Sexualisation of Childhood." Report presented to Parliament, London, 2011, 104; Standing Committee on Environment, Communications, and the Arts, "Sexualisation of Children in the Contemporary Media," Report to Parliament, Canberra, AU, 2008, 112; American Psychological Association, "Report of the APA Task Force on the Sexualization of Girls" (Washington, DC, 2007; 2010), 66.

4. World Health Organization and UNFPA, "Measuring Sexual Health: Conceptual and Practical Considerations and Related Indicators," last modified 2010, accessed March 25, 2014, http://www.who.int/reproductivehealth/public ations/monitoring/who_rhr_10.12/en/

5. Sharna Olfman, "The Sexualization of Childhood: Growing Older Younger/ Growing Younger/Older," in *The Sexualization of Childhood.* Childhood in America (Westport, CT: Praeger, 2009), 1.

6. Durham, *The Lolita Effect*.

7. Victor C. Strasburger, Barbara J. Wilson, and Amy B. Jordan, *Children, Adolescents, and the Media* (Los Angeles: Sage, 2009).

8. Deborah Schooler, L. Monique Ward, Ann Merriweather, et al., "Who's That Girl: Television's Role in the Body Image Development of Young White and Black Women," *Psychology of Women Quarterly* 28, no. 1 (2004): 38–47; Shelly Grabe and Janet S. Hyde, "Body Objectification, MTV, and Psychological Outcomes Among Female Adolescents," *Journal of Applied Social Psychology* 39, no. 12 (2009): 2840–2858; D. J. Anschutz, D. Spruijt-Metz, T. Van Strien, et al., "The Direct Effect of Thin Ideal Focused Adult Television on Young Girls' Ideal Body Figure," *Body Image* 8, no. 1 (2011): 26–33; Rebecca L. Collins, Steven Martino, Marc Elliott, et al., "Relationships Between Adolescent Sexual Outcomes and Exposure to Sex in Media: Robustness to Propensity-Based Analysis," *Developmental Psychology* 47, no. 2 (2011): 585–591; Deborah Schooler and Sarah Trinh, "Longitudinal Associations Between Television Viewing Patterns and Adolescent Body Satisfaction," *Body Image* 8, no. 1 (2011): 34–42.

9. Urie Bronfenbrenner, *The Ecology of Human Development* (Cambridge, MA: Harvard University Press, 1979); Nancy Darling, "Ecological Systems Theory: The Person in the Center of the Circles," *Research in Human Development* 4, no. 3–4 (2007): 203–217.

CHAPTER 1

1. American Psychological Association, *Report of the APA Task Force on the Sexualization of Girls* (Washington, DC: American Psychological Association, 2007; 2010), 1.

2. Ibid.

3. Ibid.

4. Jane D. Brown, Carolyn T. Halpern, and Kelly L. L'Engle, "Mass Media as a Sexual Super Peer for Early Maturing Girls," *Journal of Adolescent Health* 36, no. 5 (2005): 420–427.

5. *Merriam-Webster Online*, s.v. "mass medium," accessed March 26, 2014, http://www.merriam-webster.com/dictionary/mass%20media

6. Tom F. M. ter Bogt, Rutger C. M. E. Engels, Sanne Bogers, et al., "'Shake It Baby, Shake It': Media Preferences, Sexual Attitudes and Gender Stereotypes Among Adolescents," *Sex Roles* 63, no. 11–12 (2010): 844–859.

7. Caroline Oates, Mark Blades, and Barrie Gunter, "Children and Television Advertising: When Do They Understand Persuasive Intent?," *Journal of Consumer Behavior* 1, no. 3 (2001): 238–245; Barrie Gunter, Caroline Oates, and Mark Blades, *Advertising to Children on TV: Content, Impact, and Regulation* (Mahwah, NJ: Erlbaum, 2005); Esther Rozendaal, Moniek Buijzen, and Patti Valkenburg, "Children's Understanding of Advertisers' Persuasive Tactics," *International Journal of Advertising* 30, no. 2 (2011): 329–350.

8. Victoria Mallinckrodt and Dick Mizerski, "The Effects of Playing an Advergame on Young Children's Perceptions, Preferences, and Requests," *Journal of Advertising* 36, no. 2 (2007): 87–100; Soontae An and Susannah Stern, "Mitigating the Effects of Advergames on Children: Do Advertising Breaks Work?," *Journal of Advertising* 40, no. 1 (2011): 43–56.

9. Victoria J. Rideout, *Zero to Eight: Children's Media Use in America 2013* (San Francisco: Common Sense Media, 2013).

10. Donald F. Roberts, Ulla G. Foehr, and Victoria J. Rideout, *Generation M: Media in the Lives of 8-to-18-Year-Olds* (Menlo Park, CA: Kaiser Family Foundation,

2005); Donald F. Roberts and Ulla G. Foehr, *Kids & Media in America* (Cambridge, UK: Cambridge University Press, 2004).

11. American Psychological Association, *Report on the APA Task Force*, 2010.

12. Roberts, Foehr, and Rideout, *Generation M*; Rideout, *Zero to Eight*.

13. Ibid.

14. Ibid.

15. "Nickelodeon Is Listening, So Let's Make Even More Noise," *Campaign for a Commercial Free Childhood*, June 7, 2010, accessed September 22, 2014, http:// www.commercialfreechildhood.org/blog/nickelodeon-listening-so-lets-make -even-more-noise

16. Susan Linn, *Consuming Kids: Thomas H. Wright Lecture 2009*, video recording, 1:23, July 13, 2009, accessed September 22, 2014, http://www.slc.edu/news- events/archived/2009-2010/consuming-kids-2009-thomas-wright-lecture.html; Juliet B. Schor, *Born to Buy: The Commercialized Childhood and the New Consumer Culture* (New York: Scribner, 2004); Mark Blades, Caroline Oates, and Shiying Li, "Children's Recognition of Advertisements on Television and on Web Pages," *Appetite* 62 (2012): 190–193.

17. David Buckingham, *After the Death of Childhood: Growing Up in the Age of Electronic Media* (Cambridge, UK: Polity, 2000); Oates et al., "Children and Television Advertising."

18. Kim Campbell and Kent Davis-Packard, "How Ads Get Kids to Say, I Want It!," *Christian Science Monitor*, September 18, 2000, accessed September 22, 2014, http://www.csmonitor.com/2000/0918/p1s1.html

19. Elizabeth S. Moore and Richard J. Lutz, "Children, Advertising, and Product Experiences: A Multimethod Inquiry," *Journal of Consumer Research* 27, no. 1 (2000): 31–48.

20. Linn, *Consuming Kids*.

21. "Shut Down HappyMeal.com," 2013, Campaign for a Commercial-Free Childhood, accessed April 14, 2014, http://www.commercialfreechildhood.org /action/stop-happymeal

22. M. Carole Macklin, "Preschoolers' Understanding of the Informal Function of Television Advertising," *Journal of Consumer Research* 14, no. 2 (1987): 229–239; Eliot J. Butter, Paula Popovich, Robert Stackhouse et al., "Discrimination of Television Programs and Commercials by Preschool Children," *Journal of Advertising Research* 21, no. 2 (1981): 53–56.

23. Brian L. Wilcox, Dale Kunkel, Joanne Cantor, et al., *Report of the APA Task Force on Advertising and Children* (Washington, DC: American Psychological Association, 2004).

24. Moondore Ali, M. Blades, C. Oates, et al., "Young Children's Ability to Recognize Advertisements in Web Page Designs," *British Journal of Developmental Psychology* 27, no. 1 (2009): 71–83.

25. Rideout, *Zero to Eight*.

26. "Retouching Is 'Excessive' Says Slimline Covergirl Kate Winslet," *Hello! Magazine*, January 10, 2003, accessed September 22, 2014, http://www.hellomagazine .com/film/2003/01/10/katewinslet/

27. Duane Hargreaves, "Idealized Women in TV Ads Make Girls Feel Bad," *Journal of Social and Clinical Psychology* 21, no. 1 (2002): 287–308.

28. Sofia Fernandez and Mary Pritchard, "Relationships Between Self-Esteem, Media Influence and Drive for Thinness," *Eating Behaviors* 13 (2012): 321–325; Isabelle

H. S. Mischner, Hein T. von Schie, Daniel H. G. Wigboldus, et al., "Thinking Big: The Effect of Sexually Objectifying Music Videos on Bodily Self-Perception in Young Women," *Body Image* 10 (2013): 26–34; Michael P. Levine and Sarah K. Murmen, "'Everybody Knows that Mass Media Are/Are Not [*Pick One*] a Cause of Eating Disorders': A Critical Review of Evidence for a Causal Link Between Media, Negative Body Image, and Disordered Eating in Females," special issue: Body Image and Eating Disorders, *Journal of Social and Clinical Psychology* 28 (2009): 9–42; Shelly Grabe, L. Monique Ward, and Janet S. Hyde, "The Role of the Media in Body Image Concerns Among Women: A Meta-Analysis of Experimental and Correlational Studies," *Psychological Bulletin* 134, no. 3 (2008): 460–476; Gayle R. Bessenoff, "Can the Media Affect Us? Social Comparison, Self-Discrepancy, and the Thin Ideal," *Psychology of Women Quarterly* 30, no. 3 (2006): 239–251; Gen Kanayama, S. Barry, J. I. Hudson, et al., "Body Image and Attitudes toward Male Roles in Anabolic Androgenic Steroid Users," *American Journal of Psychiatry* 163, no. 4 (2006): 697–703.

29. Jennifer A. Harriger, Rachel Calogero, David Witherington, et al., "Body Size Stereotyping and Internalization of the Thin Ideal in Preschool Girls," *Sex Roles* 63 (2010): 609–620.

30. Marita P. McCabe, Lina A. Ricciardelli, Jacqueline Stanford, et al., "Where Is All the Pressure Coming From? Messages from Mothers and Children about Preschool Children's Appearance, Diet and Exercise," *European Eating Disorders Review* 15, no. 3 (2007): 221–230; Dara R. Musher-Eizenman, Shayla C. Holub, Amy Barnhart Miller, et al., "Body Size Stigmatization in Preschool Children: The Role of Control Attributions," *Journal of Pediatric Psychology* 29, no. 8 (2004): 613–620; Jacinta Lowes and Marika Tiggemann, "Body Dissatisfaction, Dieting Awareness and the Impact of Parental Influence in Young Children," *Journal of Health Psychology* 8, no. 2 (2003): 135–147; Samantha Williamson and Catherine Delin, "Young Children's Figural Selections: Accuracy of Reporting and Body Size Dissatisfaction," *International Journal of Eating Disorders* 29, no. 1 (2001): 80–84; Neala Ambrosie-Randic, "Perception of Current and Ideal Body Size in Preschool Age Children," *Perceptual and Motor Skills* 90 (2000): 885–889.

31. Musher-Eizenman et al., "Body Size Stigmatization."

32. Stephen R. Daniels, "The Consequences of Childhood Overweight and Obesity," *Future of Children* 16, no. 1 (2006): 47–67; Marlene B. Schwartz and Katherine E. Henderson, "Does Obesity Prevention Cause Eating Disorders?," *Journal of the American Academy of Child and Adolescent Psychiatry* 48, no. 8 (2009): 784–786.

33. Lisa Jervis, "Barbie's New Bod, BFD," *Mother Jones*, December 4, 1997, accessed September 22, 2014, http://www.motherjones.com/politics/1997/12/barbies-new-bod-bfd

34. Teresa Moore, "Barbie Doll to Get More Real/Smaller Bust, Wider Waist, Flatter Feet—Even Her Smile Is Changing," *SFGate*, November 18, 1997, accessed September 22, 2014, http://www.sfgate.com/news/article/Barbie-Doll-to-Get-More-Real-Smaller-bust-2795230.php

35. Harriger et al., "Body Size Stereotyping," 616.

36. Bianca Bush and Adrian Furnham, "Gender Jenga: The Role of Advertising in Gender Stereotypes within Educational and Non-Educational Games," *Young Consumers: Insight and Ideas for Responsible Marketers* 14, no. 3 (2013): 216–229; Stacy L. Smith, Katherine M. Piper, Amy Granados, et al., "Assessing Gender-Related Portrayals in Top-Grossing G-Rated Films," *Sex Roles* 62 (2010): 774–786.

37. George Comstock and Erica Scharrer, *Media and the American Child* (New York: Academic Press, 2007).

38. Bush and Furnham, "Gender Jenga;" Smith et al., "Assessing Gender-Related Portrayals."

39. George Comstock and Erica Scharrer, *The Psychology of Media and Politics* (San Diego, CA: Elsevier, 2005).

40. Richard M. Lerner, "Developmental Science, Developmental Systems, and Contemporary Theories," in *Theoretical Models of Human Development*, ed. Richard M. Lerner, vol. 1 of *Handbook of Child Psychology*, 6th ed. (Hoboken, NJ: Wiley, 2006), 1–17.

41. Richard M. Lerner, Alexander von Eye, Jacqueline V. Lerner, et al., "Exploring the Foundations and Functions of Adolescent Thriving within the 4-H Study of Positive Youth Development: A View of the Issues," *Journal of Applied Developmental Psychology* 30 (2009): 567–570.

42. Peter L. Benson, Peter C. Scales, Stephen F. Hamilton, et al., "Positive Youth Development So Far: Core Hypotheses and Their Implications for Policy and Practice," *Search Institute Insights and Evidence* 3, no. 1 (2006): 1–13.

43. Richard M. Lerner, Jacqueline Lerner, Alexander von Eye, et al., "Individual and Contextual Bases of Thriving in Adolescence: A View of the Issues," *Journal of Adolescence* 34 (2011): 1107–1114; Richard M. Lerner, Jacqueline Lerner, Jason Almerigi, et al., "Positive Youth Development, Participation in Community Youth Development Programs, and Community Contributions of Fifth-Grade Adolescents: Findings from the First Wave of the 4-H Study of Positive Youth Development," *Journal of Early Adolescence* 25, no. 1 (2005): 17–71.

44. Lerner et al., "Positive Youth Development," 23.

45. Mindy E. Scott, Elizabeth Wildsmith, Katie Welti, et al., "Risky Adolescent Sexual Behaviors and Reproductive Health in Young Adulthood," *Perspectives on Sexual and Reproductive Health* 43, no. 2 (2011): 110.

46. Leslie G. Simons, Callie H. Burt, and F. Ryan Peterson, "The Effect of Religion on Risky Sexual Behavior Among College Students," *Deviant Behavior* 30, no. 5 (2009): 467–485.

47. Scott et al., "Risky Adolescent Sexual Behaviors," 110.

48. Lisa M. Groesz, Michael P. Levine, and Sarah K. Murnen, "The Effect of Experimental Presentation of Thin Media Images on Body Satisfaction: A Meta-Analytic Review," *International Journal of Eating Disorders* 31, no. 1 (2002): 1–16; Doeschka J. Anschutz, D. Spruijt-Metz, T. Van Strien, et al., "The Direct Effect of Thin Ideal Focused Adult Television on Young Girls' Ideal Body Figure," *Body Image* 8 (2011): 26–33.

49. Shelly Grabe and Janet S. Hyde, "Body Objectification, MTV, and Psychological Outcomes among Female Adolescents," *Journal of Applied Social Psychology* 39, no. 12 (2009): 2840–2858.

50. Deborah Schooler and Sarah Trinh, "Longitudinal Associations between Television Viewing Patterns and Adolescent Body Satisfaction," *Body Image* 8, no. 1 (2011): 34–42.

51. Hayley Dohnt and Marika Tiggemann, "The Contributions of Peer and Media Influences to the Development of Body Satisfaction and Self-Esteem in Young Girls: A Prospective Study," *Developmental Psychology* 42, no. 5 (2006): 929–936.

52. Carol J. Pardun, Kelly L. L'Engle, and Jane D. Brown, "Linking Exposure to Outcomes: Early Adolescents' Consumption of Sexual Content in Six Media,"

Mass Communication and Society 8, no. 2 (2005): 75–91; L. Monique Ward and Rocio Rivadeneyra, "Contributions of Entertainment Television to Adolescents' Sexual Attitudes and Expectations: The Role of Viewing Amount versus Viewer Involvement," *Journal of Sex Research* 36, no. 3 (1999): 237–249.

53. Kelly L. L'Engle, Jane D. Brown, and Kristin Kenneavy, "The Mass Media Are an Important Context for Adolescents' Sexual Behavior," *Journal of Adolescent Health* 38 (2006): 186–192.

54. J. D. Brown, Kelly Ladin L'Engle, Carol J. Pardun, et al., "Sexy Media Matter: Exposure to Sexual Content in Music, Movies, Television and Magazines Predicts Black and White Adolescents' Sexual Behavior," *Pediatrics* 117 (2006): 1018–1027; Anita Chandra, Steven C. Martino, Rebecca L. Collins, et al., "Does Watching Sex on Television Predict Teen Pregnancy? Findings from a National Longitudinal Survey of Youth," *Pediatrics* 122, no. 5 (2008): 1047–1054; Rebecca L. Collins et al., "Entertainment Television as a Healthy Sex-Educator: The Impact of Condom-Efficacy Information in an Episode of 'Friends,'" *Pediatrics* 112, no. 5 (2003): 1115–1121.

55. Chandra et al., "Does Watching Sex on Television," 1047.

CHAPTER 2

1. Victoria J. Rideout, Ulla G. Foehr, and Donald F. Roberts, *Generation M2: Media in the Lives of 8-to-18-Year-Olds* (Menlo Park, CA: Kaiser Family Foundation, 2010); Donald F. Roberts, Ulla G. Foehr, and Victoria J. Rideout, *Generation M: Media in the Lives of 8-to-18-Year-Olds* (Menlo Park, CA: Kaiser Family Foundation, 2005).

2. Urie Bronfenbrenner, *The Ecology of Human Development* (Cambridge, MA: Harvard University Press, 1979); Ross Vasta, ed., *Six Theories of Child Development: Revised Formulations and Current Issues* (London: Jessica Kingsley, 1992), 187–249; Urie Bronfenbrenner, ed., *Making Human Beings Human* (Thousand Oaks, CA: Sage, 2005); Urie Bronfenbrenner and Pamela A. Morris, "The Ecology of Developmental Processes," in *Theoretical Models of Human Development*, ed. Richard M. Lerner, vol. 1 of *Handbook of Child Psychology*, 5th ed., ed. William Damon (New York: Wiley, 1998), 993–1028; Urie Bronfenbrenner and Pamela A. Morris, "The Bioecological Model of Human Development," in *Theoretical Models of Human Development*, ed. Richard M. Lerner, vol. 1 of *Handbook of Child Psychology*, 5th ed., ed. William Damon (New York: Wiley 2006).

3. Bronfenbrenner, *Making Human Beings Human*; Bronfenbrenner and Morris, "The Bioecological Model."

4. Bronfenbrenner and Morris, "The Ecology of Developmental Processes," 996.

5. Jonathan R. H. Tudge, Irina Mokrova, Bridget H. Hatfield, et al., "Uses and Misuses of Bronfenbrenner's Bioecological Theory of Human Development," *Journal of Family Theory and Review* 1, no. 4 (2009): 198–210.

6. Ibid.

7. Richard M. Lerner, Jacqueline Lerner, Jason Almerigi, et al., "Positive Youth Development, Participation in Community Youth Development Programs, and Community Contributions of Fifth-Grade Adolescents: Findings from the First Wave of the 4-H Study of Positive Youth Development," *Journal of Early Adolescence* 25, no. 1 (2005): 17–71.

8. Bronfenbrenner, *Making Human Beings Human*, 148.

9. Ibid.

10. Ibid.

11. Ibid., 150.

12. Ibid.

13. Tudge et al., "Uses and Misuses."

14. Ibid.

15. Ibid.

16. H. Hill Goldsmith, Arnold H. Buss, Robert Plomin, et al., "Roundtable: What Is Temperament? Four Approaches," *Child Development* 58 (1987): 505–529; Rebecca Shiner, Kristin A. Buss, Sandee G. McClowry, et al., "'What Is Temperament Now?': Assessing Progress in Temperament Research on the Twenty-Fifth Anniversary of Goldsmith et al. (1987)," *Child Development Perspectives* 6, no. 4 (2012): 436–444.

17. Shiner et al., "What Is Temperament Now?"

18. Ronny A. Shtarkshall, John S. Santelli, and Jennifer S. Hirsch, "Sex Education and Sexual Socialization: Roles for Educators and Parents," *Perspectives on Sexual and Reproductive Health* 39, no. 2 (2007): 116–119.

19. Kathryn Jones, Aurora Meneses da Silva, and Kristy Soloski, "Sexological Systems Theory: An Ecological Model and Assessment Approach for Sex Therapy," *Sexual & Relationship Therapy* 26, no. 2 (2011): 127–144.

20. Alex Molnar, D. R. Garcia, F. Boniger, et al., "Marketing of Foods of Minimal Nutritional Value to Children in Schools," *Preventative Medicine* 47, no. 5 (2008): 504–507.

21. Alex Molnar and Faith Boninger, "Adrift: Schools in a Total Marketing Environment," in *The Tenth Annual Report on Schoolhouse Commercialism Trends: 2006–2007* (Tempe, AZ: Commercialism in Education Research Unit, 2007); Alex Molnar, Faith Boninger, Gary Wilkinson, et al., *Effectively Embedded: The Thirteenth Annual Report on Schoolhouse Commercializing Trends: 2009–2010* (Boulder, CO: National Education Policy Center, 2010); Alex Molnar, Faith Boninger, Michael D. Harris, et al., *Promoting Consumption at School: Health Threats Associated with Schoolhouse Commercialism* (Boulder, CO: National Education Policy Center, 2013).

22. Catherine Potard, Robert Courtois, and Emmanuel Rusch, "The Influence of Peers on Risky Sexual Behaviour During Adolescence," *European Journal of Contraception and Reproductive Health Care* 13, no. 3 (2008): 264–270.

23. L. Monique Ward and Kimberly Friedman, "Using TV as a Guide: Associations Between Television Viewing and Adolescents' Sexual Attitudes and Behaviors," *Journal of Research on Adolescence* 16, no. 1 (2006): 133–156; Jones, Meneses da Silva, and Soloski, "Sexological Systems Theory," 127–144.

24. Jane D. Brown, Carolyn T. Halpern, and Kelly L. L'Engle, "Mass Media as a Sexual Super Peer for Early Maturing Girls," *Journal of Adolescent Health* 36, no. 5 (2005): 420–427; Jane D. Brown, "The Media Do Matter: Comment on Steinberg and Monahan," *Developmental Psychology* 47, no. 2 (2011): 582–584; Jane D. Brown, Kelly Ladin L'Engle, Carol J. Pardun, et al., "Sexy Media Matter: Exposure to Sexual Content in Music, Movies, Television and Magazines Predicts Black and White Adolescents' Sexual Behavior," *Pediatrics* 117, no. 4 (2006): 1018–1027.

25. Renee R. Hobbs, *Digital and Media Literacy: Connecting Culture and Classroom* (Thousand Oaks, CA: Corwin Press, 2011).

26. George Stephanopoulos, *Too Young to Be So Sexy?*, interview, October 26, 2013, *Good Morning America*, 2013.

27. Marcia S., personal communication with author, March 12, 2011.

28. Haley Whatley, personal communication with author, June 23, 2013.

29. Lerner et al., "Positive Youth Development," 17–71.

30. Albert Bandura, "Toward a Unifying Theory of Behavioral Change," *Psychological Review* 84, no. 2 (1977): 193.

31. Albert Bandura, "Regulative Function of Perceived Self-efficacy," in *Personal Selection and Classification*, eds. M. G. Rumsey, C. B. Walker, and J. H. Harris (Hillsdale, NJ: Erlbaum, 1994), 261–271; Albert Bandura, ed., *Self-efficacy in Changing Societies* (New York: Cambridge University Press, 1995); Albert Bandura, *Self-efficacy: The Exercise of Control* (New York: Freeman, 1997); Albert Bandura, "Social Cognitive Theory: An Agentic Perspective," *Annual Review of Psychology* 52, no. 1 (2001): 1–26; Viktor Gecas, "The Social Psychology of Self-efficacy," *Annual Review of Sociology* 15 (1989): 291–316.

32. Beth Bourdeau, Volker K. Thomas, and Janie K. Long, "Latino Sexual Styles: Developing a Nuanced Understanding of Risk," *Journal of Sex Research* 45, no. 1 (2008): 71–81; Sharon S. Rotosky, O. Dekhtyar, P. K. Cupp, et al., "Sexual Self-Concept and Self-Efficacy in Adolescents: A Possible Clue to Promoting Sexual Health?," *Journal of Sex Research* 45, no. 3 (2008): 277–286.

33. Christina M. Mitchell, Carol E. Kaufman, and Janette Beals, "Resistive Efficacy and Multiple Sexual Partners Among American Indian Young Adults: A Parallel-Process Latent Growth Curve Model," *Applied Developmental Science* 9, no. 3 (2005): 160–171; Renee E. Sieving, L. H. Bearinger, M. D. Resnick, et al., "Adolescent Dual Method Use: Relevant Attitudes, Normative Beliefs and Self-Efficacy," *Journal of Adolescent Health* 40, no. 3 (2007): 275e15–e22.

34. Bandura, "Regulative Function," 261–271; Bandura, *Self-Efficacy in Changing Societies*; Bandura, "Social Cognitive Theory," 1–26; Albert Bandura, "Toward a Psychology of Human Agency," *Perspectives on Psychological Science* 1, no. 2 (2006): 164–180.

35. Bandura, "Toward a Psychology of Human Agency."

36. The Steubenville Rape Case, *The Huffington Post*, last modified June 26, 2014, accessed September 23, 2014, http://www.huffingtonpost.com/news/steubenville-rape/

37. Julia Dahl, "Steubenville Rape Trial: Cell Phone Photos of Alleged Victim Discussed in Second Day of Testimony," CBS News, last modified March 14, 2013, accessed September 23, 2014, http://www.cbsnews.com/2102-504083_162_5757 4350.html

38. Ibid.

39. Lerner et al., "Positive Youth Development," 23.

40. American Psychological Association, *Report of the APA Task Force on the Sexualization of Girls* (Washington, DC: American Psychological Association, 2007; 2010), 1.

41. Cara Wallis, "Performing Gender: A Content Analysis of Gender Display in Music Videos, *Sex Roles* 64, no. 3–4 (2011): 160–172.

42. Mia A. Towbin, Shelley A. Haddock, Toni Schindler Zimmerman, et al., "Images of Gender, Race, Age and Sexual Orientation in Disney Feature-Length Animated Films," *Journal of Feminist Family Therapy* 15, no. 4 (2003): 19–44.

43. Dale Kunkel, Keren Eyal, Keli Finnerty, et al., *Sex on TV4* (Menlo Park, CA: Kaiser Family Foundation, 2005).

44. *How Teens Use Media: A Nielsen Report on the Myths and Realities of Teen Media Trends*. Nielsen Corporations, 2009.

45. Jeffrey A. Gottfried, Sarah E. Vaala, Amy Bleakley, et al., "Does the Effect of Exposure to TV Sex on Adolescent Sexual Behavior Vary by Genre?," *Communication Research* 40, no. 1 (2011): 73–95.

46. Ibid.

47. Amy Bleakley, Michael Hennessy, Martin Fishbein, et al., "Using the Integrative Model to Explain How Exposure to Sexual Media Content Influences Adolescent Sexual Behavior," *Health Education and Behavior* 38, no. 5 (2011): 530–540; Amy Bleakley, Michael Hennessy, Martin Fishbein, et al., "How Source of Sexual Information Relates to Adolescents' Belief About Sex," *American Journal of Health Behavior* 33, no. 1 (2009): 37–48; Amy Bleakley, Michael Hennessy, Martin Fishbein, et al., "It Works Both Ways: The Relationship Between Exposure to Sexual Content in the Media and Adolescent Sexual Behavior," *Media Psychology* 11, no. 4 (2008): 443–461; Annenberg Media Exposure Research Group, "Linking Measures of Media Exposure to Sexual Cognitions and Behaviors: A Review," *Communication Methods and Measures* 2, no. 1–2 (2008): 23–42; Rebecca L. Collins, Marc N. Elliott, Sandra H. Berry, et al., "Entertainment Television as a Healthy Sex-Educator: The Impact of Condom-Efficacy Information in an Episode of 'Friends,'" *Pediatrics* 112, no. 5 (2003): 1115–1121; Rebecca L. Collins, Steven Martino, Marc N. Elliott, et al., "Relationships Between Adolescent Sexual Outcomes and Exposure to Sex in Media: Robustness to Propensity-Based Analysis," *Developmental Psychology* 47, no. 2 (2011): 585–591; Jennifer S. Aubrey, Kristin Harrison, Leila Kramer, et al., "Variety Versus Timing: Gender Differences in College Students' Sexual Expectations as Predicted by Exposure to Sexually Oriented Television," *Communication Research* 30, no. 4 (2003): 432–460.

48. Michael Hennessy, D. Romer, R. F. Valois, et al., "Safer Sex Media Messages and Adolescent Sexual Behavior: 3 Year Follow-up Results from Project iMP-PACS," *American Journal of Public Health* 103, no. 1 (2013): 134–140; Jennifer L. Walsh and Monique Ward, "Magazine Reading and Involvement and Young Adults' Sexual Health Knowledge, Efficacy, and Behaviors," *Journal of Sex Research* 47, no. 4 (2010): 285–300.

49. Duane Hargreaves, "Idealized Women in TV Ads Make Girls Feel Bad," *Journal of Social and Clinical Psychology* 21, no. 1 (2002): 287–308.

50. Elizabeth A. Daniels, "Sex Objects, Athletes, and Sexy Athletes: How Media Representations of Women Athletes Can Impact Adolescent Girls and College Women," *Journal of Adolescent Research* 24, no. 4 (2009): 399–422; Elizabeth A. Daniels and Heidi Wartena, "Athlete or Sex Symbol: What Boys Think of Media Representations of Female Athletes," *Sex Roles* 65, no. 7–8 (2011): 566–579.

51. Elizabeth Daniels, personal communication with author, July 1, 2013.

52. Carol J. Pardun and Kathy B. McKee, "Strange Bedfellows: Symbols of Religion and Sexuality on MTV," *Youth & Society* 26, no. 4 (1995): 438–449; L. Monique Ward and Rocio Rivadeneyra, "Dancing, Strutting, and Bouncing in Cars: The Women of Music Videos," presentation, Chicago, IL, August 2002; American Psychological Association, *Report of the APA Task Force*, 2007, 2010; Kathryn McMahon, "The Cosmopolitan Ideology and the Management of Desire," *Feminist Perspectives on Sexuality* 27, no. 3 (1990): 381–396.

53. Rashida Jones, "Why Is Everyone Getting Naked? Rashida Jones on the Pornification of *Everything*," *Glamour*, December 5, 2013, accessed September 22, 2014, http://www.glamour.com/entertainment/2013/12/rashida-jones-major -dont-the-pornification-of-everything

54. Daniels and Wartena, "Athlete or Sex Symbol," 566–579.

55. Daniels, personal communication, 2013.

56. Donald R. McCreary, T. B. Hildebrandt, L. J. Heinberg, et al., "A Review of Body Image Influences on Men's Fitness Goals and Supplement Use," *American Journal of Men's Health* 1, no. 4 (2007): 307–316; Lina A. Ricciardelli, Marita P. McCabe, Alexander J. Mussap, et al., "Body Image in Preadolescent Boys," in *Body Image, Eating Disorders, and Obesity in Youth*, ed. Linda Smolak and J. Kevin Thompson, 2nd ed. (Washington, DC: American Psychological Association, 2009), 77–96.

57. Linda Smolak and Jonathan Stein, "A Longitudinal Investigation of Gender Role and Muscle Building in Adolescent Boys," *Sex Roles* 63, no. 9 (2010): 738–746.

58. "Top 10 Xbox 360 Games for Teens," Squidoo, LLC, last modified 2013, accessed May 15, 2014, http://www.squidoo.com/xbox-360-games-for-teens

59. Trevor Thieme, "Sculpt a Monster 6-Pack: *New Moon* Star Taylor Lautner's Secret Formula for Big Screen Abs," *Men's Health*, May 21, 2013, accessed September 23, 2014, http://menshealthmags.com/fitness/taylor-lautners-ab-workout?page=7

CHAPTER 3

1. Benda Surminski and Jeff McDougal, *Onslaught*, directed by Tim Piper (West Hollywood: Worldwide Productions, 2007).

2. AdRelevance Intelligence Report, "The ABCs of Advertising to Kids Online," Nielsen/Net Ratings AdRelevance, 2000.

3. Sharon Beder, "'A Community View,' Caring for Children in the Media Age," ed. John Squires and Tracy Newlands (paper presentation, New College Institute for Values Research, Sydney, 1998), 101–111.

4. Mark C. Miller, "'Demonopolize Them!' A Call for a Broad-Based Movement against the Media Trust," *Extra!* (November–December 1995): 9.

5. "History and Highlights," Campaign for a Commercial-Free Childhood, accessed May 2, 2014, http://www.commercialfreechildhood.org/history-and-highlights

6. Brooks Barnes, "Disney Looking into Cradle for Customers," *New York Times*, February 6, 2011, accessed September 24, 2014, http://www.nytimes.com/2011/02/07/business/media/07disney.html?_r=2&sq=Disney&st=cse&scp=2?&pagewanted=print

7. Ibid.

8. Andrea Chang, "Mattel Reports Strong Profits for 2010 and Holiday Period," *Los Angeles Times*, February 3, 2011, accessed September 24, 2014, http://articles.latimes.com/print/2011/feb/03/business/la-fi-mattel-earnings-20110202

9. "Disney: 'Cars 2' Franchise Earns $2 Billion in Annual Global Retail Sales," *Huffington Post*, February 14, 2012, accessed September 24, 2014, http://www.huffingtonpost.com/2011/02/14/disney-consumer-products-_n_822972.html

10. The Walt Disney Company, "The Walt Disney Company Reports Fourth Quarter and Full Year Earnings for Fiscal 2011," accessed May 2, 2014, http://thewaltdisneycompany.com/sites/default/files/reports/q4-fy11-earnings.pdf

11. The Walt Disney Company, "The Walt Disney Company Reports Fourth Quarter and Full Year Earnings for Fiscal 2013," accessed May 2, 2014, http://thewaltdisneycompany.com/sites/default/files/reports/q4-fy13-earnings.pdf

12. Media Awareness Network, "How Marketers Target Kids," 2010, accessed September 24, 2014, http://mediasmarts.ca/marketing-consumerism/how-marketers-target-kids

13. Soontae An and Hannah Kang, "Do Online Ad Breaks Clearly Tell Kids that Advergames Are Advertisements that Intend to Sell Things?," *International Journal of Advertising* 32, no. 4 (2013): 655–678.

14. MediaSmarts, "Young Canadians in a Wired World, Phase III: Talking to Youth and Parents about Life Online," 2012, accessed September 24, 2014, http://mediasmarts.ca/sites/default/files/pdfs/publication-report/full/YCWWIII-youth-parents.pdf

15. Jennifer L. Harris, Megan E. Weinberg, Marlene B. Schwartz, et al., *Trends in Television Food Advertising: Progress in Reducing Unhealthy Marketing to Young People?* (New Haven, CT: Yale Rudd Center, 2010).

16. Andrew Lipsman, Graham Mudd, Mike Rich, et al., "The Power of 'Like': How Brands Reach (and Influence) Fans Through Social-Media Marketing," *Journal of Advertising Research* 52, no. 1 (2012): 40–52.

17. Ibid.

18. An and Kang, "Do Online Ad Breaks," 655–678.

19. Federal Trade Commission, *Marketing Violent Entertainment to Children: A Review of Self-Regulation and Industry Practices in the Motion Picture, Music Recording & Electronic Game Industries* (Washington, DC: Federal Trade Commission, 2000), 1, accessed September 24, 2014, http://www.ftc.gov/sites/default/files/docum ents/reports/marketing-violent-entertainment-children/vioreport_0.pdf

20. Alex Pham, "Parent Advocacy Group Hates EA's 'Your Mom Hates Dead Space 2' Ads," *Los Angeles Times*, February 4, 2011, accessed September 24, 2014, http://latimesblogs.latimes.com/entertainmentnewsbuzz/2011/02/your-mom-hates-dead-space-2-advert-stirring-controversy.html

21. Center for Science in the Public Interest, "Open Letter to McDonald's Vice Chairman, CEO, & President Jim Skinner," Center for Science in the Public Interest, 2010, accessed September 24, 2014, http://cspinet.org/new/pdf/mcdonalds-dem and-062210.pdf

22. "McDonald's Threatened with Happy Meals Lawsuit," CBC News, last modified June 22, 2010, accessed May 5, 2014, http://www.cbc.ca/news /mcdonald-s-threatened-with-happy-meals-lawsuit-1.939735

23. Campaign for a Commercial-Free Childhood, "Toy Industry Execs Hijack the Tooth Fairy; CCFC Launches Campaign to Save Childhood Icon," press release, July 16, 2013, accessed September 24, 2014, http://www.commercialfreechildhood.org /toy-industry-execs-highjack-tooth-fairy-ccfc-launches-campaign-save-childhood -icon

24. Vindu Goel, "Facebook Deal on Privacy is Under Attack," *New York Times*, February 13, 2014, accessed September 24, 2014, http://www.nytimes .com/2014/02/13/technology/facebook-deal-on-privacy-is-under-attack.html? _r=0

25. Carl Erik Fisher, Lisa Chin, and Robert Klitzman, "Defining Neuromarketing: Practices and Professional Challenges," *Harvard Review of Psychiatry* 18, no. 4 (2010): 230–237.

26. Nick Lee, Amanda J. Broderick, and Laura Chamberlain, "What Is 'Neuromarketing'? A Discussion and Agenda for Future Research," *International Journal of Psychophysiology* 63 (2007): 199–204, quote on 200.

27. Fern L. Johnson and Karren Young, "Gendered Voices in Children's Television Adlvertising," *Critical Studies In Media Communication* 19, no. 4 (2002): 461–480; John R. Rossiter, Richard B. Silberstein, Philip G. Harris, et al., "So What? A Rejoinder to the Reply by Critics and Aikman-Eckenrode to Rossiter et al," *Journal of Advertising Research* 41, no. 3 (2001): 59–61.

28. Tim Ambler, Andreas Ioannides, and Steven Rose, "Brands on the Brain: Neuro-Images of Advertising," *Business Strategy Review* 11, no. 3 (2000): 17.

29. Dan Ariely and Gregory S. Berns, "Neuromarketing: The Hope and Hype of Neuroimaging in Business," *Nature Reviews Neuroscience* 11, no. 4 (2010): 284–292; Ambler et al., "Brands on the Brain."

30. Donald Kennedy, "Neuroethics: An Uncertain Future," presentation, Society for Neuroscience Annual Conference. New Orleans, LA, November 8–12, 2003.

31. Clive Thompson, "There's a Sucker Born in Every Medial Prefrontal Cortex," *New York Times Magazine* 153, no. 52648 (2003): 54–57.

32. "Leading Edge: Neuromarketing: Beyond Branding," *Lancet Neurology* 3, no. 2 (2004): 71–132.

33. Emily R. Murphy, Judy Illes, and Peter B. Reiner, "Neuroethics of Neuromarketing," *Journal of Consumer Behaviour* 7, no. 4–5 (2008): 293–302; Deblina Saha Vashishta and B. Balaji, "Social Cognitive Neuroscience, Marketing Persuasion and Customer Relations," *Procedia—Social and Behavioral Sciences* 65 (2012): 1033–1039.

34. Natasha Singer, "Making Ads that Whisper to the Brain," *New York Times*, November 13, 2010, accessed September 24, 2014, http://www.nytimes.com/2010/11/14/business/14stream.html?_r=0

35. Ibid.

36. Allen Kanner, "The Piracy of Privacy: Why Marketers Must Bare Our Souls," *Campaign for a Commercial Free Childhood*, July–August 2009, accessed September 24, 2014, http://www.commercialfreechildhood.org/sites/default/files/kanner_piracyprivacy.pdf

37. Susan Linn, *Consuming Kids: 2009 Thomas H. Wright Lecture*, film, 2009, accessed September 24, 2014, http://www.slc.edu/news-events/archived/2009-2010/consuming-kids-2009-thomas-wright-lecture.html; Adriana Barbaro and Jeremy Earp, *Consuming Kids: The Commercialization of Childhood*, film, Media Education Foundation, 2008.

38. Linn, *Consuming Kids*.

39. American Academy of Pediatrics. "Children, Adolescents, and Advertising," *Pediatrics* 118 (2006; 2010): 2563.

40. Jim Geoghan, Danny Kallis, and Valerie Ahern, "Kisses and Basketball," *The Suite Life of Zack and Cody*, television, Disney Channel, 2006.

41. Danny Kallis, Jim Geoghan, Valerie Ahern, et al., "The Fairest of Them All," *The Suite Life of Zack and Cody*, television, Disney Channel, 2005.

42. Todd J. Greenwald, Gigi McCreery, and Perry M. Rein, "I Almost Drowned in a Chocolate Fountain," *The Wizards of Waverly Place*, television, Disney Channel, 2007.

43. Kevin Kopelow, Heath Seifert, and Teresa Ingram, "Couples and Careers," *Austin & Ally*, television, Disney Channel, 2013.

44. Pamela Eells, Valerie Ahern, and Christian McLaughlin, "Trashin' Fashion," *Jessie*, television, Disney Channel, 2012.

45. Ashton Gerding and Nancy Signorielli, "Gender Roles in Tween Television Programming: A Content Analysis of Two Genres," *Sex Roles* 70, no. 1–2 (2014): 43–56.

46. Ibid., 52.

47. Samantha M. Goodin, Alyssa Van Denburg, Sarah K. Murnen, et al., "'Putting on' Sexiness: A Content Analysis of the Presence of Sexualizing Characteristics in Girls' Clothing," *Sex Roles* 65, no. 1–2 (2011): 1–12; J. Auster and Claire S. Mansbach, "The Gender Marketing of Toys: An Analysis of Color and Type of Toy on the Disney Store Website," *Sex Roles* 67, no. 7–8 (2012): 375–388; Elizabeth V. Sweet, "Boy Builders and Pink Princesses: Gender, Toys, and Inequality over the Twentieth Century,'" doctoral dissertation, University of California, Davis, 2013.

48. Ibid.; Judith E. Owen Blakemore and Renee E. Centers, "Characteristics of Boys' Toys and Girls' Toys," *Sex Roles* 53 (2005): 619–633; Isabelle D. Cherney and Kamala London, "Gender-linked Differences in the Toys, Television Shows, Computer Games, and Outdoor Activities of 5-to 13-year Old Children," *Sex Roles* 54 (2006): 717–726.

49. L. Monique Ward and Rocio Rivadeneyra, "Dancing, Strutting, and Bouncing in Cars: The Women of Music Videos," presentation, annual convention of the American Psychological Association, Chicago, IL, 2002.

50. Carol J. Pardun, Kelly Ladin L'Engle, and Jane D. Brown, "Linking Exposure to Outcomes: Early Adolescents' Consumption of Sexual Content in Six Media," *Mass Communication & Society* 8, no. 2 (2005): 75–91.

51. Justin Bieber, "First Dance," digital download, Island and RBMG, 2009.

52. Chynanny, "3 year old crying over Justin Bieber," film, 2010, accessed September 24, 2014, http://www.youtube.com/watch?v=dTCm8tdHkfI

53. Miley Cyrus, "Can't Be Tamed," digital download, Hollywood, 2010.

54. Kaitlin A. Graff, Sarah K. Murnen, and Anna K. Krause, "Low-Cut Shirts and High-Heeled Shoes: Increased Sexualization Across Time in Magazine Depictions of Girls," *Sex Roles* 69 (2013): 571–582.

55. "Hook-up Handbook," Seventeen.com, accessed May 13, 2014, http://www.seventeen.com/love/advice/hooking-up-tips

CHAPTER 4

1. Adrian Grumbein and Robyn J. Goodman, "The Good, the Bad and the Beautiful: How Gender Is Represented on Reality Television," in *Media Disparity: A Gender Battleground*, ed. Cory L. Armstrong (New York: Lexington Books, 2013), 99–114.

2. Yalda T. Uhls and Patricia M. Greenfield, "The Value of Fame: Preadolescent Perceptions of Popular Media and Their Relationship to Future Aspirations," *Developmental Psychology* 48 (2012): 315–326.

3. Victoria J. Rideout, Ulla G. Foehr, and Donald F. Roberts, *Generation M2: Media in the Lives of 8-to-18-Year-Olds* (Menlo Park, CA: Kaiser Family Foundation, 2010).

4. George Gerbner, Larry Gross, Nancy Signorielli, et al., "Aging with Television: Images on Television Drama and Conceptions of Social Reality," *Journal of Communication* 30 (1980): 37–47.

5. George Gerbner, Larry Gross, Michael Morgan, et al., "Growing Up with Television: The Cultivation Perspective," in *Media Effects: Advances in Theory and Research* (Hillsdale, NJ: Erlbaum, 1994), 17–41.

6. Ibid.

7. Ibid.

8. John Maltby, Lynn E. McCutcheon, and Robert Jay Lowinger, "Brief Report: Celebrity Worshipers and the Five-Factor Model of Personality," *North American Journal of Psychology* 13, no. 2 (2010): 343–348; Dara Greenwood, Christopher R. Long, and Sonya Dal Cin, "Fame and the Social Self: The Need to Belong, Narcissism, and Relatedness Predict the Appeal of Fame," *Personality and Individual Differences* 55 (2013): 490–495; John Maltby, "An Interest in Fame: Confirming the Measurement and Empirical Conceptualization of Fame Interest," *British Journal of Psychology* 101 (2010): 411–432.

9. Maltby, "An Interest in Fame."

10. David C. Giles, "Parasocial Interaction: A Review of the Literature and a Model for Future Research," *Media Psychology* 4, no. 3 (2002): 279–305.

11. Reed Larson, "Secrets in the Bedroom: Adolescents' Private Use of Media," *Journal of Youth and Adolescence* 24, no. 5 (1995): 535–550; David C. Giles and John Maltby, "The Role of Media Figures in Adolescent Development: Relations between Autonomy, Attachment, and Interest in Celebrities," *Personality and Individual Differences* 36, no. 4 (2004): 813–822; Adrian C. North, Lorraine Sheridan, John Maltby, et al., "Attributional Style, Self-Esteem, and Celebrity Worship," *Media Psychology* 9, no. 2 (2007): 291–308.

12. Marc Sestir and Melanie C. Green, "You Are Who You Watch: Identification and Transportation Effects on Temporary Self-concept," *Social Influence* 5, no. 4 (2010): 272–288; Teresa Beth Bell and Helga Dittmar, "Does Media Type Matter? The Role of Identification in Adolescent Girls' Media Consumption and the Impact of Different Thin-Ideal Media on Body Image," *Sex Roles* 65 (2011): 478–490; Uhls and Greenfield, "The Value of Fame"; Keren Eyal and Tali Te'eni-Harari, "Explaining the Relationship between Media Exposure and Early Adolescents' Body Image Perceptions: The Role of Favorite Characters," *Journal of Media Psychology: Theories, Methods, and Applications* 25, no. 3 (2013): 129–141; Christopher J. Ferguson, Kimberlee Salmond, and Kamla Modi, "Reality Television Predicts Both Positive and Negative Outcomes for Adolescent Girls," *Journal of Pediatrics* 162, no. 6 (2013): 1175–1180.

13. Tricia Romano, "'Blurred Lines,' Robin Thicke's Summer Anthem, Is Kind of Rapey," *Daily Beast*, August 13, 2013, accessed September 24, 2014, http://www .thedailybeast.com/articles/2013/06/17/blurred-lines-robin-thicke-s-summer -anthem-is-kind-of-rapey.html

14. Robin Thicke, "Blurred Lines," digital download, Star Trak Interscope, 2013.

15. "Twerk" *OxfordDictionaires.com*, accessed September 24, 2014, http://www .oxforddictionaries.com/us/definition/american_english/twerk

16. Stuart Elliot, "The Media Business: Advertising: MTV's Sponsors Hope the Video Music Awards Can Draw a Crowd, without Wardrobe Malfunctions," *New York Times*, August 20, 2004, accessed September 24, 2014, http://www.nytimes .com/2004/08/20/business/media-business-advertising-mtv-s-sponsors-hope -video-music-awards-can-draw-crowd.html

17. Jacqueline Lambiase, "Codes of Online Sexuality: Celebrity, Gender and Marketing on the Web," *Sexuality & Culture* 7, no. 3 (2003): 57–78.

18. Susan Lewis and Jennifer Shewmaker, "Considering Age and Gender: A Comparative Content Analysis of Sexualization of Teen Celebrity Websites," *International Journal of Interdisciplinary Social Sciences* 5, no. 12 (2011): 215–224.

19. Maltby et al., "Celebrity Worship"; Maltby, "An Interest in Fame."

20. Ibid.

21. Maltby et al., "Celebrity Worship."

22. Ibid.

23. Ibid.

24. Ibid.

25. John Maltby, James Houran, and Lynn E. McCutcheon, "A Clinical Interpretation of Attitudes and Behaviors Associated with Celebrity Worship," *Journal of Nervous and Mental Disease* 191, no. 1 (2003): 25–29.

26. Ibid.

27. Louise Shorter, Stephen L. Brown, Stephanie J. Quinton, et al., "Relationships between Body-Shape Discrepancies with Favored Celebrities and Disordered Eating in Young Women," *Journal of Applied Social Psychology* 38, no. 5 (2008): 1364–1377.

28. Bell and Dittmar, "Does Media Type Matter."

29. Stella C. Chia and Yip Ling Poo, "Media, Celebrities, and Fans: An Examination of Adolescents' Media Usage and Involvement with Entertainment Celebrities," *Journalism & Mass Communication Quarterly* 86, no. 1 (2009): 23–44.

30. Miley Cyrus, "Just Like You," digital download, Walt Disney, 2006.

31. Jon M. Chu, *Justin Bieber: Never Say Never*, film, Paramount Pictures, 2011.

32. Jennifer Pozner, *Reality Bites Back: The Troubling Truth about Guilty Pleasure TV* (Berkeley, CA: Seal Press, 2010).

33. Eileen J. Zurbriggen and Elizabeth M. Morgan, "Who Wants to Marry a Millionaire? Reality Dating Television Program, Attitudes toward Sex, and Sexual Behaviors," *Sex Roles* 54 (2006): 1–17.

34. Laura Vandenbosch and Steven Eggermont, "Temptation Island, The Bachelor, Joe Millionaire: A Prospective Cohort Study on the Role of Romantically Themed Reality Television in Adolescents' Sexual Development," *Journal of Broadcasting and Electronic Media* 55, no. 4 (2013): 563–580.

35. Bradley J. Bond and Kristin L. Drogos, "Sex on the Shore: Wishful Identification and Parasocial Relationships as Mediators in the Relationship Between Jersey Shore Exposure and Emerging Adults' Sexual Attitudes and Behaviors," *Media Psychology* 17, no. 1 (2014): 102–126.

36. Joshua Fogel and Lyudmila Kovalenko, "Reality Television Shows Focusing on Sexual Relationships Are Associated with College Students Engaging in One-Night Stands," *Journal of Cognitive and Behavioral Psychotherapies* 13, no. 2 (2013): 321–331.

37. Emily Moyer-Guse, Adrienne H. Chung, and Parul Jain, "Identification with Characters and Discussion of Taboo Topics After Exposure to an Entertainment Narrative about Sexual Health," *Journal of Communication* 61 (2011): 387–406.

CHAPTER 5

1. R. A. Shtarkshall, J. S. Santelli, and J. S. Hirsch. "Sex Education and Sexual Socialization: Roles for Educators and Parents," *Perspectives on Sexual & Reproductive Health* 39, no. 2 (2007): 116–119.

2. Nielsen Corporations, "How Teens Use Media: A Nielsen Report on the Myths and Realities of Teen Media Trends," June 2009, accessed September 25, 2014,

http://www.nielsen.com/us/etc/medialib/nielsen_dotcom/en_us/documents/
pdf/white_papers_and_reports.Par.48571.File.dat/Nielsen_HowTeensUseMedia_
June2009.pdf

3. Amy I. Nathanson, "Identifying and Explaining the Relationship between
Parental Mediation and Children's Aggression," *Communication Research* 26, no. 2
(1999): 124.

4. Melina Bersamin, Michael Todd, Deborah A. Fisher, et al., "Parenting
Practices and Adolescent Sexual Behavior: A Longitudinal Study," *Journal of
Marriage and Family* 1 (2008): 97.

5. Amy I. Nathanson, Jocelyn McGee, and Barbara J. Wilson, "Counteracting
the Effects of Female Stereotypes on Television via Active Mediation," *Journal of
Communication* 52, no. 4 (2002): 922–937.

6. Ibid.

7. Rebecca L. Collins, Marc N. Elliott, Sandra H. Berry, et al., "Entertainment
Television as a Healthy Sex Educator: The Impact of Condom-Efficacy Information
in an Episode of Friends," *Pediatrics* 112, no. 5 (2003): 1115.

8. Brent C. Miller, Brad Benson, and Kevin A. Galbraith, "Family Relationships
and Adolescent Pregnancy Risk: A Research Synthesis." *Developmental Review* 21,
no. 1 (2001): 1–38; M. Diane McKee and Alison Karasz, "'You Have to Give Her
that Confidence': Conversations about Sex in Hispanic Mother-Daughter Dyads,"
Journal of Adolescent Research 21, no. 2 (2006): 158–184.

9. Taya Cromley, Dianne Neumark-Sztainer, Mary Story, et al., "Parent and
Family Associations with Weight-Related Behaviors and Cognitions among
Overweight Adolescents," *Journal Of Adolescent Health* 47, no. 3 (2010): 263–269.

10. Rachel F. Rodgers, Karine Faure, and Henri Chabrol, "Gender Differences
in Parental Influences on Adolescent Body Dissatisfaction and Disordered Eating,"
Sex Roles 61, no. 11–12 (2009): 837–849.

11. Cromley et al., "Parent and Family Associations"; Rodgers et al., "Gender
Differences in Parental Influences."

12. Haleama Al Sabbah, A. Vereecken Carine, J. Elgar Frank, et al., "Body
Weight Dissatisfaction and Communication with Parents among Adolescents in 24
Countries: International Cross-Sectional Survey," *BMC Public Health* 1 (2009): 52.

13. Erin Calhoun Davis and Lisa V. Friel, "Adolescent Sexuality: Disentangling
the Effects of Family Structure and Family Context," *Journal of Marriage and Family*
63, no. 3 (2001): 669–681; Kimberly K. Usher-Seriki, Mia Smith Bynum, and Tamora
A. Callands, "Mother-Daughter Communication about Sex and Sexual Intercourse
among Middle- to Upper-Class African American Girls," *Journal of Family Issues* 29,
no. 7 (2008): 901–917.

14. Triece Turnbull, Anna van Wersch, and Paul van Schaik, "A Review of
Parental Involvement in Sex Education: The Role for Effective Communication in
British Families," *Health Education Journal* 67, no. 3 (2008): 182.

15. Tamara D. Afifi, Andrea Joseph, and Desiree Aldeis, "Why Can't We Just
Talk About It? An Observational Study of Parents' and Adolescents' Conversations
about Sex," *Journal of Adolescent Research* 23, no. 6 (2008): 689–721.

16. S. Shirley Feldman and Doreen A. Rosenthal, "The Effect of Communication
Characteristics on Family Members' Perceptions of Parents as Sex Educators,"
Journal of Research on Adolescence 10, no. 2 (2000): 119–150; Mark D. Regnerus,
"Talking about Sex: Religion and Patterns of Parent-Child Communication about
Sex and Contraception," *Sociological Quarterly* 1 (2005): 79.

17. Magaly Marques and Nicole Ressa, "The Sexuality Education Initiative: A Programme Involving Teenagers, Schools, Parents and Sexual Health Services in Los Angeles, CA, USA," *Reproductive Health Matters* 21, no. 41 (2013): 124–135.

18. James Jaccard and Patricia J. Dittus, "Adolescent Perceptions of Maternal Approval of Birth Control and Sexual Risk Behavior," *American Journal of Public Health* 90, no. 9 (2000): 1426–1430; Susan M. Blake, Linda Simkin, Rebecca Ledsky, et al., "Effects of a Parent-Child Communications Intervention on Young Adolescents' Risk for Early Onset of Sexual Intercourse," *Family Planning Perspectives* 2 (2001): 52; Douglas Kirby, "Abstinence, Sex, and STD/HIV Education Programs for Teens: Their Impact on Sexual Behavior, Pregnancy, and Sexually Transmitted Disease," *Annual Review of Sex Research* 18, no. 1 (2007): 143–177; Vincent Guilamo Ramos, James Jaccard, Patricia Dittus, et al., "A Comparative Study of Interventions for Delaying the Initiation of Sexual Intercourse among Latino and Black Youth," *Perspectives on Sexual And Reproductive Health* 43, no. 4 (2011): 247–254.

19. Miller et al., "Family Relationships and Adolescent"; McKee and Karasz, "You Have to Give Her that Confidence."

20. Laura D. Pittman and P. Lindsay Chase-Lansdale, "African American Adolescent Girls in Impoverished Communities: Parenting Style and Adolescent Outcomes," *Journal of Research on Adolescence* 11, no. 2 (2001): 199–224; Allyssa L. Harris, Melissa A. Sutherland, and M. Katherine Hutchinson, "Parental Influences of Sexual Risk among Urban African American Adolescent Males," *Journal of Nursing Scholarship* 45, no. 2 (2012): 141–150; Kirby, "Abstinence, Sex, and STD/HIV Education."

21. Kirby, "Abstinence, Sex, and STD/HIV Education."

22. Rebekah Levine Coley, Bethany L. Medeiros, and Holly S. Schindler, "Using Sibling Differences to Estimate Effects of Parenting on Adolescent Sexual Risk Behaviors," *Journal of Adolescent Health* 43, no. 2 (2008): 133–140.

23. Kathleen M. Roche, Saiffudin Ahmed, and Robert W. Blum, "Enduring Consequences of Parenting for Risk Behaviors From Adolescence into Early Adulthood," *Social Science & Medicine* 66 (2008): 2023–2034.

24. Allison Rose, Helen P. Koo, Brinda Bhaskar, et al., "The Influence of Primary Caregivers on the Sexual Behavior of Early Adolescents," *Journal of Adolescent Health* 37 (2005): 135–144.

25. Scott Edward Rutledge, Darcy Clay Siebert, Jill Chonody, et al., "Information about Human Sexuality: Sources, Satisfaction, and Perceived Knowledge among College Students," *Sex Education* 11, no. 4 (2011): 471–487.

26. Christine M. Markham, Donna Lormand, Kari M. Gloppen, et al., "Review Article: Connectedness as a Predictor of Sexual and Reproductive Health Outcomes for Youth," *Journal of Adolescent Health* 46 (Suppl. 2010): S23–S41; Kirby, "Abstinence, Sex, and STD/HIV Education."

27. Michael Bleakley Hennessy, Amy Fishbein, and Amy Martin Jordan, "Estimating the Longitudinal Association between Adolescent Sexual Behavior and Exposure to Sexual Media Content," *Journal of Sex Research* 46, no. 6 (2009): 586; Scott Edward Rutledge, Darcy Clay Siebert, Jill Chonody, et al., "Information about Human Sexuality: Sources, Satisfaction, and Perceived Knowledge among College Students," *Sex Education* 11, no. 4 (2011): 471–487.

28. Albert Bandura, "Efficacy," *Behaviour Therapist* 17, no. 6 (1994): 127; Albert Bandura, "Reflections on Human Agency," in *Contemporary Psychology in Europe:*

Theory, Research, and Applications (Ashland, OH: Hogrefe & Huber Publishers, 1996), 194–210; Albert Bandura, *Self-Efficacy: The Exercise of Control* (New York: Freeman, 1997); Albert Bandura, "Social Cognitive Theory: An Agentic Perspective," *Annual Review of Psychology* 52 (2001): 1–26; Viktor Gecas, "The Social Psychology of Self-Efficacy," *Annual Review of Sociology* 15 (1989): 291–316.

29. Bianca L. Guzmán and M. E. Dello Stritto, "The Role of Socio-psychological Determinants in the Sexual Behaviors of Latina Early Adolescents," *Sex Roles* 66, no. 11–12 (2012): 776–789.

30. Sabine Elizabeth French and Kathryn J. Holland, "Condom Negotiation Strategies as a Mediator of the Relationship Between Self-efficacy and Condom Use," *Journal of Sex Research* 50, no. 1 (2013): 48–59; Kali S. Van Campen and Andrea J. Romero, "How Are Self-Efficacy and Family Involvement Associated with Less Sexual Risk Taking among Ethnic Minority Adolescents?," *Family Relations* 61, no. 4 (2012): 548–558; Sharon Scales Rostosky, Olga Dekhtyar, Pamela K. Cupp, et al., "Sexual Self-Concept and Sexual Self-Efficacy in Adolescents: A Possible Clue to Promoting Sexual Health?," *Journal of Sex Research* 45, no. 3 (2008): 277–286; Renee E. Sieving, Linda H. Bearinger, Michael D. Resnick, et al., "Adolescent Dual Method Use: Relevant Attitudes, Normative Beliefs and Self-Efficacy," *Journal of Adolescent Health* 40, no. 3 (2007): e15–e22.

31. E. A. Borawski, C. E. Ievers-Landis, L. D. Lovegreen, et al., "Parental Monitoring, Negotiated Unsupervised Time, and Parental Trust: The Role of Perceived Parenting Practices in Adolescent Health Risk Behaviors," *Journal of Adolescent Health* 33, no. 2 (2003): 60–70.

32. Feldman and Rosenthal, "The Effect of Communication Characteristics"; Rostosky et al., "Sexual Self-Concept and Sexual Self-Efficacy."

33. Dae C. Sheridan, Rob Tremp, and Scott Merritt, "Have a Daughter, Be a Man," in press.

34. Dae Sheridan, personal communication with author, August 3, 2013.

35. Ibid.

36. Ibid.

37. Ibid.

38. Ibid.

39. Ibid.

40. M. Joycelyn Elders and Barbara Kilgore, "The Dreaded 'M' Word," *Nerve*, June 26, 1997, accessed September 25, 2014, http://www.nerve.com/dispatches/elders/mword

41. Sheridan, personal communication, 2013.

42. Ibid.

43. Ibid.

44. Ibid.

45. Ibid.

46. Ibid.

47. Ibid.

48. Ibid.

CHAPTER 6

1. May Ling Halim, Kristina M. Zosuls, Diane N. Ruble, et al., "Pink Frilly Dresses and the Avoidance of All Things "Girly": Children's Appearance Rigidity

and Cognitive Theories of Gender Development," *Developmental Psychology* 50, no. 4 (2014): 1091–1101.

2. Kristina M. Zosuls, Diane N. Ruble, Catherine S. Tamis-Lemonda, et al., "The Acquisition of Gender Labels in Infancy: Implications for Gender-Typed Play," *Developmental Psychology* 45, no. 3 (2009): 688–701.

3. Laura E. Berk, *Child Development*, 9th ed. (New York: Pearson, 2013), 652; May Ling Halim, Diane N. Ruble, and David M. Amodio, "From Pink Frilly Dresses to 'One of the Boys': A Social-Cognitive Analysis of Gender Identity Development and Gender Bias," *Social & Personality Psychology Compass* 5, no. 11 (2011): 933–949.

4. George Gerbner, Larry Gross, Nancy Signorielli, et al., "Aging with Television: Images on Television Drama and Conceptions of Social Reality," *Journal of Communication* 30 (1980): 37–47.

5. Ibid.

6. L. Monique Ward, "Does Television Exposure Affect Emerging Adults' Attitudes and Assumptions about Sexual Relationships? Correlational and Experimental Confirmation," *Journal of Youth and Adolescence* 31 (2002): 1–15; L. Monique Ward. "Understanding the Role of Entertainment Media in the Sexual Socialization of American Youth: A Review of Empirical Research," *Developmental Review* 23 (2003): 347–388.

7. Rocio Rivadeneyra, L. Monique Ward, and Maya Gordon, "Distorted Reflections: Media Exposure and Latino Adolescents' Conceptions of Self," *Media Psychology* 9 (2007): 261–290.

8. Elizabeth V. Sweet, "Boy Builders and Pink Princesses: Gender, Toys, and Inequality over the Twentieth Century," doctoral dissertation, University of California, Davis, 2013.

9. Rebecca Collins, "Content Analysis of Gender Roles in Media: Where Are We Now and Where Should We Go?," *Sex Roles* 64, no. 3–4 (2011): 290–298.

10. Stacy Smith, Katherine Pieper, Amy Granados, et al., "Assessing Gender-Related Portrayals in Top-Grossing G-Rated Films," *Sex Roles* 62, no. 11–12 (2010): 774–786.

11. Mark B. Tappan, Lyn Mikel Brown, and Sharon Lamb, *Packaging Boyhood: Saving Our Sons from Superheroes, Slackers, and Other Media Stereotypes* (New York: St. Martin's, 2009).

12. Avi Ben-Zeev, Liz Scharnetzki, Lann K. Chan, et al., "Hypermasculinity in the Media: When Men 'Walk Into the Fog' to Avoid Affective Communication," *Psychology of Popular Media Culture* 1, no. 1 (2012): 53–61.

13. Rosemary Ricciardelli, Kimberly A. Clow, and Phillip White, "Investigating Hegemonic Masculinity: Portrayals of Masculinity in Men's Lifestyle Magazines," *Sex Roles* 63 (2010): 64–78; Rosalind Gill, "Beyond the Sexualization of Culture. An Intersectional Analysis of Sixpacks, Midriffs, and Hot Lesbians in Advertising," *Sexualities* 12 (2009): 137–160; Laura Vandenbosch and Steven Eggermont, "Sexualization of Adolescent Boys: Media Exposure and Boys' Internalization of Appearance Ideals, Self-Objectification, and Body Surveillance," *Men and Masculinities* 16 (2013): 283–306.

14. Dawn Elizabeth England, Lara Descartes, and Melissa A. Collier-Meek, "Gender Role Portrayal and the Disney Princesses," *Sex Roles* 64, no. 7–8 (2011): 555–567.

15. Shelly Grabe, L. Monique Ward, and Janet Shibley Hyde, "The Role of the Media in Body Image Concerns Among Women: A Meta-analysis of Experimental and Correlational Studies," *Psychological Bulletin* 134, no. 3 (2008): 460–476.

16. Smith et al., "Assessing Gender-Related Portrayals."

17. L. Monique Ward and Kimberly Friedman, "Using TV as a Guide: Associations between Television Viewing and Adolescents' Sexual Attitudes and Behavior," *Journal of Research on Adolescence* 16, no. 1 (2006): 133–156; Jochen Peter and Patti Valkenburg, "Adolescents' Exposure to a Sexualized Media Environment and Their Notions of Women as Sex Objects," *Sex Roles* 56, no. 5–6 (2007): 381–395.

18. Lisa M. Groesz, Michael P. Levine, and Sarah K. Murnen, "The Effect of Experimental Presentation of Thin Media Images on Body Satisfaction: A Meta-analytic Review," *International Journal of Eating Disorders* 31, no. 1 (2002): 1–16.

19. Beth Bell and Helga Dittmar, "Does Media Type Matter? The Role of Identification in Adolescent Girls' Media Consumption and the Impact of Different Thin-Ideal Media on Body Image," *Sex Roles* 65, no. 7–8 (2011): 478–490.

20. Ibid.; Stephen C. Want, "Meta-analytic Moderators of Experimental Exposure to Media Portrayals of Women on Female Appearance Satisfaction: Social Comparisons as Automatic Processes," *Body Image* 6, no. 4 (2009): 257–269.

21. Want, "Meta-analytic Moderators," 265.

22. Kimberly K. Powlishta, "The Effect of Target Age on the Activation of Gender Stereotypes," *Sex Roles* 42, no. 3–4 (2000): 271–282.

23. Ruchi Bhanot and Jasna Jovanovic, "Do Parents' Academic Gender Stereotypes Influence whether They Intrude on Their Children's Homework?," *Sex Roles* 52, no. 9–10 (2005): 597–607.

24. Halim et al., "From Pink Frilly Dresses to 'One of the Boys'"; Halim et al., "Pink Frilly Dresses and the Avoidance of All Things 'Girly'."

25. Lynn S. Liben, Rebecca S. Bigler, and Holleen R. Krogh, "Language at Work: Children's Gendered Interpretations of Occupational Titles," *Child Development* 73, no. 3 (2002): 810–828.

26. Sweet, "Boy Builders and Pink Princesses."

27. Susan Kahlenberg and Michelle Hein, "Progression on Nickelodeon? Gender-Role Stereotypes in Toy Commercials," *Sex Roles* 62, no. 11–12 (2010): 830–847.

28. Fern L. Johnson and Karren Young, "Gendered Voices in Children's Television Advertising," *Critical Studies in Media Communication* 19, no. 4 (2002): 461–480.

29. Ibid., 477.

30. Brad Weiners, "Lego Is for Girls," *Bloomberg Businessweek,* December 14, 2011, accessed February 8, 2011, http://www.businessweek.com/magazine/lego-is-for-girls-12142011.html

31. Cindy Faith Miller, Leah E. Lurye, Kristina M. Zosuls, et al., "Accessibility of Gender Stereotype Domains: Developmental and Gender Differences in Children," *Sex Roles* 60, no. 11–12 (2009): 870–881.

32. George A. Comstock and Erica Scharrer, *Media and the American Child* (Burlington, MA: Elsevier, 2007), 392.

33. Jane P. Sheldon, "Gender Stereotypes in Educational Software for Young Children," *Sex Roles* 51, no. 7–8 (2004): 433–444.

34. Jennifer J. Pike and Nancy A. Jennings, "The Effects of Commercials on Children's Perceptions of Gender Appropriate Toy Use," *Sex Roles* 52, no. 1–2 (2005): 83–91.

35. Aysen Bakir, Jeffrey G. Blodgett, and Gregory M. Rose, "Children's Responses to Gender-Role Stereotyped Advertisements," *Journal of Advertising Research* 48, no. 2 (2008): 255–266.

36. Lacey J. Hilliard and Lynn S. Liben, "Differing Levels of Gender Salience in Preschool Classrooms: Effects on Children's Gender Attitudes and Intergroup Bias," *Child Development* 81, no. 6 (2010): 1787–1798.

37. Leonard Sax, *Why Gender Matters: What Parents and Teachers Need to Know about the Emerging Science of Sex Differences* (New York: Three Rivers Press, 2006), 336.

38. Janet Shibley Hyde, "The Gender Similarities Hypothesis," *American Psychologist* 60, no. 6 (2005): 581–592.

39. Sax, *Why Gender Matters*.

40. Lise Eliot, *Pink Brain Blue Brain* (New York: Mariner Books, 2009), 432.

41. Christina Hoff Sommers, "You Can Give a Boy a Doll, but You Can't Make Him Play with It," *The Atlantic*, December 6, 2012, accessed September 25, 2014, http://www.theatlantic.com/sexes/archive/2012/12/you-can-give-a-boy-a-doll -but-you-cant-make-him-play-with-it/265977/

42. Lise Eliot, "The Myth of Pink and Blue Brains," *Educational Leadership* 68 (2010): 32–37.

43. Ibid., 33.

44. Claude M. Steele, *Whistling Vivaldi and Other Clues to How Stereotypes Affect Us* (New York: Norton, 2010).

45. Ibid.

46. Ibid.

47. Yuko Yamamiya, Thomas F. Cash, Susan E. Melnyk, et al., "Women's Exposure to Thin-and-Beautiful Media Images: Body Image Effects of Media-Ideal Internalization and Impact-Reduction Interventions," *Body Image* 2, no. 1 (2005): 74–80.

48. Amy I. Nathanson, Jocelyn McGee, and Barbara J. Wilson, "Counteracting the Effects of Female Stereotypes on Television via Active Mediation." *Journal of Communication* 52, no. 4 (2002): 922–937.

49. Carlo Tomasetto, Francesca Romana Alparone, and Mara Cadinu, "Girls' Math Performance Under Stereotype Threat: The Moderating Role of Mothers' Gender Stereotypes," *Developmental Psychology* 47, no. 4 (2011): 943–949.

50. Steele, *Whistling Vivaldi*.

51. Ibid.

52. Melanie C. Steffens, Petra Jelenec, and Peter Noack, "On the Leaky Math Pipeline: Comparing Implicit Math-Gender Stereotypes and Math Withdrawal in Female and Male Children and Adolescents," *Journal of Educational Psychology* 102, no. 4 (2010): 947–963.

53. Jennifer Siebel Newsom, *Miss Representation*, Documentary (Ross, CA: Girls' Club Entertainment, 2011).

54. Sapna Cheryan and Victoria C. Plaut, "Explaining Underrepresentation: A Theory of Precluded Interest," *Sex Roles* 63, no. 7–8 (2010): 475–488.

CHAPTER 7

1. Martin E. P. Seligman, *Flourish : A Visionary New Understanding of Happiness and Well-Being* (New York: Free Press, 2011), 368.

2. Stephen M. Schueller and Martin E. P. Seligman, "Pursuit of Pleasure, Engagement, and Meaning: Relationships to Subjective and Objective Measures of Well-Being," *Journal of Positive Psychology* 5, no. 4 (2010): 253–263.

3. Mihaly Csikszentmihalyi, *Flow: The Psychology of Optimal Experience* (New York: Harper & Row, 1990), 336.

4. Michael F. Steger, Todd B. Kashdan, and Shigehiro Oishi, "Being Good by Doing Good: Daily Eudaimonic Activity and Well-Being," *Journal of Research In Personality* 42, no. 1 (2008): 22–42.

5. Schueller and Seligman, "Pursuit of Pleasure."

6. Ibid.

7. For a thorough discussion of eudaimonic theory and positive psychology, see Alan S. Waterman, *The Best Within Us: Positive Psychology Perspectives on Eudaimonia* (Washington, DC: American Psychological Association, 2013), 304.

8. Steger et al., "Being Good by Doing Good."

9. Michael S. Dunn, Cathy Kitts, Sandy Lewis, et al., "Effects of Youth Assets on Adolescent Alcohol, Tobacco, Marijuana Use, and Sexual Behavior," *Journal of Alcohol & Drug Education* 55, no. 3 (2011): 23–40.

10. Jane E. Myers, John T. Willise, and José A. Villalba, "Promoting Self-Esteem in Adolescents: The Influence of Wellness Factors," *Journal of Counseling & Development* 89, no. 1 (2011): 28–36.

11. Lisa Kort-Butler and Kellie Hagewen, "School-Based Extracurricular Activity Involvement and Adolescent Self-Esteem: A Growth-Curve Analysis," *Journal of Youth & Adolescence* 40, no. 5 (2011): 568–581.

12. Margaret M. Dolcini, Gary W. Harper, Susan E. Watson, et al., "Friends in the 'Hood': Should Peer-Based Health Promotion Programs Target Nonschool Friendship Networks?," *Journal of Adolescent Health* 36 (2005): 267.e6–267.e15; Angela Chen, Chia-Chen, Elaine Adams Thompson, et al., "Multi-system Influences on Adolescent Risky Sexual Behavior," *Research in Nursing & Health* 33, no. 6 (2010): 512–527.

13. M. Margaret Dolcini, Gary W. Harper, Cherri B. Boyer, et al., "Preliminary Findings on a Brief Friendship-based HIV/STI Intervention for Urban African American Youth: Project ORE," *Journal of Adolescent Health* 42, no. 6 (2008): 629–633.

14. Farzana Kapadia, Victoria Frye, Sebastian Bonner, et al., "Perceived Peer Safer Sex Norms and Sexual Risk Behaviors among Substance-Using Latino Adolescents," *AIDS Education & Prevention* 24, no. 1 (2012): 27–40.

15. Shannon Gadbois and Anne Bowker, "Gender Differences in the Relationships between Extracurricular Activities Participation, Self-description, and Domain-specific and General Self-esteem," *Sex Roles* 56, no. 9–10 (2007): 675–689.

16. Christy Greenleaf, Elizabeth M. Boyer, and Trent A. Petrie, "High School Sport Participation and Subsequent Psychological Well-Being and Physical Activity: The Mediating Influences of Body Image, Physical Competence, and Instrumentality," *Sex Roles* 61, no. 9–10 (2009): 714–726.

17. Tonya Dodge and Sharon F. Lambert, "Positive Self-beliefs as a Mediator of the Relationship Between Adolescents' Sports Participation and Health in Young Adulthood," *Journal of Youth and Adolescence* 38, no. 6 (2009): 813–825.

18. Bree D. Abbott and Bonnie L. Barber, "Differences in Functional and Aesthetic Body Image between Sedentary Girls and Girls Involved in Sports and

Physical Activity: Does Sport Type Make a Difference?," *Psychology of Sport & Exercise* 12 (2011): 333–342.

19. Ibid.

20. Michael C. Reichert and Peter Kuriloff, "Boys' Selves: Identity and Anxiety in the Looking Glass of School Life," *Teachers College Record* 106, no. 3 (2004): 544–573; Michael Reichert and Peter Kuriloff, "A New Look at BOYS," *Independent School* 64, no. 2 (2005): 88.

21. Trisha E. Mueller, Lorrie E. Gavin, and Aniket Kulkarni, "The Association between Sex Education and Youth's Engagement in Sexual Intercourse, Age at First Intercourse, and Birth Control Use at First Sex," *Journal of Adolescent Health* 42, no. 1 (2008): 89–96; Kristin A. Haglund and Richard J. Fehring, "The Association of Religiosity, Sexual Education, and Parental Factors with Risky Sexual Behaviors among Adolescents and Young Adults," *Journal of Religion and Health* 49, no. 4 (2010): 460–472; Lisa M. Edwards, Kristin Haglund, Richard J. Fehring, et al., "Religiosity and Sexual Risk Behaviors among Latina Adolescents: Trends from 1995 to 2008," *Journal of Women's Health* 20, no. 6 (2011): 871–877; Laura Durberstein Lindberg and Isaac Maddow-Zimet, "Consequences of Sex Education on Teen and Young Adult Sexual Behaviors and Outcomes," *Journal of Adolescent Health* 51 (2012): 332–338; R. Vivancos, I. Abubakar, P. Phillips-Howard, et al., "School-based Sex Education Is Associated with Reduced Risky Sexual Behaviour and Sexually Transmitted Infections in Young Adults," *Public Health* 127 (2013): 53–57.

22. Lise M. Youngblade, Laura A. Curry, Maureen Novak, et al., "The Impact of Community Risks and Resources on Adolescent Risky Behavior and Health Care Expenditures," *Journal of Adolescent Health* 38 (2006): 486–494.

23. Douglas Kirby, "Strong Religious Views Decrease Teens' Likelihood of Having Sex; Teens' Attitudes Towards Sex Hold More Sway than Religious Views," National Institutes of Health Report (Washington, DC: National Institutes of Health, 2002), 31.

24. Leslie Gordon Simons, Callie Harbin Burt, and F. Ryan Peterson, "The Effect of Religion on Risky Sexual Behavior among College Students," *Deviant Behavior* 30, no. 5 (2009): 467–485; Raffy Luquis, Gina Brelsford, and Liliana Rojas-Guyler, "Religiosity, Spirituality, Sexual Attitudes, and Sexual Behaviors Among College Students," *Journal of Religion & Health* 51, no. 3 (2012): 601–614; Brenna C. LeJeune, Gregory D. Zimet, Faouzi Azzouz, et al., "Religiosity and Sexual Involvement within Adolescent Romantic Couples," *Journal of Religion and Health* 52, no. 3 (2013): 804–816.

25. Kirby, "Strong Religious Views Decrease Teens' Likelihood of Having Sex."

26. Haglund and Fehring, "The Association of Religiosity."

27. Antoinette Landor, Leslie Gordon Simons, Ronald L. Simons, et al., "The Role of Religiosity in the Relationship between Parents, Peers, and Adolescent Risky Sexual Behavior," *Journal of Youth and Adolescence* 40, no. 3 (2011): 296–309.

28. Haglund and Fehring, "The Association of Religiosity."

29. Mark D. Regenurus, "Talking about Sex: Religion and Patterns of Parent-Child Communication about Sex and Contraception," *Sociological Quarterly* 46 (2005): 79–105.

30. Haglund and Fehring, "The Association of Religiosity"; Landor et al., "The Role of Religiosity."

31. Jeremy E. Uecker, "Alternative Schooling Strategies and the Religious Lives of American Adolescents," *Journal for the Scientific Study of Religion* 47, no. 4 (2008): 563–584.

32. Csikszentmihalyi, *Flow*.

33. W. C. Howard and Mary Rice-Crenshaw, "No Child Left Behind: A Successful Implementation," *Education* 126, no. 3 (2006): 403.

34. Barbara Buck, Sheila R. Carr, and Jan Robertson, "Positive Psychology and Student Engagement," *Journal of Cross-Disciplinary Perspectives in Education* 1, no. 1 (2008): 28–35.

CHAPTER 8

1. Jennifer H. Pfeifer, Carrie L. Masten, III, William E. Moore, et al., "Entering Adolescence: Resistance to Peer Influence, Risky Behavior, and Neural Changes in Emotion Reactivity," *Neuron* 69 (2011): 1029–1036.

2. Renee Hobbs, *Digital and Media Literacy: Connecting Culture and Classroom* (Thousand Oaks, CA: Corwin, 2011), 232.

3. "CML Media Lit Kit," Center for Media Literacy, accessed June 18, 2014, http://www.medialit.org

4. Hobbs, *Digital and Media Literacy*.

5. "2010 Press Release," Monster High Wiki, accessed May 20, 2011, http://monsterhigh.wikia.com/wiki/2010_Press_Release

6. "Monster High Doll Description," Amazon, accessed May 7, 2012, http://www.amazon.com/Mattel-N5946-Monster-High-Draculaura/dp/B0037V0PDG/ref=sr_1_6?ie=UTF8&qid=1348873719&sr=8-6&keywords=monster+high+dolls

7. "Monster High Clothing Description," Kmart, accessed May 12, 2012, http://www.kmart.com/search=monster%20high%20clothes?storeId=10151&catalogId=10104&vName=Clothing&cName=Girls&viewItems=25&autoRedirect=true&redirectType=CAT_REC

8. "Monster High Dolls," Target, accessed May 14, 2012, http://www.target.com/sb/toys-dolls-fashion-dolls/-/N-5xt8uZ5zl3x

9. "Monster High and the Kind Campaign Bring the Power of Kindness to Girls," released May 18, 2011, accessed September 17, 2014, http://news.mattel.com/News/Monster-High-and-the-Kind-Campaign-Partner-to-Bring-the-Power-of-Kindness-to-Girls-da.aspx

10. Ibid., 1.

11. Elizabeth Ellery, Morgan Myer, Jennifer W. Shewmaker, et al., "Social Modeling in Media from Aardvarks to Zombies: A Comparison of Prosocial and Aggressive Themes in Mattel's Monster High and Public Broadcasting System's Arthur," poster presented at the Texas Association of School Psychologists Annual Conference, Houston, TX, October 6–8, 2012.

12. Hobbs, *Digital and Media Literacy*.

13. Leonard Armato, "Skechers: Setting the Record Straight," *Huffington Post, Style,* posted May 12, 2011, accessed September 27, 2014, http://www.huffingtonpost.com/leonard-armato/skechers-setting-the-reco_b_861302.html

14. Hobbs, *Digital and Media Literacy*; "CML Media Lit Kit," Center for Media Literacy.

15. Ibid.

16. Jonathan McIntosh, *Buffy vs Edward: Twilight Remixed*, YouTube, Rebellious Pixels, 2009.

17. "Gender Remixer," Rebellious Pixels, accessed May 12, 2012, http://www.genderremixer.com

18. "Shed a Tear," higatv.com, accessed May 20, 2014.

19. Jennifer Pozner, "Reality Rehab," Reality Bites Back, accessed May 25, 2014, http://www.realitybitesbackbook.com/about-reality-bites-back/reality-rehab-with-dr-jenn/

20. Lauren Parsekian, *Finding Kind*, Indieflixs, 2011.

21. "Girl-Caught!" New Moon Girls, accessed May 14, 2013, http://www.newmoon.com/girl-caught/

22. Smita C. Banerjee and Kathryn Greene, "Analysis Versus Production: Adolescent Cognitive and Attitudinal Responses to Antismoking Interventions," *Journal of Communication* 56, no. 4 (2006): 773–794.

23. "Girl-Caught!" New Moon Girls.

Index

About the Author

Jennifer W. Shewmaker, PhD, is an associate professor of psychology at Abilene Christian University in Abilene, Texas. She is a nationally certified school psychologist who has worked with hundreds of families, children, teachers, and community organizations in her career. She is a founding board member of the Brave Girls Alliance, an international partnership of parents, professionals, and small business owners advocating for healthy, empowering media for children.

About the Series Editor and Advisors

SERIES EDITOR

Sharna Olfman, PhD, is a clinical psychologist and professor of psychology in the Department of Humanities at Point Park University in Pittsburgh, Pennsylvania. Her books include *The Science and Pseudoscience of Children's Mental Health* (2015), *Drugging Our Children* (2012), *The Sexualization of Childhood* (2008), *Bipolar Children* (2007), *Child Honoring: How to Turn This World Around* (coedited with Raffi Cavoukian, 2006), *Childhood Lost . . . How American Culture Is Failing Our Kids* (2005), and *All Work and No Play . . . How Educational Reforms Are Harming Our Preschoolers* (2004). She has written and lectured internationally on the subjects of children's mental health and parenting. She was the founder and director of the annual Childhood and Society Symposium, a multidisciplinary think tank on childhood advocacy from 2001 to 2008.

ADVISORS

Joan Almon is coordinator of the U.S. branch of the Alliance for Childhood, and cochair of the Waldorf Early Childhood Association of North America. She is internationally renowned as a consultant to Waldorf educators and training programs, and she is the author of numerous articles on Waldorf education.

Jane M. Healy has appeared on most major media in the United States and is frequently consulted regarding the effects of new technologies on the developing brain. She holds a PhD in educational psychology from Case Western University and has done postdoctoral work in developmental neuropsychology. Formerly on the faculties of Cleveland State University and John Carroll University, she is internationally recognized as a lecturer and a consultant with many years experience as a classroom teacher, reading and learning specialist, and elementary administrator. She is author of numerous articles, as well as the books *Endangered Minds: Why Our Children Don't Think and What We Can Do About It* (1999), *How to Have an Intelligent and Creative Conversation with Your Kids* (1994), *Your Child's Growing Mind: A Guide to Learning and Brain Development from Birth to Adolescence* (1994), and *Failure to Connect: How Computers Affect Our Children's Minds—For Better or Worse* (1998).

Stuart Shanker, PhD Oxon, is a distinguished professor of philosophy and psychology at York University in Toronto. He is, with Stanley Greenspan, codirector of the Council of Human Development and associate chair for Canada of the Interdisciplinary Council of Learning and Developmental Disorders. He has won numerous awards and currently holds grants from the Unicorn Foundation, the Templeton Foundation, and Cure Autism Now. His books include *The First Idea: How Symbols, Language, and Intelligence Evolved from Our Primate Ancestors to Modern Humans* (2004), *Toward a Psychology of Global Interdependency* (2002), and *Wittgenstein's Remarks on the Foundations of Animal Intelligence* (1998).

Meredith F. Small, PhD, is a writer and professor of anthropology at Cornell University. Trained as a primate behaviorist, she now writes about all areas of anthropology, natural history, and health. Besides numerous publications in academic journals, she contributes regularly to *Discover* and *New Scientist*, and she is a commentator on National Public Radio's *All Things Considered*. She is the author of five books, including *What's Love Got to Do With It? The Evolution of Human Mating* (1996), *Our Babies, Ourselves; How Biology and Culture Shape the Way We Parent* (1999), and *Kids: How Biology and Culture Shape the Way We Parent* (2001, paperback 2002).